Annie Horniman

SHEILA GOODDIE

Annie Horniman

A PIONEER IN THE THEATRE

Methuen

'There's always something one's ignorant of
About anyone, however well one knows them;
And that may be something of the greatest importance.
It's when you're sure you understand a person
That you're liable to make the worst mistake about him.

T. S. Eliot *The Confidential Clerk*

First published in Great Britain in 1990
by Methuen London
Michelin House, 81 Fulham Road, London SW3 6RB
Distributed in the USA by HEB Inc, 361 Hanover St
Portsmouth, New Hampshire 03801

A CIP catalogue record for this book
is available from the British Library
ISBN 0 413 17330 5

Printed in Great Britain
by St Edmundsbury Press, Bury St Edmunds, Suffolk
and bound by Hunter & Foulis Ltd, Edinburgh

Contents

Acknowledgements

There are many people who have helped me over the past four years as I have sought information for this book and I am most grateful to them.

First of all I must thank my dear friend Vera Sarkis who gave me the idea of writing a book on Annie Horniman.

I am indebted to Michael Horniman, Annie's great nephew, who from the start was most welcoming and gave me every assistance on family matters.

Ellic Howe and R. A. Gilbert gave me valuable help in my search for information on Annie's mystical years and Dr Paul Mortimer kindly lent me his doctoral thesis on Stanley Houghton for help on the Gaiety years.

I should like to thank Senator Michael Yeats for his kind permission to consult Yeats material at the National Library of Ireland.

I am very grateful to the staff of the following libraries and institutions for their co-operation and patient help in my research: Bodleian Library, Oxford; British Theatre Association; Central Library of Manchester; Fawcett Library; Horniman Museum; John Rylands University Library of Manchester; Manchester City Art Library; Raymond Mander and Joe Mitchenson Theatre Collection; National Library of Ireland; National Theatre Society Ltd of the Abbey Theatre, Dublin; Religious Society of Friends; Slade School of Art, University College of London; Tate Gallery; Theatre Museum; Trinity College, Dublin; Warburg Institute, University of London.

Last and most of all I wish to thank my partner David Rheubottom whose loving encouragement gave me the confidence to believe that I could do it.

List of Illustrations

The Avenue Theatre, 1894

Saturday evening, 21 April 1894

It will not be a dull evening. London's literati are sure of this as they make their way to the Avenue Theatre (now the Playhouse) in Northumberland Avenue. There is a buzz of conversation drifting through the theatre foyer. Fabians mingle with feminists, critics rub shoulders with first-nighters and all are asking the same questions. Will there be boos and hisses or shouts of hurray? Will they be shocked and outraged? They rather hope so, for they have come to witness the first public performance of a play by Bernard Shaw, that angry young Irishman who has every intention of becoming the new standard-bearer for Ibsenite ideas. It is his second play to be staged but you can hardly count the first. *Widowers' Houses* had only two performances eighteen months ago by the Independent Theatre Society. It could only be seen by subscription members and there were never more than a hundred and fifty.

Tonight, *Arms and the Man* is being performed at a West End theatre and the doors are open to everyone who is looking for more than mere entertainment. This is experimental theatre, aiming to present thought-provoking issues and controversial ideas in a new way. At eight-o'clock the programme opens with a one-act trifle by the dashing young Irish poet William Butler Yeats. *The Land of Heart's Desire* has already been running at the Avenue for three weeks and doing quite nicely, unlike the fate of the other plays with which it shared the original bill. *A Comedy of Sighs*, yet another new play by an Irishman, Dr John Todhunter, barely survived its first performance. It is anyone's bet how long tonight's play will run. One thing is certain: the management is not expecting a commercial success. There is no money to be made in this new kind of theatre which seeks not to give the public what they want but to educate them to want what it gives. A minimum of £400 a week is needed to meet the expenses and the run must last for at least fifty nights before it can be called anything other than 'an ignominious and probably ruinous failure'.

Where has the money come from for the Avenue season? Bernard Shaw and W.B. Yeats are two fortunate young men to have found a backer with a small fortune to risk and probably lose. An anonymous backer. How mysterious! The playwrights protest that not even they know to whom their grateful thanks belong – and they remain in the dark for the next ten years.

In April 1894 Annie Horniman was an unmarried woman of thirty-three, four years younger than Shaw and nearly five years older than Yeats. She was tall and slender, not unattractive and with a quiet wit, hiding her intensely shy and private nature beneath a forthright and sharply intelligent tone that often terrified less able people and kept men at a safe distance. Bernard Shaw recognised her shyness and frankness and to these two qualities he added a third – originality. It was true, Annie Horniman was a woman of her own making. She certainly did not belong with those Victorian spinsters who by their thirties were faced with two choices. They could either eke out a miserable existence in a lowly paid job or devote themselves to charitable works while dependent on family for a home and financial support. About the only respectable job on offer in late Victorian England that secured a small income and a home was that of governess.

Miss Horniman could enjoy the luxury of independence. Her only brother, three years her junior, had married in 1886, leaving her at home as companion for her mother whenever her father was travelling abroad on business and pleasure – which was often. But this did not mean that Annie was frustrated and restricted; far from it. Her father, brought up in the Quaker faith, had encouraged his two children to think for themselves, to keep their minds open to new ideas and to lead responsible lives. She had a private income from legacies, she had her own rooms at home where she could entertain her friends free from parental supervision and, as long as she did not openly defy her parents' religious beliefs or flout conventional forms of respectability, she was free to come and go as she pleased.

Annie valued her freedom. She saw her friends being tied down in matrimony. She observed the difference in her parents' lifestyles, her mother stifled at home while her father roamed far and wide. 'When I was young,' she once told a friend, 'I never said I won't marry just because of the idea that people who talked so were really about to plunge into matrimony. If people like to give up Liberty, let them.'[1] Annie wanted to be free to indulge her rebellions. She smoked, she bicycled, she went to theatres, she belonged to a secret mystical society, she studied astrology – all signs in the 1890s of an unconformist, emancipated young lady.

The previous year, on 12 August 1893, Annie's grandfather had died. He was in his ninetieth year and all his life had been a devoted Quaker. He had worked hard and lived modestly, establishing an increasingly successful business in tea, and by his death he had amassed a vast fortune. He left over £300,000, worth today roughly £24 million, great wealth by any standards. One third of his fortune and the family business went to Annie's father; another third went to charities of all kinds, from Friends' mission societies to temperance unions, from the Peace Society to prison reform; and the last third was shared in annuities and bequests to his dear wife, his loved friends and relations and his two cherished grandchildren. Annie's share amounted to about £40,000. Overnight she became the equivalent of a millionairess. Her lifestyle changed not one iota and her friends were quite unaware of the extent of her private income. She had always been generous and she continued to be so. She had always lived modestly and she continued to do so. A leg of mutton would continue to last her for three or four days. As long as she could drink as many cups of tea as she liked at tea-time and as many tumblers of whisky-flavoured water at night, she was content. Money was important to her only for the uses she could make of it and her greatest loves were travel and art (and on this broad canvas she placed music and theatre). From her late teens she had holidayed regularly in Europe, soaking up as much of the culture as she could. She travelled very simply, staying in small hotels and leaving the high style to brother Emslie who liked to motor with Rolls and chauffeur.

It was on one of her continental holidays that Annie had seen her first Ibsen play, *The Enemy of the People*, in 1889 at the Residenz Theater in Munich. She came back to the same theatre in 1891 for the first performance of *Hedda Gabler*, and this time she

was in the audience with the great playwright himself. Munich was
Europe's centre of art, music and drama, and the German people
were enjoying the new controversial plays. Subsidised municipal
theatres were springing up in many German towns, free from
censorship, free from the old dramatic conventions, free from
commercial restraints, while London's literary avant-garde could
only wish for such theatres. In England there had been one
performance of Ibsen's *Ghosts* by the Independent Theatre Society
in March 1891, when there had been such a storm of protest and
abuse from actor-managers, theatre-owners and old-fashioned critics that the dust had still not settled. 'Ninety-seven per cent of the
people who go to see *Ghosts* are nasty-minded people who find the
discussion of nasty subjects to their taste in exact proportion to
their nastiness', declared the *Sporting & Dramatic News*.[2] The Lord
Chamberlain and his Chief Examiner, who licensed new plays,
gave their judgement that 'all the characters in Ibsen's plays appear
to be morally deranged'.[3]

With many similar opinions being voiced it is not surprising that
the commercial theatres were unwilling to risk losing their theatre
licence by putting on an Ibsen play. A few brave souls dared to
lease a theatre and finance their own season – like Charles Charrington and his actress-wife Janet Achurch, who had put on *A Doll's
House* at the Avenue Theatre in April 1892, and Elizabeth Robins,
who had produced *A Master Builder* for a three-week run in 1893.
But these were professionals in the theatre business with a vested
interest in trying to change the climate of the British theatre. What
chance was there for Annie Horniman whose knowledge of the
theatre had been learnt from her theatre seat to make the contacts
that she would need to put on the first performance of Ibsen's *The
Wild Duck*? This is what she really wanted to do with some of her
grandfather's money.

Ever since a child Annie had dreamed of having her own theatre.
She often said that she was first attracted to the idea by one of her
favourite Hans Andersen fairy stories about a puppet-showman
who dreams of managing a great theatre and discovers that leading
actors are far more troublesome than puppets. When he wakes up
he is so thankful it was only a dream that he remains content to be
a puppet-player for ever. Annie had thought him a coward and
decided that when she grew up she would have 'a real theatre and

even if the actors came to blows, I would not lose heart'.[4] She kept
her dream a secret, for her parents did not regard the theatre as a
place for respectable people. She had to wait until she was free to
lead her own life and make her own decisions before she was able
to go to the theatre as often as she wished – and the restriction now
was the availability of the sort of theatre that she wanted. Not for
her the popular melodrama, spectacle and music-hall. Annie
wanted to see the new plays that presented serious ideas on stage,
that confronted the Victorian ideals of manly superiority and
womanly subservience. Her only chance was to find a club performance in a suburban hall or at a commercial theatre between its long
runs. She became a member of the Independent Theatre Society
which had put on *Ghosts* in a hall on Tottenham Court Road before
being able to lease the Royalty Theatre. Its principal maxim was
that the play was the thing. Elaborate scenery and 'star' treatment
were out. In December 1892 there had been the opportunity to see
Widowers' Houses, when the part of Blanche Sartorius was played
by a beautiful actress called Florence Farr.

Annie and Florence were friends. Since 1890 they had both been
members of a secret occult society called the Order of The Golden
Dawn. They were about the same age, both with a private income,
both rebels and both intent on self-knowledge and self-fulfilment.
In May 1890 Florence had played the lead in John Todhunter's *A
Sicilian Idyll* at the little red-brick Bedford Park Playhouse in
Hammersmith. Yeats had seen her there and had fallen in love
with her beautiful speaking voice. Florence had been briefly and
unhappily married to Edward Emery, an actor who went off to
America and never returned. She had great talent and enormous
energy which she poured into many creativities. Since her failed
marriage, she had vowed never to give her heart to any man but to
enjoy love and sexual adventures, the only rules being not to be
bored and not to be serious. Sex 'gives us every happiness we
know', she said, 'on condition that we never give way to it in our
serious relations.' Of course it was necessary to produce heirs but
sex was a game, 'a hygienic gymnastic'. Florence's sister Henrietta
had married into the Paget family and lived in Bedford Park, as
did the Todhunters and the Yeats. Through the Pagets Florence
had met May Morris and through the Morrises had met Bernard
Shaw, with whom she enjoyed a brief passionate affair until each

moved on, in Florence's case, to an even briefer fling with Yeats. One positive result from these affairs was that her lovers became her life-long friends.[5]

Annie had no creative talents to impress and no great beauty to entrance; she was neither an artist nor an actress. Her contribution to this circle of brilliant individualists would be made in the service of Art. If Florence would find a theatre and organise the plays, she would provide the finance, but it would have to remain their secret. If the news got out and her parents discovered what she was doing, there would be a terrible row. Helping the deserving poor was a worthy cause and bringing culture and art to the common people was a worthwhile crusade but pouring money into the theatre for the new iconoclastic drama would definitely not be considered suitable. At this time Annie was as keen to promote Florence's acting career as she was to stage an Ibsen play and both could be achieved together. But she left these professional decisions to Florence. The money was there for Florence to use as she saw fit.

W.B. Yeats had just written a one-act curtain-raiser for Florence with a part for her eleven-year-old niece Dorothy Paget. It was *The Land of Heart's Desire*. John Todhunter had another play ready for her called *A Comedy of Sighs*. The two playwrights had much in common. They were both Irish, both poets, both founder members of the Irish Literary Society in London, both intellectuals with dramatic ambitions and both were members of the Order of The Golden Dawn, where they joined with Annie and Florence to make magic. John Todhunter was, however, older and wiser than Yeats. Moreover, he had been brought up in the Quaker faith, which made Annie feel that he could be trusted with the knowledge that she would be the backer of their theatre adventure. She was not so sure of Yeats, who had an easy Irish charm and a way of tumbling out words when he became excited or wanted to impress. As well as being a poet, he acted the part of a poet and Annie, not taken in by his posturings, kept her secret from him.

Having taken a lease on the Avenue Theatre, Florence asked Aubrey Beardsley to design a theatre poster for the event. He had recently designed a book cover for her first novel, *The Dancing Faun*, published by John Lane in his 'Keynotes' series, and had drawn a saucy devilish creature, a caricature of Whistler with whom he was joined in battle over a snub. Florence was hoping for a highly original, possibly *risqué* poster that would shock and startle, and she was not disappointed. Annie said that even the cab horses shied at it!

On Thursday, 29 March 1894, at eight o'clock, the curtain rose at the Avenue Theatre on *The Land of Heart's Desire*. It was a delightful, poetical romance of faery folk that pleased the artistic audience, although there were jokes from a few philistines about preferring London fog to Celtic twilight. G. K. Chesterton thought that it was a very good play. 'There is only one thing wrong with *The Land of Heart's Desire*: the heart does not desire it.'[6] Todhunter's *A Comedy of Sighs* followed and was a complete disaster. Although Florence Farr struggled valiantly with her part, its overlong Ibsenite message on modern woman dragged wearily on to boos and jeers and emptying seats. The author sat through the four acts 'listening to the howling of his enemies'. George Moore, who was in the audience, described Yeats striding 'to and forth at the back of the dress circle, a long black cloak drooping from his shoulders, a soft black sombrero on his head, a voluminous silk tie flowing from his collar, loose black trousers dragging untidily over his long, heavy feet.'[7] Annie was not there, for she had decided to remove herself from London so that there was no danger of her name being linked with the plays. She was away on holiday.

The next morning *A Comedy of Sighs* was savaged by the critics. A post-mortem was held at the Avenue and Bernard Shaw came hurrying over in response to Florence's telegram for help. When he arrived he found her poring over *Widowers' Houses* with her theatre manager, hoping it might replace Todhunter's play. Florence knew that Shaw was working on a new play for her and here was his chance of a West End showing. He offered his new play, Florence accepted and he dashed home to finish writing it. He had called his first draft *Alps and Balkans*, reflecting the geographical setting of the Serbo-Bulgarian war which had been suggested to him by Sydney Webb. Now he changed the title to *Arms and the Man* and called it 'A Romantic Comedy'. It seemed just the thing to follow Yeats' fairy story.

For two more weeks the Avenue limped along until Shaw's play was ready, even increasing its audiences as news of the first-night fracas and Beardsley's startling poster brought in the curious. The poster received almost as much adverse comment as Todhunter's play, the *Globe* describing it as 'an ingenious piece of arrangement, attractive by its novelty and cleverly imagined. The mysterious female who looms vaguely through the transparent curtain is, however, of an unnecessarily repulsive facial type.'[8] After the Saturday night performance on 14 April the theatre closed for a week to rehearse Shaw's play, with the author taking full responsibility for choosing the cast and directing. This was the one and only time that Annie had not read the play that her money was backing. The second first-night was scheduled for 21 April and Shaw made sure that all the right people were invited. In the audience were Oscar Wilde, George Moore, Pinero, Henry Arthur Jones, Sydney Webb, the Charringtons. It was a 'boisterous' evening. Yeats described the scene: 'the whole pit and gallery, except certain members of the Fabian Society, started to laugh at the author, and then, discovering that they themselves were being laughed at, sat there not converted – their hatred was too bitter for that – but dumbfounded, while the rest of the house cheered and laughed.' At his curtain call Shaw responded to one loud hiss with the now legendary remark, 'I quite agree with you, sir, but what can two do against so many.'[9]

The critic William Archer urged his readers not to miss the chance to see *Arms and the Man*, 'one of the most amazing entertainments at present before the public. It is quite as funny as *Charley's Aunt* or *The New Boy*; we laughed at it wildly, hysterically.' The hysteria could well have been bewilderment, for most of the audiences could not understand what the play was about, and it was no help when Shaw said that he had invented nothing, it was all true. The Prince of Wales and the Duke of Edinburgh, Queen Victoria's two eldest sons, came along to see for themselves one night. 'Very pleasant,' murmured the Prince. The Duke was more outspoken. 'The man is mad,' he said, and repeated himself loudly so that the whole of the stalls could hear.[10]

When Annie returned to London the Avenue season was still making headlines. Yeats was there every night, bewitched and bewildered by the wit, ecstatic about this new talent. He believed that Shaw had become 'the most formidable man in modern letters'. But the theatre seats were not being filled, it was not what the general public wanted. The Avenue season ran on for eleven weeks, costing Annie about £4,000, with the total receipts amount-ing to £1,777. There was much speculation about who had given the money for the first public staging of a Shaw play and Annie was amused by a story in the magazine *Truth* that behind the Avenue project was 'an invalid woman living somewhere in Bedford Square'. Years later she looked back to these days and spoke of her 'fruitful failure'.

It was certainly fruitful for some of the players, who went on to make names for themselves in the theatre. One of the youngest was sixteen-year-old Granville Barker who made sixteen shillings a week as an understudy. Shaw opened his first bank account with about a hundred pounds and sold the American rights of his play to an actor called Richard Mansfield. Annie was not yet a business woman and had only secured the London rights. But she was not downhearted by losing money in the venture and looked for further ways of working with Florence Farr. In March 1895, Bernard Shaw wrote to Charles Charrington: 'I am told, not at first hand though, that the capital which the mysterious backer of *Arms and the Man* proposes to put down for four years hence is no less than quarter of a million. We had better all spend the interim in writing plays with magnificent parts for Miss F. F. . . .'[11] Florence, like Annie, dreamt of a theatre of her own, and Bernard Shaw promised her 'the most brilliant play of the century' for it. Perhaps this is where Annie was thinking of putting her money.

After the Avenue season Bernard Shaw disappeared from Annie's life and it was ten years before he knew for sure that she was the one who should be thanked for starting him on the road to success and fame. Yeats wondered from time to time but when he put the possibility to Annie, he was 'pulverised for hinting at such a possibility'. Shaw's enlightenment came, so he said, in a dream, when the solution suddenly flashed before him. 'The matter went no further,' he wrote to Annie in 1904, 'and the only effect of it was to suggest to me that I might be under a considerable obligation to a person whom I had met once or twice, and to whom I was perfectly content to be under an obligation.'[12] He appreciated that she must have weighty reasons for wanting secrecy, but he won-dered if she had appreciated sufficiently the weighty reasons against. If her contribution had become known, would she not have received her fair share of the respect and recognition that had been woefully lacking over the years? Her later efforts in the theatre would have been seen as professional business ventures and not spoken of so scathingly by certain men of the theatre.

Annie had never wished her secret to be exposed and she played down her part. In June 1907 she wrote:

> Dear Mr Shaw,
>
> . . . You are inclined to make too much of my connection with the Avenue affair . . . I used to be a little ashamed that I had given no personal efforts to the scheme . . .
>
> With kind regards,
Yours sincerely,
A. E. F. Horniman[13]

By then Bernard Shaw knew her name but that was all. Two years later he teasingly tried to learn more. He wanted to send her a copy of one of his plays with a personal inscription, but how should he address her? 'Miss Horniman is a mere address and A. E. F. Horniman is dreadful.' He came up with various witty combinations, from Annie Elsie Feeby to Aphrodite Evadne Fedora, and wrote that, if she did not confess, he would call her Anonyma Egregia Fantastica. Annie was not to be drawn and suggested playfully that he wanted to know her names in order to include her in his will. She would rather have fresh plays from him than any other legacy, so he must go on living for many more years.

Once the secret was out Annie was willing to acknowledge the truth. She wrote to Florence in December 1905, 'My circumstances in life have so changed that secrecy is no longer necessary.'[14] By then she was forty-five. Her 'circumstances' must have been overwhelmingly powerful to have held her bound in silence by complex family ties of duty, loyalty, privacy and love for so many years.

2

The Horniman Family

'Circumstances shut me off from other girls and I was very lonely then,' Annie told her distant cousin Marjorie, trying to explain how she had become friendly with someone with whom she had little in common and whose friendship she later regretted.[1] Annie's 'circumstances' were that she was born into a very wealthy, very pious home in the middle of Queen Victoria's reign, a combination that could hardly make for a more restricted, suffocating situation.

Her parents, Frederick John Horniman and Rebekah Emslie, had married in 1859 at Finsbury Congregational Chapel in North London. Frederick had been brought up and educated in the Quaker faith but he changed to Congregationalism for his wife's sake and to gain the approval of her Scottish parents. As he rose in wealth and social status, so he moved further along the Nonconformist line until, when Annie was eighteen, 'we had a handsome carriage and pair and that (in a London suburb) took us automatically to church'.[2]

Within sixteen months of marriage their first child was born and was christened after her two grandmothers, two of her aunts and her father. Annie Elizabeth Fredericka arrived at thirty-five minutes past seven o'clock on the evening of 3 October 1860. It was the feast of Saint Candidus and later she joked that she might have been christened Candida if she had been born into a different religion, but with one grandfather a devout Quaker and the other a pious deacon, her path was clearly marked. On Annie's third birthday Emslie John was born and the family was complete, small compared with many Victorian households where infants often arrived annually. But Rebekah was not a young mother. She was thirty-five when Annie was born, and ten years older than her husband. It must have been sterling qualities of character that had attracted Frederick, who was a particularly eligible bachelor, good-looking, rich and dependable. Perhaps his Quaker upbringing strongly influenced his choice, urging him to perpetuate the sober, serious side of his home.

Annie's paternal grandfather, John Horniman, was a self-made man. Born in Reading in 1803, the son of a cabinet-maker turned umbrella-fashioner, he had been sent to Ackworth Boarding School in Yorkshire. The school had been established in the late eighteenth century by the Society of Friends for children whose parents were 'not in affluence', and charged eight guineas a year for education, board and clothing. Here John learnt the principles of hard work, thrift and charity, and upon this solid foundation he built when he went out into the world to seek his fortune. He was twenty-one when he married Ann Smith of Witney, Oxfordshire. Annie's rather patronising memory of her grandmother was that 'she never had much of a brain but she was a good little woman, a strict Quakeress, so plain that she never had a wedding ring'.[3]

John and Ann Horniman started married life in Northampton, where John became a grocer, a Liberal and a councillor. He had no intention of staying there long and after six years and two children he moved to Bristol, then Reading, and by 1835, when Annie's father was born, was making cheese in Bridgewater, Somerset. From cheese he turned his attention to tea, and took his family to Newport on the Isle of Wight. By now six children had been born, two girls and four boys, although only two survived beyond childhood, Frederick John and his brother William Henry, who was four years his senior.

There was money to be made in selling tea and John had the brilliant idea of selling it in packets, sealed and clearly marked with the weight and price. He staked his reputation on its purity and he was soon known in the trade as 'Honest John'. His business expanded faster than hands could pack the tea leaves into packets, so he invented a machine to do the job. His packets of tea, 'the Black not artificially coloured, the Green a natural dark olive leaf', were in demand throughout the British Isles and were despatched to more and more countries around the world. Newport became too small for his needs and he took his business and his family to London. In 1854 Horniman & Company, which now included his two sons, had offices and warehouses in Philpot Lane on the south side of the River Thames. Mrs Horniman set up home at Coombe

Cliffe House, Croydon, a large solid mansion with a fashionable eastern-style tower and beautiful grounds from which the country-side around them could be enjoyed. Here Annie's grandparents lived in quiet respectability, scarcely known outside their gates except to fellow Friends to whose charities they gave thousands of pounds every year.

In 1868, when Annie was eight years old and her father was thirty-three, her grandfather handed over the family business to his two sons and gave his attention to travel. He took with him his favourite nephew, Henry, recently returned from a successful life in America and doubly related to him as his father was John's brother and his mother was Ann's sister. Together the two gentlemen, sixty-five and forty-one years respectively, wintered in Egypt, Rome, Naples and Nice, while back at home Messrs W. H. & F. J. Horniman expanded into Nos 29 to 32 Wormwood Street with warehouses at Hay's Wharf, nicely situated between Tower and London Bridge. The chests of tea leaves arrived on the wharf and were taken to the warehouses, where the leaves were emptied out, blended, sampled, re-packed in airtight tinfoil packets, labelled and duly despatched back in the same fragrantly tea-scented chests to the four corners of the world. Horniman's tea emporium stretched from shore to shore. Agents in every country were appointed to promote Horniman interests and Annie's father took every opportunity to make personal contacts. He travelled to India, Ceylon, China, Japan, Africa, America and Canada, using his position of influence and wealth to further a hobby which had absorbed him from boyhood.

Frederick's bedroom had always been the despair of the house-maids, for it was full of collections of beetles, butterflies, birds' eggs, insects of all kinds. Now, on his travels around far-away places, he was always on the lookout for additions to his entomolog-ical, archaeological and cultural treasures. By the time that Annie was sixteen, he had become a fellow of the Royal Geographical Society and member of the Linnaean Society, the Zoological Society, the Entomological Society and the Royal History Society. In 1879 he had the distinction of having a butterfly named after him. He had discovered a new variety in Africa and brought it back to be catalogued as 'Papilio Hornimani' in 'The Proceedings of The Zoological Society of London, 17 June'. His enthusiasm was taken up by many who met him – like the agent in Darjeeling who wrote that he had found a Tibetan teapot, and the member of Stanley's Relief Expeditionary Force who looked out for rare beetles while searching for Livingstone.

There was no question of Annie's mother accompanying him on his travels. For women of her class and background such an idea was simply not socially acceptable. Partnership in marriage was then a very different concept. The worlds of the sexes were separate, different and autonomous. Rebekah organised the household, gave orders to the servants and instructed her children in their duties with the help of a governess and a tutor, for Annie and Emslie were educated privately at home. It was a privileged, carefully correct world, loving yet stern, described by G. K. Chesterton as one 'in which nobody was any more likely to drop an "h" than to pick up a title'.[4] Annie's father had been educated at the Friends' College at Croydon but, no longer being of their religious persuasion, he could not have sent his son to such a school. Perhaps he decided on private education because he wanted no discrimination between daughter and son, or maybe because the family wealth had been made in trade which did not easily open doors into the public schools of the upper and professional classes. Whatever the reasons, Annie benefited from sharing some of Emslie's lessons. She became fluent in French and German, studied music and painting, read suitable literature and history, and was taught the socially desirable accomplishment of dancing. She was never given cause to think that she was inferior to Emslie, 'except that he was better looking', she fondly remembered.

The family home, Surrey Mount in Forest Hill, was one of the 'detached villa residences with extensive prospects' which had sprung up in this south-east suburb on the direct railway line to the city. Between 1854 and 1866 the parish population grew from 1,500 to 10,000. The Hornimans, however, were well sheltered within their fifteen acres of grounds, which included a second house and a lodge. They lived at the highest point of Forest Hill overlooking the tree-lined avenues that were being laid down to the neighbouring residences, while beyond stretched the green fields of Sydenham and Lewisham. To outward eyes, Annie's home was a typical Victorian statement of success, comfortable and complacent, reflecting the priorities of its owners. Annie liked to describe it as a 'middle-class, dissenting, suburban home' but it was much more than this.

Over the years her father brought home from distant lands crate-loads of treasures, from moths and mummies to musical instruments and medieval armour. Rebekah Horniman gave up one room after another to her husband's trophies, which gradually filled the conservatory, the stables and the outbuildings, and crept into the spare rooms and corridors, eventually taking over the house next door to the family home. Once through the door, the visitor stepped into an Aladdin's cave, a wonderland of oriental mystery, with statues of Egyptian deities, Chinese dragons, Venetian glassware, French porcelain, tapestries, snuff boxes, tobacco pipes, shells, fossils – a cornucopia of magic and delight garnered from exotic places.

Instead of girl friends of her own age Annie had Emslie. Any advantage that he might have by virtue of his sex was cancelled out by her three years' seniority, so they were equal at work and play. But this did not quite compensate for her lack of girl friends. Until she was old enough to share confidences with her governess, Annie had only her dolls to whisper her secrets to, and the company of the life-size statues that her father had brought back home. Osiris, Egyptian god of the Nile, sun god and ruler over the kingdom of the dead, was as tall as her father, and by his side sat the moon goddess Isis, his sister and his wife. Ganesha, Hindu god of wisdom, was an enormously fat man with an elephant's head who, Annie learnt, had the power to remove all obstacles. As the son of Shiva, the agent of destruction and recreation, he was of major importance in the Hindu belief that the soul continued to be reborn until it was united with God. 'Before I ever heard the word "reincarnation" I believed that I had lived in this world long ago; it is the only theory by which we can even try to account for the various happenings in life,' she wrote to a friend many years later, and asked him if he had ever wondered whether he had once been an Egyptian and whether that was why he was so attracted to the idea of learning what was once his life and habit. 'In considering reincarnation one must remember the future as well as the past,' she told him.[5]

Surrey Mount offered a rich mixture of fantasy and reality and, as a child, Annie could wander effortlessly between the two. She much preferred the strange romances of the gods and goddesses to the gloom and doom that the Presbyterians offered at Sunday worship. She even endured this in her own home when her parents invited the local fellowship to meet at Surrey Mount until the local hall was built. When Annie grew older, she rejected her parents' strict Nonconformist faith and turned for answers to life's mysteries in theosophy and the occult, in ancient religions and astrology. Religious doubt was fashionable in late Victorian years and Annie, having discovered attractive alternatives at an early age, had more reason than many for turning from conventional beliefs.

Annie left very few reminiscences of her parents and what her mother thought of the encroachment into her home of her husband's ancient and oriental fantasies, as well as thousands of insects, can only be imagined. Perhaps she was relieved that her much younger husband could burn up his energies in travel and the pursuit of art and science, leaving her to her quiet round of church and charity. Annie remembered only one outburst from her mother, after she had opened a letter addressed to her husband on some business matter from young cousin Sophie, who had been staying for a short time. The tone was evidently too intimate for her mother's liking as she read out loud 'Dear Frederick', followed by the whole letter, to Annie's nurse. Annie was seven at the time, and she was mortified that her mother should open a letter not addressed to her and read it out to the nurse. Even in her seventies the scene had the power to disturb her. In a letter of 16 February 1932 she asked a relation, 'I don't think that Bella opened your letters, if she did, *could* she have read them out to a servant?'[6]

Mrs Horniman had broken one of the strict rules of social etiquette, of much more importance in her daughter's eyes than the many finely drawn rules of dress and appearance. When Annie looked back to her girlhood she remembered that it had been considered presumptuous for a clerk in her father's office to sport a moustache, unmanly for him to part his hair in the middle, to comb it back or to cut it very short; he was expected to wear a tall hat and a black coat. These were the days when ladies wore hooped petticoats and tightly corseted their bodies. When Emslie had left behind his nursery dresses Annie had to submit to frills and flounces that seriously restricted her activities. She had many battles with her mother over what was considered suitable wear for a young lady. One of her earliest memories was of wearing her newest, most uncomfortable dress to present a purse to the Princess of Wales, later Queen Alexandra, who had come to lay the foundation stone at Farningham Home for Little Boys, a home in which her father took a charitable interest, giving every boy a new suit each year.

Annie often sat quietly listening to the grown-ups in conversation. She remembered one such time when she was nursing her doll on her lap while matters of the day were being discussed – the rights of women and the place of women in the home. Voices were raised as tempers grew short. Her father was voicing his support for Jacob Bright, the Liberal politician who was promoting a Parliamentary Bill which would give women the vote. Annie remembered that her mother and aunt were tearful. Why was this? Were the other gentlemen in the room objecting strongly to the thought of their bastion of male supremacy being scaled or were the ladies afraid that their safe secure world might fold overnight like a pack of cards? Whatever the adults thought, Annie resolved that one day she would have a vote.

There were plenty of 'dos' and 'don'ts' for Annie and Emslie at Surrey Mount in spite of their father's liberal views. One subject on which he kept to a puritanical attitude was the theatre, which was generally regarded as a sinful place. This made the idea seem all the more desirable to Annie, who found an ally in her German governess. The Crystal Palace, which was considered more respectable than the average theatre because of its association with the Prince Consort, was conveniently close to Surrey Mount and when Annie was fourteen she and Emslie were taken there by her governess to a Saturday matinee performance of *The Merchant of Venice*. The trip was successfully made without parental knowledge and it may have been only the first. It could well be that they also saw 'Pepper's Ghost Show' there. This show, which was very popular in the early 1870s, was the creation of Professor Pepper of the Royal Polytechnic Institution in Regent Street, who had patented a magical trick using a piece of glass that was transparent and reflective at the same time, so that characters appeared to walk through doors and walls and disappear into furniture. Back home Annie and Emslie made their own little theatre with the help of the governess, building scenery and props and putting on their own plays, of which Annie remembered that their favourite was 'Pepper's Ghost'.

The German governess was a considerable influence. Mr Horniman was away for months on his world travels, while Mrs Horniman was bound in narrow domesticity, and as she passed through her rebellious teens Annie was held within the family home yet isolated from her parents. Her confidante was her German governess, who told her about life in her home town, about its cleanliness and its culture, in particular its new theatre which was open to everyone and which was one of many being built in towns all over Germany. Annie was determined to see for herself when she was old enough to be free from the petty restrictions of home life. For the moment, however, she was a lonely little rich girl.

Annie was indeed particularly isolated. The Hornimans had accumulated so much wealth that it placed them outside their own middle class. (Before her grandfather died he was giving away £100,000 every year to charity, in today's currency £8 million.) But those who made money in trade were not welcomed in the upper classes; and besides the Hornimans had the social handicap of being Nonconformist. Annie detested these social distinctions that created misery for so many who happened to be on the wrong side of the social divide. When she became famous in her own right she often made clear her own views on social snobbery. A typical comment was, 'I don't see why the *trading* classes should imitate the upper classes by sacrificing their daughters.'[7]

Mrs Horniman must have hoped for a suitable marriage for her daughter but Annie's immediate desires lay in quite another direction. Fortunately, Emslie's interests and ambitions ran along similar lines to hers and he could be her passport to freedom. They both delighted in art and beauty, encouraged by their father, one of whose favourite sayings was that those who used their eyes obtain the most enjoyment and knowledge. No doubt his children reminded him of this when they told him that they wanted to become art students. They persuaded him to give them both the opportunity to discover whether they had any real talent. Eventually Emslie would go into the family tea business but first he would accompany Annie as they set out on new and exciting experiences. It was 1881. Their first stop was Paris and a chance to see the new Impressionist paintings that were the talk of London, although there had not yet been any exhibitions of what some were calling scandalous works. Annie was twenty-one and Emslie eighteen. Whatever impressions they formed of life and art on their trip, they came home determined to become art students, to continue along their chosen path of self-discovery.

3

Student Years

The Victorian London into which the student Annie plunged in 1882 'had all the vices that are now called virtues: religious doubt, intellectual unrest, a hungry credulity about new things, a complete lack of equilibrium. It also had the virtues that are now called vices: a rich sense of romance, a passionate desire to make the love of man and woman once more what it was in Eden, a strong sense of the absolute necessity of some significances in human life' – so wrote G. K. Chesterton in 1936.[1] Annie had her share of these virtues and vices.

The date of 3 October 1882 was memorable in the Horniman household. Not only was it Annie's twenty-second birthday and Emslie's nineteenth, but it was also the beginning of student life for them both. Together they walked through the gates of the honey-stone building in Gower Street that housed the Slade School of Art and made their way to the north wing where they signed the register, a daily ritual for all students. In 1868 Sir Felix Slade, wealthy art connoisseur and collector, had died, leaving £35,000 to found and endow art faculties at Oxford, Cambridge and University College, London, and a further £10,000 to endow six scholarships at University College. The college had responded by giving £5,000 from its own funds and in 1871 the Slade School of Art had opened its doors to male and female students – the first Fine Art School in Europe to make its courses available to both sexes. Professor Alphonse Legros was its head, an avant-garde teacher and a respected artist who had come from Paris with a wide experience of French Impressionist painting.

Annie enrolled for classes in drawing and painting, which Professor Legros taught from the examples of Antiquity and the Old Masters. Emslie signed for the course in architecture as well. Legros' philosophy was 'Do as I do' not 'Do as I say', and he would wander among his students, encouraging them and seizing a brush to show them what he meant. Annie tried hard to follow his lead of creating a picture with a few deft strokes instead of taking hours laboriously striving for perfection, but the hardest lesson she had to learn was that she was never going to be a very good painter. Her achievements were never more than modest. Not for her the gold medal and the first prize of £5 which in her first year were carried off by Eleanor Halle, daughter of the creator of Manchester's famous orchestra. Annie managed to gain a second class certificate and so did Emslie.

She was not going to excel in her studies but there were compensations. She was one of nearly a hundred and fifty students, equally divided male and female, and for the first time in her life she was free to make her own friends. She soon found the special friend that she had wanted during her lonely years at home: Mina Bergson, a talented French girl a year ahead of Annie, and sister of the later well-known philosopher Henri. The two girls liked each other at once and soon entered into an intense romantic relationship, then fashionable among the young women artists. In these pre-Freudian days such friendships were regarded as quite normal, and many women had been brought up to consider sex as something bestial. Annie decided to have her long golden hair cropped, which prompted a fellow student to tell her that she looked like a cat from the back and to christen her 'Tabbie'. She was delighted and 'Tabbie' she became to her closest friends. She cultivated cat-like behaviour, purring when she was pleased, hissing and scratching when she was annoyed, stretching her long slim fingers like a cat unsheathing her claws. 'Tabbie' and 'Bergie' swore to be true to one another and to have nothing to do with the opposite sex.

As a student of the Slade Annie qualified for a reader's ticket at the British Museum. Her hands would never be able to create what her soul was struggling to articulate but, in the domed circular reading room, she could study the Old Masters and worship at the shrine of Art and Beauty. She could wander among the wonders of the centuries and learn about music and mysticism, astrology and Egyptology. The British Museum was a meeting place of like and unlike minds, attracting people from the many strands of London life. At one table she saw 'a pale-faced tall man with beard and hair the colour of a newly painted pillar box'.[2] Bernard Shaw was studying the score of *Tristan and Isolde* in one hand and *Das Kapital* in the other. Nearby sat the music and drama critic William Archer, translating Ibsen. In another chair sat William Ashton Ellis working on one of his books on Wagner. Florence Farr spent her days here, becoming 'erudite in many heterogeneous studies, moved by an insatiable, destroying curiosity'.[3] W.B. Yeats was researching Celtic folklore for his book on fairy stories. He sported a little beard that was soon replaced by a drooping moustache and later by a lock of hair that curled in studied negligence on to his brow. Frequently to be seen under a load of books on mysticism, symbolism and early religions was a handsome athletic figure by the name of Samuel Liddell Mathers. He confided to a passing colleague, 'I have clothed myself in hieroglyphics as with a garment.'[4]

Annie was one of these earnest searchers after life's hidden truths. They met on the steps of the Museum, gossiped in the corridors, made assignations in remote corners, met for tea and toast, at soirées and dinner parties, public meetings and concerts. In the summer of her first year at the Slade, Angelo Neumann's touring company arrived at Her Majesty's Theatre with Wagner's *The Ring*, bringing scenery from the original Bayreuth production. Wagner, nearly seventy, supervised the event. The company then moved on to the Drury Lane Theatre and, with Hans Richter conducting, gave a season of Wagner's operas. Annie and Emslie became disciples of Wagner. Their childhood spent among their father's fantastic treasures and exotic creatures had been but an overture to the supernatural world of gods, giants and mythical beings that Wagner's heroes encountered on stage.

For the next thirty years Annie was a devoted pilgrim to Bayreuth's summer festival, only missing one year. Here she found the ultimate theatrical experience, embracing art, music and drama in one world that glowed with romantic and mystical intensity. She was transported by the overwhelming music while her eyes feasted on the costumes and scenery that formed an artistic and dramatic unity. It was not just the theatre that called her back year after year. She loved the country, its sunshine, its cleanliness, its beer. Munich was perhaps her favourite city. 'If circumstances ever take you to Munich,' she once wrote to a friend, 'you will see a *clean* city with a clean river, too lively to freeze completely and a certain picturesqueness quite different from other places. I have lived there and – oh the "Bier". Don't be frightened, it is not a dangerous drink, but very refreshing!'[5]

In the little town of Bayreuth she would walk the cobbled streets, ride in carriages pulled by long-tailed Bavarian horses, visit the Master's home and gaze at his writing table and books. She sat in the cafes amid the beer and the cigars and the actors, while endless discussions went on of singers, conductors and performances. Then she would pack away her memories and carry them back to London to filter through her dreams until the next year. She became friendly with William Ashton Ellis, who was equally passionate about Wagnerian opera and was translating Wagner's *Prose Works* and several volumes of his letters. In 1888 he edited *Meister*, a new Wagner journal. Annie, fluent in German, offered to help him with his translations, which led to their going to concerts together and even holidaying together to take in more concerts.

During her student days Annie discovered the bicycle. It was the latest toy for dashing young men and emancipated young women. Annie, adventurous and fearless, chose a light-weight man's bicycle. 'Ladies' bicycles are mere hen-roosts,' she declared, 'the gears are so low that any serious travelling on them is ridiculous.'[6] She was open to ridicule and even hostility from men who objected to such flagrant acts of female defiance but she was not in the least daunted. When she got tired of such calls as 'I've seen better legs on a table' she took to wearing trousers and went on cycling. Bernard Shaw said that to ride as she did was 'monstrous and unheard of'. Perhaps he was jealous of Annie's prowess, for he had some horrifying smashes. After one of these he wrote: 'Still I am not thoroughly convinced yet that I was not killed. Anybody but a vegetarian would have been. Nobody but a teetotaller would have faced a bicycle again for six months.'[7] Annie herself had her share of cycling accidents and when Shaw first met her at a social occasion she was nursing a black eye. They travelled home together by public transport and Annie was secretly amused by what she interpreted as pitying glances from fellow-travellers who thought her black eye had been given to her by her husband at her side.

Annie's cycling was not just in and around London. She went on weekend excursions into Hampshire and Surrey, and in a few years was taking her bicycle on holidays on the Continent. Twice she cycled over the Alps, once with a friend and once alone, sending her luggage in advance to her hotel to await her arrival. On one occasion she arrived so dirty and dishevelled that she was nearly turned away by the horrified hotelier, who could not believe that she could be one of his clientele. Only on producing the key that unlocked her case was she able to prove that she was indeed Miss Horniman from London.

After two years at the Slade Emslie left to spend a year at the Académie des Beaux Arts in Antwerp. Like Annie, he was no great artist, but he learnt a great appreciation of beauty and in later life, whenever he was able to help those with more talent by a recommendation or a commission, he did so. At the Académie, Vincent van Gogh was a fellow-student, ill at ease with the other students, having nothing in common with them, set apart by his genius. Many years later Emslie told his nephew William Plomer how van Gogh 'worked very rapidly in charcoal, looking steadfastly at the plaster cast of an antique figure and then at a great pace making a strong black drawing of, say, a landscape with peasant figures in a storm . . . We thought him mad and were in awe of him.'[8]

Annie missed Emslie's companionship at home and for the first time she was really alone apart from her new friends. While he was abroad, she took a year off from her art studies. This was quite common for students to do, some of them needing to earn money for the next year's fees. Finance, however, was no problem for Annie and there are no clues as to what she did in this year. But she was back at The Slade for the start of the autumn term in 1886 and before the term was over Emslie, not yet twenty-three, had returned home to marry.

His bride was Laura Plomer, a high-spirited, attractive young woman, daughter of a colonel with conventional views. When Emslie first brought her to Surrey Mount, she and Annie became friends, but the step from friend to sister-in-law was too large for Annie's liking. Neither did Laura's parents approve of the idea of the marriage. They had tried hard to discourage the relationship between their daughter and the handsome young man who professed to be an artist, an aesthete and an atheist. Mrs Plomer, whose husband had reached the rank of colonel in the Indian Army before they retired home to England, had every intention that her lovely daughter should make a good match, which meant marrying into a higher social class as well as money. Emslie might be very wealthy but his money had been made in trade. Parental disapproval only intensified Laura's love. On 16 November 1886 Emslie married Laura despite Colonel Plomer's threat to disown his daughter. Mrs Plomer showed her disapproval by giving her daughter only one of everything for her bottom drawer, rather than the customary two, leaving Mrs Horniman to provide the second of the pair. Emslie gave his profession as artist on his marriage certificate but his time was running out. He was assuming the responsibilities of a married man and from now on he would follow the path mapped out by his father – tea merchant and traveller, collector and connoisseur, philanthropist and politician.

Annie was losing a brother and fellow-artist, and perhaps her disapproval of the marriage was because she thought he was giving up too much too soon. However, she kept her feelings to herself on the wedding day, when, looking like an Arcadian shepherdess in a gown designed by Emslie from a William Morris brocade – rich crimson and gold with green leaves over a satin petticoat, the bodice and sleeves trimmed with flounces of Flanders lace and an antique clasp at her waist – she almost outshone the bride. Laura now became the main influence in Emslie's life and as the years went by she and Annie grew increasingly less friendly to the point of enmity. There is a family story that they once sat side by side in a theatre and refused to acknowledge each other. This may be apocryphal, but in a letter that Annie wrote when she was in her seventies she is bitingly critical of her sister-in-law: 'she has *no* imagination at all, on the other hand she has a more ruthless power of getting her own way than a clever (more intellectual) woman would *dare* to use.'[9]

Another event in 1886, though of less immediate importance than the wedding, also had an effect on Annie's home life. In May people flocked to the Albert Hall to gaze at the wonders of the Colonial and Indian Exhibition, sponsored by a number of wealthy travellers with business acumen, among them Annie's father. At the close of the exhibition Frederick Horniman took the advantage to buy a number of exhibits to add to his own collection, which was becoming well known in his locality. Perhaps inspired by the success of the Colonial and Indian, he decided to have his own exhibition and invited all the local dignitaries to tour his treasures. This was a prelude to inviting interested parties (up to thirty in number) to visit his home to view his exhibits, as long as it was by prior arrangement.

Frederick's private dream was gradually turning into a public pleasure. Over the next two years he worked on preparing his displays so that any number of people would be able to wander freely through his exhibits. On Boxing Day 1889, Surrey House Museum was declared open to the people of London, free of charge from 10 a.m. to 9 p.m. – and again on Friday and Saturday. It could never be just the family home again. The next year the Horniman Free Museum opened every Monday, Wednesday and Saturday. Frederick Horniman's idea was to bring science and art to the common people and from the numbers who responded he was giving them what they wanted – they could have a day out and go home happier and wiser. There was even a live monkey called Nellie and two bears, Alice and Jumbo, to entertain the children. On the first Boxing Day opening in 1889 nearly two thousand people came to see Mr Horniman's exhibits. The *Forest Hill News* sent along a reporter and gave him a whole column, every inch of which was needed to describe all that he saw as he wandered up and down stairs, in and out of rooms, peering into showcases and display cabinets. He was particularly impressed by an automatic organ. 'Suddenly there boomed out what I at first thought was the music of a complete orchestra, but afterwards found was a wonderful automatic organ which was stated to contain 352 metal and wood pipes and 78 brass instruments, besides drums, cymbals, and other adjuncts.'[10] The list of treasures was endless, from a four-poster bedstead 'of hearse-like proportions and suggestive of any amount of nightmares' to a fine stuffed lion from South Africa which might have had the same effect as the bed . . . and every year Annie's father added more so that in 1893 an extension had to be built.

If back in 1886 Frederick Horniman had discussed his plans with his family, Emslie and Annie would doubtless have encouraged them, praising his foresight and generosity. Meanwhile Annie carried on with her art studies at the Slade until the summer of 1888 and as these came to an end another absorbing interest began to take over. Her dear friend Bergie had met one of the earnest

British Museum habituées and introduced him to Tabbie as 'an interesting man whom she did *not* want to marry'. Samuel Liddell Mathers was a natural leader with a magnetic personality that attracted many young romantics in search of life's secrets. Tabbie, Bergie, W.B. Yeats and Florence Farr were some of the first to fall under his spell. When Yeats first met him in the reading room he saw 'a man of thirty-six or thirty-seven, in a brown velveteen coat, with a gaunt resolute face and an athletic body . . . his studies were two only – magic and the theory of war'.[11] As well as writing and publishing books on these subjects, he was a physical fitness fanatic, boxing and fencing nightly to keep his body at such a pitch of vitality that it would never fall prey to illness or weakness. He was a Rosicrucian and a Freemason, and was now immersing himself in mysticism and symbolism, Eastern, Egyptian and Christian religion, and occult rituals.

In the London of the 1880s mysticism was being taken up by the young and enquiring. A. P. Sinnett's books, *The Occult World* and *Esoteric Buddhism*, were immensely popular and occult groups were forming, splintering and re-forming, as one mystical philosophy faded or melted into another. There was a Theosophical Society, founded by Madame Blavatsky, a Rosicrucian Society, a Hermetic Society, a Society for Psychical Research and, the most exclusive and secret of them all, the Hermetic Order of the Golden Dawn, which came into existence on 1 March 1888. It was introduced by Mathers (who had dropped his other two names and adopted MacGregor in memory of his Scottish ancestors) after he had decided not to take up Madame Blavatsky's invitation to join her society but but to create his own with the help of two of his Rosicrucian brothers.

The Russian-born Madame Blavatsky had arrived in London from India to try to regain her reputation after being denounced by the Society for Psychical Research as 'one of the most accomplished, ingenious and interesting imposters of history'. She claimed to have received wisdom and knowledge from Mahatmas under whom she had studied in Tibet and India, and had written *Isis Unveiled* and *The Secret Doctrine* to explain these mysteries. She was fifty-six, weighed seventeen stone, and smoked hashish and numerous cigarettes, which she rolled herself from very strong tobacco. She favoured hashish, believing that under its influence previous existences could be recollected and profound mysteries plumbed. On the other hand, 'sex,' she declared – after one real and two bigamous marriages – 'is a beastly appetite that should be starved into submission'.[12]

G. K. Chesterton thought her 'a coarse, witty, vigorous, scandalous old scallywag', while to Yeats she was 'a sort of female Dr Johnson' with an imagination that 'contained all the folk-lore of the world'. He liked her gaiety and humour, finding an evening at her home good entertainment.

Annie knew about the multifarious groups all seeking salvation through occult knowledge but Madame Blavatsky's particular blend of theosophy did not appeal to her. She was closely involved with the setting up of the Golden Dawn, although at the very beginning she watched from the sidelines as rituals and rules were created and examinations and instructions were written. Bergie drew the occult symbols on the Golden Dawn Charter while Mathers worked on the authoritative antecedents that would give respectability and credence to his new Order. It was a hierarchical society with all members starting at the lowest grade and working their way up by dint of serious study. Secret loyalties gave the members a status and importance, and the society attracted a lot of women, who were often denied these qualities in the real world.

By Christmas 1889 Annie was in her thirtieth year and wanted desperately to have a worthwhile role in life. She was flattered to be asked to be a candiate for serious occult study, feeling that Mathers must have detected rather special qualities in her. She had been going through a painful time and Bergie, with Mathers' help, had been particularly kind and considerate, which she gave as her reason for joining the Golden Dawn. Her initiation ceremony took place at Bergie's studio in Fitzroy Street in January 1890. Annie described the rituals as a necessary discipline that treated each new neophyte exactly alike. Every member took on a new name, signifying a casting off of the old worldly persona and an act of rebirth, and Annie chose Fortiter et Recte (Bravely and Justly). She was welcomed with the words, 'Child of Earth, long hast thou dwelt in darkness. Quit the night and seek the day.'[13] She entered into the first grade of the Order and at once poured all her energies into this new commitment. One of her favourite Biblical verses was Ecclesiastes, 9, verse 10: 'Whatever your hand finds to do, do it with all your might'. It was not long before she was one of the most learned and experienced of all the members of the Golden Dawn.

Mathers had taken as his motto Deo Duce Comite Ferro (With God as my leader and the sword as my companion) and Bergie became Vestigia Nulla Retrorsum (No trace left behind). It was the custom to use the initials or the first word of these names to address each other, so Mathers, for example, became DDCF and Annie Fortiter. Two months after Annie had joined, Yeats was initiated, taking the motto Demon est Deus Inversus (The devil is the converse of God). He described the rituals as beautiful and profound, not unlike those in Masonry. In June he brought along Florence Farr, who chose to be named Sapientia Sapienti Dono Data (Wisdom is given to the wise as a gift).

It was at this time that Bergie married Mathers and Annie found him a job as caretaker at her father's museum. A house went with the job, and there they were able to meet to further their occult activities under Mathers' guidance. Yeats later recalled that his house was 'on the edge of some kind of garden or park belonging to an eccentric rich man, whose curiosities he arranged and dusted'.[14] DDCF taught them how to harness their imagination and will power so that they could experience a different plane of reality. The idea was to concentrate exclusively on a symbol until it was transformed into a vast door through which one could pass and the vision could unfold. There were five Mother-symbols of Fire, Earth, Water, Air and Spirit used to summon their visions. 'Believe thyself there and thou art there' was an old proverb that they earnestly believed.

In December 1891 Fortiter was the first to be initiated into a new higher Order created by DDCF for advanced students who in his opinion were ready for instruction in ritual magic. He gave the new group the impressive title of Ordo Rosae Rubeae et Aureae Crucis, which, as with most of their titles, was known to them by its initials. Strict secrecy was impressed on all the advanced students. The ability to be silent and to be discreet were qualities that Fortiter thought particularly important, showing a seriousness of purpose. Any questions were to be answered thus: 'If you belonged to the second Order, you would know what you ask me; if you do not know, you do not belong – and if I did know, I could no more tell you than a $1=10$ can tell anything about it to a $0=0$.'

($1=10$ and $0=0$ were the highest and lowest grades in the Golden Dawn.)[15]

On 1 December Annie had written from her home at Surrey Mount a formal application for entry into the Order of R. R. et A. C.

> Care et G. H. Frater
>
> I have already passed through the Grades of the First Order & in addition there has been conferred on me the Grade of Lady of the Paths in the Portal of the Vault of the adepts. I now write to ask that I may be admitted to a full participation in the Mysteries of the Grade of Adeptus Minor.
>
> I have received so much hope and satisfaction from the knowledge which has been given me that I am most anxious to be allowed to go on when it is considered fit for me. I hope to be able in the future to be of more service in the society as well as to gain personally in Strength and Knowledge. Hoping that my sincere request may be granted.
>
> Yours fraternally,
soror 'Fortiter et Recte' 5–6
s.u.a.t.[16]
>
> [s. u. a. t. Stood for 'sub umbra alarum tuarum
Jehovah', meaning 'under the shadow of thy wings
Jehovah'.]

Annie's initiation went through increasingly complex ritualistic procedures revolving around the symbols of the red rose and the golden cross. The bizarre climax was the submission of the candidate within a seven-sided vault painted with Egyptian and Eastern symbols set in rectangles. Drawing on all his Masonic and Hermetic lore, DDCF had created a tomb 'symbolically situated in the Centre of the Earth, in the Mountain of the Caverns, the Mystic Mountain of Abiegnus'. It could have come straight off a Wagnerian set to the rather dirty, noisy and cheaply rented room at Thavies Inn off Holborn Circus where the order's meetings were held after DDCF and Vestigia had moved from the lodge at Surrey Mount.

There were good practical reasons for giving Fortiter the honour of being first inside the Rose and Crown vault, apart from her talents for magical practices. Her ability to read horoscopes, understand the messages of the tarot cards and project her mind on to the astral plane was not unique, but she had the bonus of wealth and a generous nature. DDCF had not lasted long in his caretaker's job, which left him and Vestigia without a home, and it was Fortiter who helped them to find lodgings and gave them money for rent and living expenses. It is uncertain whose idea was Paris but it obviously suited the married pair: DDCF had contacts there for his occult business, while Vestigia could take up her art studies again. Fortiter persuaded her to do this and to count on her dear Tabbie for financial support, but first they would take a holiday together in Venice, all expenses paid by Fortiter.

By September 1892 the Mathers had set up home in Paris. 'I arranged with them both to give them £200 a year so that they should be able to study and work for the Order.' Back in London Fortiter was one of a handful of senior officials at their new meeting rooms, up a back-street off Great Portland Street but with the grand title of the Isis-Urania Lodge. They could boast a membership of over a hundred. Fortiter was their Sub-Praemonstrator, directly responsible to their Chief, DDCF, and she held the post for four years before handing over to her close friend Helen Rand, who was known in the Golden Dawn as Vigilate (Be Watchful). Florence Farr – Sapientia – was another of the order's important officials, taking over as Praemonstrator of the London Lodge in 1893, and in January of that year Yeats – DEDI – also joined this senior Order. London was the head of activities and remained so but there were lodges set up in Weston-super-Mare, Bradford, Edinburgh and soon in Paris. DDCF managed to commute between Paris and London but he had to delegate some responsibilities for the provincial lodges. Fortiter was appointed as his ambassador to the Horus Temple at Bradford to adjudicate over a disciplinary matter and report back. Her place of special privilege was marked by an invitation to consecrate the new temple in Paris in January 1894, a temple that her money had more than likely helped furnish.[17]

Annie's loyalty to her Supreme Chief was absolute but her loyalty to him as a private individual was not so intact. She was aware of extravagances in his nature, of which she was particularly sensitive because she was paying for them. She called these extravagances 'MacGregor Foolishness' and she was not the only one to notice them. When Yeats stayed with the Mathers in Paris he noted: 'At night he would dress himself in Highland dress, and dance the sword dress, and his mind brooded upon the ramifications of clans and tartans . . . I think that he lived under some great strain, and presently I noted that he was drinking too much neat brandy, though not to drunkenness.' Mathers was fantasising over a 'Napoleonic role for himself, a Europe transformed according to his fancy, Egypt restored, a Highland Principality'.[18] Annie was growing uneasy over these Parisian political activities with revolutionary elements but felt unable to speak out openly about Mathers' behaviour because she was subsidising his life style and any criticism was taken to mean that she grudged the money. She was not happy about his position of moral and spiritual authority over her in the Order and she resolved that, despite her oath of allegiance, she would make her own decisions on magical practices in the future. At the same time she would keep her eyes open to the uses made of her money and be on her guard against Bergie's effusive letters of friendship. Time would tell on whom she could trust.

4

The Years of Mystery, 1893–1903

The exact date that Annie left home and set up on her own is unknown, but she had established her own pattern of independence from the time that she went off to become an art student in 1882. She had her own rooms at Surrey Mount where she could entertain her friends with a remarkable degree of freedom for the late Victorian years, and she spent more and more time away from home, travelling around Europe – France, Germany, Italy, Holland, Norway. Only the occasional letter remains to tell where she went.

In the summer of 1893, while at Trondheim in western Norway, she wrote a document for the Golden Dawn on the way that the Order's students progressed through the various grades towards the true enlightenment. She wanted to help and encourage those who were finding the rules and rituals difficult or incomprehensible and, no doubt drawing on her own experiences, she told the initiates that they must be very determined to pursue this chosen path: usually 'the necessity of overcoming opposition at the outset is a test in itself which shows individuality and fixity of purpose'. Perhaps she was recalling her parents' frank disapproval of their only daughter joining an Order to delve into mysticism and search deliberately for supernatural visions. J. B. Yeats certainly tried hard to wean his son from his love of magic, describing William's mysticism as 'a rank vegetation destroying the vital principle', quite unlike the visions of his psychic daughter Lily which came to her without her looking for them. Annie believed that difficulties along the way had only spurred her on to greater efforts. 'The uncongenial spiritual surroundings in which most of us are obliged to live out our lives have their uses,' she told her young adepts.[1]

Why she was in Trondheim in 1893 is a mystery. She may have been on holiday and her choice of the medieval city may well have been connected with her close friendship with Clement Oswald Skilbeck. Five years younger than Annie, he was an artist of the Pre-Raphaelite school, a friend of William Morris and Burne-Jones, and particularly interested in medieval ecclesiastical art, stained glass and the peasant crafts and customs of Western Norway. How or when he met Annie is another mystery, as is their relationship, but his significance in her life is evident from her will, which she made in 1932. On her death in 1937 he would benefit by about £30,000, the residue of her estate after various bequests. He was the main beneficiary, yet there is no mention of him in any of the letters that remain. Annie learnt well the Golden Dawn discipline of secrecy.

The year 1894 was that of the Avenue Theatre project, which in retrospect was an important landmark in Annie's life, although at the time she was just as concerned with her magical revelations as her theatrical hopes. She was now one of the five top officials in the Isis-Urania Lodge of the Hermetic Order of the Golden Dawn. There was a further landmark the next year, on 14 February 1895, when Annie's mother died. She was seventy and had only been ill for three weeks with what was described as a spinal complaint. Annie's father was away from home on one of his customary travels, this time to Ceylon and Egypt. A telegram was sent to Aden as soon as there seemed to be cause for alarm, but he reached home too late. By the time that he arrived at Surrey Mount, his wife was dead and the funeral arrangements were in hand. Annie was thirty-five.

After her mother's death, her father went into politics, accepting an invitation to stand as Liberal MP for Falmouth in Cornwall, and he spent even less time at the home which he had made into a museum. In June he opened his lovely grounds at Surrey Mount for the enjoyment of the people who came three days a week to look at his exhibits. His new life took him increasingly to the West Country, where his ancestors had lived and which he knew well. He had often gone there to visit Sir Richard Burton's private collection, buying from him exhibits to add to his own collection. According to a family story, he loved rice pudding, insisting on eating a bowl a day, and on his many trips from London to Falmouth he would take with him in a hay-box enough rice pudding to last the journey. Perhaps this was what gave him the vitality to become Liberal Member of Parliament for Falmouth for the first time at the age of sixty and to hold the seat for the next ten years.

With father and brother busily engaged in their own pursuits, Annie was able to devote her energies even more to the Golden Dawn. She had time and money to spare and was continuing to fund the Mathers in their Parisian flat. In July 1895 they asked for £100 to entertain important visitors, whom Annie took to be occultists. When she visited them in September, however, she found that the guests had been a duke and his hangers-on and that money was again in short supply. It was not surprising, for there was a constant stream of visitors from England, but when she returned to London Annie was troubled and letters of friendship from dearest Bergie did not soothe or placate her.

Nor was money the only worry. There were also Mathers' strange political posturings and she was now concerned too about the way that some of the rituals were being turned into sexual activities. It was a small step from mental and spiritual union to bodily union and as long as pure and honourable thoughts were behind the actions, the Higher Authorities seemed satisfied. Fortiter was not. When she objected to what was called 'Elemental Marriage' she was told that all that was disgusting and obscene was in her own mind. She was at fault for not leaving her worldly self outside the Order. 'If, on the contrary, you are not "Miss Horniman" but an initiate striving after Light, the Evil Persona cannot arise,' Mathers wrote to her, and suggested that on all matters of sex she should refer to his greater wisdom and understanding. Bergie wrote letters of loving chastisement: 'As to exaggeration in you, you distinctly have a fad as regards sexual subjects.' She reminded dear Fortiter that she and her husband had 'always kept perfectly clean . . . as regards the human, the elemental and any other thing whatever'. She urged her to trust in her Chief who was becoming increasingly annoyed with Fortiter for sowing seeds of rebellion against his authority.[2]

Restlessness in the Order grew over the next twelve months, with Fortiter as the prime mover. In September 1896 she resigned from her office as Sub-Praemonstrator and stopped all further payments to Paris. She decided that she would no longer accept Mathers's authority on what was moral and decent when she

believed that her self-respect was threatened. Mathers strove to
keep control of the London Lodge with long letters from Paris
condemning 'intolerance, intermeddling and malicious self-
conceit'. He thundered: 'Of what use are the Second Order Centres
if they are not places where the Gods and Angelic Forces are
involved in Spirit and Truth and where Mystic Powers have their
abode, and where petty social gossip can find no place.' Fortiter,
however, would not bow the knee to his authority any longer and
when she also ignored Bergie's plea for more money, he snapped
into action. On 19 December 1896 Annie was expelled from the
Order, accused of 'intense arrogance, narrowness of judgement and
self-conceit'. She was told that her behaviour had been below
standard and that she was unable to leave her worldly persona
behind when she entered into her mystical exercises so that she was
putting her own impure interpretations on others' actions.[3]

In February 1897, almost exactly two years after the death of her
mother, her father remarried. He was sixty-one and his new bride
was twenty-one and beautiful. Annie was appalled. She was in
Florence when news of the wedding reached her and she made no
attempt to return home for the celebrations; neither did she send a
present. There seemed to be indecent haste about the marriage. At
the wedding reception even the groom's best friend who proposed
the health of the newly weds made the point that a week had not
elapsed since he had first been introduced to the bride so he was
unable to speak of her many good qualities which he felt sure from
her appearance she must possess. If he had known that she were
pregnant, he might have chosen other words to express his
sentiments. Whatever Emslie and Laura thought privately about
the marriage, they gave it their public support – their daughter was
a bridesmaid and their son helped to cut the wedding cake.

The next year, in May 1898, Annie's old home was pulled down
to make way for a striking new building to house the Horniman
Museum and in November the foundation stone was laid by the
new Mrs Horniman. There were two large halls at different levels
to take account of the hill slope and they were linked inside by a
wide staircase. Across the facade Robert Anning-Bell designed a
decorative mosaic panel which depicted, in larger than life-size
allegorical figures, man's progress through life, dependent on the
circumstances of his birth, his education and his environment,

against a background of the eternal truths. Inside the two halls many of Annie's father's exhibits were displayed in mahogany-lined bays and showcases. The work was reputed to have cost Mr Horniman £40,000 and when it was completed he offered the Museum to the people of London as a free gift for ever. Emslie was in charge of all the necessary formalities and in February 1901 London County Council unanimously accepted the offer on behalf of the people of London. They received the Museum, a library of over five thousand volumes of travel, natural history and science, and a Biblical library of seven hundred volumes that included many early and rare editions, along with nine acres of grounds which included a bandstand where a band played on Sundays and a pond where children could sail their boats. There were six other residences, set in a further five acres of ground, which were let and the income from which helped towards the upkeep of the Museum – a very necessary provision, for over a fourteen-month period in 1897 and 1898 alone, two hundred thousand people had visited the Museum.

Perhaps it was on her father's remarriage that Annie set up a home of her own. She found an apartment in Portman Square, in central London, conveniently placed for theatres and railway stations but not so convenient for her bicycle, which was not allowed in the lift so she had to carry it up three flights of stairs. She furnished her one and only home, which she kept for the rest of her life, in simple taste, choosing large, comfortable armchairs and a few good pictures and sculptures. She loved Rossetti's works, the intensity of his form and colour, and chose one drawing and one painting by him to hang on her myrtle-green walls. The painting 'Jolie Coeur' is of a sensual red-haired beauty in an unbuttoned chemise, one hand folded round her necklace with its opal heart pointing invitingly downwards. Annie's one extravagance was books, which spilled off tables and over carpets, and were piled high on her chairs. Stepping over and round them on to the plump cushions were her only companions, two tabby cats.

Her taste was very different from that of Emslie and Laura, who had asked Charles Annesley Voysey to design their first home. 'Garden Corner', next to the Physic Garden on the Chelsea Embankment, was a light, airy house with natural oak panelling

and plain soft carpets, and colourful wallpapers of birds and trees
that seemed to bring sunshine right inside the rooms. Their nephew
William Plomer stayed there many times and described the drawing-room with its 'row of softly coloured flower paintings let into a
high dado of dove-grey slate. In every room could be found writing-
paper die-stamped in black or green mannered lettering to match
that on the front door and in the lift.' Their second home in
Hampshire, also designed by Voysey, he found:

> equally beguiling, and seemed even more idiosyncratic,
> partly because everything was either very high or very
> low. The roof came down steeply, almost to the ground;
> the casement windows were wide and low, the window
> seats very low; but the latches on the doors were so high
> that to open them one had to make the gesture of
> someone proposing a toast to the architect. High-backed
> chairs, like those at Chelsea, were pierced with heart-
> shaped openings, and on high shelves near the ceiling
> stood vases of crafty green pottery filled with peacock's
> feathers in defiance of the superstition that they
> shouldn't be brought indoors. Coal scuttles, hotwater
> cans, and electroliers were made of beaten or hammered
> brass or copper.[4]

Annie never visited these homes. She broke off communications
with Emslie and Laura because they had supported her father's
remarriage. She did not believe in half-measures. If you were not
with her, you must be against her. She never spoke to her father
again after his second marriage, although she once called at his
London home in Hyde Park Terrace when she heard that he was
ill, sending her driver in to enquire after his health while she
remained in the taxi outside. When her father died nine years later
Emslie wrote her a kindly letter:

> My dear Annie
> Our father died I believe peacefully at 3.50 this
> morning. I saw him in Friday evening and Sat.
> afternoon . . . I did not think his state serious – so
> Laura and I went to our cottage at Frensham on Sunday

. . . by his will the ashes are to be buried in the grave at Honor Oak . . .

Your affectionate brother,
Emslie J. Horniman[5]

Annie's reply was polite but formal. She sent no love or warm regards, signing her short letter, 'Yours sincerely, A. E. F. Horniman'. She could not forget and she could not forgive. One of her close friends who knew her strengths and her weaknesses wrote: 'When anyone fell below her standard of right and wrong, she definitely quarrelled with them and closed the book as far as they were concerned.' Annie had closed the book on her family.

By 1897 she was out of the Golden Dawn but her interest in all things magical remained as strong as ever. She met regularly with a group of occult friends at her home or theirs. Yeats, now in his early thirties and conscious of his chosen role as a poet and prophet, made detailed notes of all his visions and kept all his documents for posterity. There are hundreds of notebooks and records, some in Annie's handwriting, some typed by her. Their practices and beliefs were secret and never to be told but Yeats published an essay on magic in 1901, admitting that he was a little uneasy about some of his revelations. 'Yet I must write or be of no account to any cause good or evil.' His essay opens with his creed, in which Annie wholeheartedly shared: 'I believe in the practice and philosophy of what we have agreed to call magic, in what I must call the evocation of spirits, though I do not know what they are, in the power of creating magical illusions, in the visions of truth in the depths of the mind when the eyes are closed . . .' He goes on to describe events 'too private or too sacred for public speech' when an individual imagination or the shared group imagination moved by its own will through space or time.[6]

He kept a record of Annie's 'Remembrances', a journey that she made through the visionary door into a different time dimension to meet characters from past centuries. In his essay on magic he writes of a similar vision in time, as a meeting with a Fleming of the sixteenth century. Between September and December 1898 Annie entered into a series of visions with an occult friend called Frederick Leigh Gardner who had taken the name De Profundis Ad Lucem (from the deep into light) and was known as DPAL. It was considered important to make detailed notes after every experiment and, under her occult initials of FER, Annie recorded as much information as she could of these astral journeys, of the inhabitants, plants, animals and minerals on the planets they visited, the extent of a particular planet's influence on man and the rest of the universe.

First she explained how, by chanting a form of words and by concentrating on a visual symbol, she put herself into a state whereby her unconscious took over from the physical body and moved freely in space. Yeats described the very similar ritual used by Mathers: 'He held a wooden mace in his hand, and turning to a tablet of many-coloured squares, with a number on each of the squares, that stood near him on a chair he repeated a form of words. Almost at once my imagination began to move of itself and to bring before me vivid images that, though never too vivid to be imagination, as I had always understood it, had yet a motion of their own, a life I could not change or shape.'[7] Once through the visionary door, FER and DPAL were met by a guide who flew with them through space to their destined planet. Sometimes they were left alone once they had alighted, sometimes they were escorted across the unfamiliar terrain and were able to question their guide.

On Jupiter she and her companion travelled to the Holy Mountain and were rowed in a wooden boat to the Temple. As they wandered through it, she was able to observe the marble pillars and the richly coloured walls inlaid with enamel. In this peaceful country there was no sickness or disease. FER felt secure and her woman guide told her that this was because of the strength of the planet in her horoscope.

On Mercury, which they reached in bright yellow radiance, they alighted in a market place where the inhabitants were dressed in tunics like ancient Greeks. They saw bushes with berries like yellow strawberries that reminded FER of berries she had seen in Norway. This too was a pleasant land where science, art and knowledge were valued. They were able to talk to the inhabitants, but it was not always so. On Mars they were invisible and were told to cover themselves with a white substance to prevent detection. First they had alighted in a volcanic area but did not stay here. They flew on over vineyards. The land was divided into small warring kingdoms that reminded FER of thirteenth-century Italy. Men fought for the love of it and she was glad when it was time to leave.

The journey to Mercury had not been easy for there had been strong wind resistance but the journey to the Sun was a great strain. They could only achieve it by losing their individuality into a flame of white light. The Sun was on a higher plane than ever before and as they travelled to it they became aware of a cross stretching across the sky. They too were hung on crosses; everywhere was lightness and brightness. How different was their travel to and on Venus on green leaf-like rays. They crossed a lake by sail-boat. The seasons were gentle and the countryside was green and fertile. There was little difference between soul and body. Time and space were acknowledged but of a different scale from on Earth.

Annie must have entered into many visions with her occult friends over a period of years. The very few remaining records of hers are written in a language that mixes factual description of normal travel with religious images of light, paths, doors and gates. It was in many ways a spiritual quest and at the same time a creative act of the imagination shared by all creative artists. 'Have not poetry and music risen, as it seems, out of the sounds the enchanters made to help their imagination to enchant, to charm, to bind with a spell themselves and the passers-by?' Yeats wrote in his essay.[8]

However, when Annie and her friends stepped down from their higher plane, they became immersed in petty squabbles, bickering, back-biting and blackening of character. Annie had been fighting for four years to get back into the Golden Dawn. Frederick Leigh Gardner had gathered signatures on a petition to reinstate her. Yeats was anxious to help and wrote that he would go a long way to do anything for Fortiter as long as it met with her approval. In March 1900 one of Mathers' most dedicated followers arrived in London from Paris with an occult sister (who was also his mistress). Aleister Crowley, known in the Golden Dawn as Perdurabo (I will last through) was determined to take over the London Lodge and introduce more severe tests for the initiates. Everyone would wear masks so that no one would know the identity of anyone. He broke into the committee rooms, which were now over a shop in Blythe

Road, and only left after Florence Farr arrived on the scene and called a policeman. Yeats, wearing his occult mantle of DEDI, took charge and arranged for new locks to be put on the doors. The next day the scene at Blythe Road was farcical. Perdurabo arrived in Highland dress, a black mask and a tartan thrown over his shoulders, an enormous golden cross on his breast and a dagger at his side. DEDI met him and barred his way. This time Perdurabo called a policeman but he was not allowed in. He left, threatening legal action.

A General Meeting was urgently called, with DEDI taking control as Imperator and Fortiter at his side as Scribe. It had been learnt that the Order of the Golden Dawn had been founded on forged documents and fraudulent claims. Mathers, their Supreme Chief, was a fraud. In April 1900 he was ousted from his own Order. 'I arraigned Mathers on Saturday last before a chapter of the Order. I was carefully polite and I am particularly pleased at the fact that in our correspondence and meetings not one word has been written or said which forgot the past and the honour that one owes even to a fallen idol,' DEDI wrote on 25 April.[9] For a brief while Yeats took over complete responsibility. For three nights he said that he only had four and a half hours sleep. He could not possibly keep going at such a pace and besides, he was busy with other, mainly Irish, activities. It was time for Annie to stage her comeback. On 26 April she wrote a formal letter 'To the Governing Body'

> C. et V. H. Fratres & Sorores,
>
> I wish to apply to you for my reinstatement into my old position in the Order. I have always kept all my Obligations & I have always maintained that my expulsion was illegal. Vale, s. u. a. t.
>
> Fortiter et Recte 5=6 T. A. M.[10]

It was a great happiness to be back but first she had to deal with an adept who was threatening to expose Mr Horniman's daughter as a dabbler in magic. Annie asked her solicitor to write an official warning to shut him up. 'I only want to frighten him. He has a terror of publicity & I have nothing in my life of which I am ashamed . . . He must be made to understand that such libellous statements about me must stop. He would look very foolish when asked to publicly explain what "magic" means'[11] Then she set out to make 'a perfectly honest order, with no false mystery and no mystagogues of any kind'[12] of which DEDI would approve. There were wearisome details of organisation and administration that had been allowed to lapse and Annie was just the meticulous person to set the records straight. 'Our Scribe's sense of law is almost too great,' DEDI commented, and he was not surprised when she took to task the unmethodical Florence Farr who as Sapientia was now the Moderator in the new Order and who had been in charge of keeping the records up to date. Sapientia had also formed her own secret group for magic and meditation, and had encouraged others to do the same. DEDI and Fortiter were in firm agreement that these secret groups must be disbanded, for inner loyalties led to outer suspicions.

Annie's obsession with accuracy made her increasingly unpopular with the adepts, who accused her of 'everlasting fact-finding', 'an extraordinary attitude of suspicion' and 'having a warped mind'. Her 'Demon' had warned her 'that in every society or movement that succeeds there is some person that is built into it, as in old times a sacrificial victim was built alive into the foundations of a bridge'.[13] He was well aware, in giving such a warning, that Fortiter would work with zealous energy with no thought for herself. One member described her as 'an irate whale' that should be allowed to blow but otherwise not heeded. It was, however, difficult to ignore her constant criticisms. At a council meeting in February 1901 she and her DEDI found themselves isolated. They were outvoted on the matter of secret groups and Fortiter was accused of absurdly persecuting other members. DEDI, like a knight of old in shining armour, tried hard to defend her honour. He called upon her accuser, 'who has never past an examination in the Second Order, who has not even consecrated his implements', to resign his official position as Sub-Imperator until he had apologised to the Scribe. But Fortiter's accuser was an old enemy; he had once circulated a piece of doggerel against her that had deeply wounded her:

> Oh! F. E. R. you should not let
> Your angry passions rise.

> Your feline claws were never meant
> To scratch a Frater's eyes.[14]

Yeats had only one word to describe the meeting – chaos. Both he and Annie resigned from their official positions and he made his final flourish with an essay entitled, 'Is the Order of R. R. & A. C. to remain a Magical Order?' It ended with a plea not to leave undone the work which had been set before them, work 'of incalculable importance in the change of thought that is coming upon the world . . . because the creed of the triflers is being cried into our ears'. He signed it with his occult initials, DEDI, 'In the Mountains of Abiegnos' – the holiest of holies in their rituals, within the seven-sided vault. Yeats saw himself as the prophet who had received the tablets of wisdom for his people, but the people chose to ignore them.

Annie did not give up a fight easily. For two more years she battled against the secret groups who, she believed, by their careless practices had let loose magical presences harmful to the Order. She saw herself as the only one who could perform the ritualistic banishing ceremony and she campaigned tirelessly for a public ceremony to be performed before all the members. They grew ever more weary of her demands. Annie, who often complained that others had no sense of humour, seemed to have lost her own at a time when it was badly needed. At last, after irritating Florence Farr beyond measure and losing for a while her friendship with Helen Rand, she admitted defeat. But before she reached this point the Order had been shaken by a public scandal that led to the resignation of twenty senior members. In September 1901 a couple who went by the bogus name of Mr and Mrs Horus were arrested and tried for the rape of a sixteen-year-old during so-called initiation rites. At the trial at the Old Bailey they were found guilty and sentenced to fifteen years and seven years respectively.

Annie's time-wasting personal crusade to save the Golden Dawn was based on her belief that she was receiving authority from a Greater Being known as the Purple Adept. In the power struggle going on at the top, she was making a bid to be the new Chief, but by February 1903 she was weary of it all. Sapientia had resigned long ago and DEDI was no longer actively involved, and Fortiter finally handed in her resignation and turned to other means of salvation. Her Demon had been burying himself in Celtic mysteries for a number of years and she had been helping him in his work to create new rituals based on the symbols and dramatic ceremonies of the Golden Dawn literature. Yeats constantly suffered from bad eyesight, forcing him to lay aside his reading and writing. Annie had been working as his unpaid secretary for about ten years, writing his letters, documents and manuscripts. Her knowledge and experience of occult matters were equal to his and she was a useful editor and commentator. A young friend described how Yeats would

> burst into the flat, disturb Tabbie at her own task and dictate his inspiration with no thought for her strength. Over and over he mulled over what he had composed, and over and over she would rewrite it until she dropped from exhaustion. When he had tired himself out, he would gather up the papers with barely a word of thanks. More likely he would issue instructions for her to be at his beck and call next day to finish off the poem he was working on.

It was little wonder that her friend thought Tabbie was treated 'unmercifully'.[15]

There were two other feminine minds at work on the Celtic mysteries, helping Yeats in their different ways and with differing ulterior motives. Lady Augusta Gregory had entered his life in 1896 and had recognised at once her need in him, 'foreseeing that he would help her out of conventions and prejudices, and give her wings to soar in the free air of ideas and instincts'.[16] Yeats had seen only 'a plainly dressed woman of forty-five, without obvious good looks, except the charm that comes from strength, intelligence and kindness'.[17] Lady Gregory was thirteen years his senior, nearly eight years older than Annie, and had been a widow for four years. Sir William Gregory had been Member of Parliament for Galway and Governor of Ceylon when in 1890, aged sixty-three and a widower he had married twenty-seven-year-old Augusta. Their marriage produced one son. On his death she took to mourning dress and ever afterwards made a virtue of her widowhood, using it as a protective cloak to take her freely into male society. Her bold approach and persuasive tones could not be misunderstood

because of her appearance. One less than kind observation of her
was of 'that monumental widow who went about swathed in weeds
and crape as if she were Queen Victoria's understudy'.[18]

The other woman who joined Yeats briefly in his Celtic mysteries
was Maud Gonne. She saw them as a means towards Irish
nationhood. From the moment that she burst into his life in 1889
like a goddess of springtime with a complexion 'like that of apple-
blossom through which the light falls', he was captive to her
beauty, doomed to love her with an unrequited love, for she had
given her heart to Ireland. For a while she entered into his dreams
of a mystic sanctuary on a real island, tiny and mist-shrouded, set
in an Irish lake. Here there was a castle with a natural stone
platform, an ideal stage 'where meditative persons might pace to
and fro'. Yeats' Uncle George Pollexfen, who lived in the west of
Ireland and was a member of the Golden Dawn for a time, helped
with the rituals.

Annie was useful for writing up the words and actions that grew
into dramatic mysteries: one-act plays in which the central character, a voyager, was given a series of tests which he had to pass in
order to attain his goal of self-knowledge. It was a kind of Celtic
Pilgrim's Progress with overtones of medieval romance and Wagnerian symbolism; the language culled from the Old Testament, Greek
drama and Celtic folklore. A typical passage which Annie wrote
out and underlined for its importance was: 'I promise in the
presence of the Rose of the World and of my own secret Imagination; that I shall be a faithful labourer, and that I shall keep the
name and knowledge of this Rite from all who have not laid their
hands, as I have, upon this emblem of the hidden truth.'[19] Their
philosophy, Yeats wrote, 'though made by many minds, would
seem the work of a single mind, and turn our places of beauty or
legendary association into holy symbols.' He did not think this
philosophy would be altogether pagan, for 'its symbols must be
selected from all those things that had moved men most during
many, mainly Christian centuries'.[20]

Annie was caught up in a dream and a drama that was, in every
way, Irish. All the protagonists save her were Irish. She was not in
the slightest degree political and she had no idea of the depth of
nationalist feeling that lay beneath the actions of the other partici-

pants. She was looking through the Irish mist to a world of perfect light and perfect beauty, a world of the imagination that had nothing to do with the real world. She had not yet set foot in Ireland.

5

Dublin, 1903

The arrival of Miss Horniman in Dublin in 1903 signalled more than her first crossing of the Irish Sea. Annie had at last stepped from the obscurity and anonymity which she had sought over the Avenue Theatre venture in 1894 into an open commitment to Art. On the threshold of her forty-third birthday she was making a bold move into a strange new world. Here was an English woman with no credentials of creative achievement ready to place her artistic efforts on the stage of the new-born Irish theatre to be scrutinised and judged by critics and public alike. She had come as costume and scenic designer and it was the first time she had ever attempted such work.

What had brought her to this moment? With hindsight there is an unfolding logic to the events, mainly Irish, that took place in London during the preceding years when Annie had been tied to her magic and mystery. The central figure, linking them all, pushing them forward, creating publicity for himself and the movements, was W. B. Yeats. He had been responsible back in 1892 for the founding of the Irish Literary Society in London at a meeting at his father's home in Blenheim Road, Bedford Park, that had brought together the London-Irish and provided a centre for Irish literature, drama and politics. It was a companion to Dublin's Irish National Literary Society founded in the same year and sharing Yeats' efforts. But the two were very different. The Dublin society, for which Maud Gonne was a passionate worker, was trying to create a national network of lending libraries so that ordinary people might discover through literature their nationhood. The London society was a much more intellectual and social affair.

In the same year of 1892 Yeats' play *The Countess Kathleen* (changed to *Cathleen* in 1895) had a copyright performance at the Athenaeum Theatre in Shepherd's Bush. After being passed by the Censor the play had 'to be gabbled through on a properly licensed

stage . . . There must be a bill outside – the smallest – and one
person must pay for admission. Money handed back afterwards.'
Yeats explained the procedure to his friend, poet and artist Sturge
Moore, a few years later when he was wanting his help in getting
more of his plays copyrighted. It was, he thought, 'a rather
troublesome affair' and he suggested that 'Miss Horniman, who
knows I think about stage matters, will I have no doubt help'.[1] He
desperately wanted a theatre of his own and the odds on whether
he might find one in Dublin or London were about even. In 1896
he confided to a friend that Miss Horniman had given away most
generously 'thousands to help certain artistic purposes which she
loves most passionately'.[2] By this time Annie was helping him as
an unpaid secretary and he knew that she shared his vision of an
intellectual theatre that would also be a home for his heroic
romances and poetical visionary plays that were rooted in the
mystical rituals which they were creating. Perhaps one day she
would help him financially to realise his dreams.

By 1897, however, he had met three Anglo-Irish who were
seeking to begin in Ireland a theatre for the people, to promote
good Irish drama in the European tradition of France, Germany
and Scandinavia. Lady Gregory, George Moore and Edward
Martyn were very different individuals. The first two, like Yeats
himself, were of Protestant stock, the last was a fervent Catholic.
All had homes on both sides of the Irish Sea and were constantly
crossing to and fro on social, intellectual, literary, dramatic and
political business. Lady Gregory was persuading him that he should
look to Dublin for his theatre, pointing out that she had many
friends in high places to whom she could turn to set up a guarantee
fund of £300 for a three-year experiment. She set about changing
the law of the land that only allowed performances for money in
Dublin's three licensed theatres. With the help of the Right
Honourable William Lecky, Unionist MP for Ireland, the law was
changed to allow performances for money in an unlicensed hall and
in 1899 the Irish Literary Theatre gave their first performances.
They were six months ahead of the Stage Society in London, which
had taken over where the Independent Theatre had left off. Both
were set on encouraging new plays that would never get a staging
in the commercial theatre.

The Irish Literary Theatre's aims were entirely Irish but they had to turn to England for actors and theatre professionals because they had none of their own. They booked the Antient Concert Rooms in Dublin for the week of 8 May but casting and rehearsals took place in London. Annie's friend Florence Farr was signed up as General Manager and for the part of Aleel, the Bard in Yeats' *The Countess Cathleen*. Florence's niece Dorothy Paget, who had played the fairy child in *The Land of Heart's Desire*, had a similar part again. The play alternated with *The Heather Field* by Edward Martyn. There was considerable London interest in what was happening in Dublin and Max Beerbohm was just one of the critics who made the journey and lauded Yeats' morality play with its tapestry of Christian, Golden Dawn, pagan Irish and Pre-Raphaelite imagery. He wrote in the *Saturday Review*, 'Despite the little cramped stage, and the scenery, which was as tawdry as it should have been dim, I was, from first to last, conscious that a beautiful play was being enacted, and I felt that I had not made a journey in vain.'[3]

The pattern of London rehearsals with English actors for performances in Dublin was repeated for two more seasons. In the third and final season F. R. Benson's company came over from England to Dublin's Gaiety Theatre to perform *Diarmid and Grania*, on which Yeats and George Moore had collaborated at Lady Gregory's stately home at Coole Park and at their London rooms. 'Collaborating with Moore must be like fighting for your life,' remarked Yeats senior,[4] and certainly the collaborators withdrew to lick their wounds after the event. The three-year experiment ended and Yeats wanted to get back to what he called 'primary ideas'. He was, he felt, wasting his time in stage management. Yet within a few months a new company had been formed which by the time of its first visit to London to play at Queen's Gate Hall in May 1903 had the grand title of the Irish National Theatre Society and he was its president. This was the company that Annie had come to help with costumes and scenery.

She arrived in Dublin with bales of richly coloured materials and half-finished costumes to dress the seventeen characters in *The King's Threshold*, Yeats' poetic drama based on the folk tale of Seanchan the Bard who goes on hunger strike to draw public attention to the wrongs he has suffered at the king's court. She stayed at the Standard Hotel, a quiet temperance hotel in Harcourt

Street. It was less showy than the Nassau Hotel where Maud Gonne stayed when she came over from England and France and where Lady Gregory held court when she came in from Coole Park in County Galway.

In the early 1900s Dublin was small enough for everyone to know everyone else, and anyone who mattered was Anglo-Irish and Protestant. This small, select group considered themselves separate and apart from the majority of the Dubliners, who were Catholic. Yeats and Lady Gregory were part of this privileged group both in the city and in the Irish National Theatre Society which now had its own resident group of local actors. It was one of the few meeting places between the classes but there was still a definite line drawn between, in Lady Gregory's words, 'those who use a toothbrush and those who don't.'[5] All the members would have claimed that they were working to make Ireland great again but their loyalties and objectives tugged in many directions even if they were centred in one large melting pot of literary, dramatic, political and national hopes.

Talent and enthusiasm were in abundance but resources were meagre and money was non-existent. Annie was therefore doubly welcome with her free costumes and more time than most to give to rehearsals, for the actors came after a full day's work to meet her at Camden Street Hall. This cold, draughty, leaky hall, squeezed in between a butcher's shop and a general provisioner's, had been hired in December for a year, with the sole virtue of its cheapness. It had room for an audience of only fifty and they had to make do with school benches for seats. One indignant supporter wrote to the local paper:

> Why should the Muse of Irish Drama . . . declaim from
> a stage which is not a stage, surrounded with scenery
> which is not scenery to an audience that is cultivating
> rheumatism or pains in the spinal column on seats that
> have no back? I may be told that it is classic simplicity.
> I answer it is merely downright commonplace
> discomfort, which not even a red-hot enthusiast would
> endure for long.[6]

All agreed that the Camden Street premises were not suitable, and the Molesworth Hall with seating for three hundred and a proper stage with proscenium arch was rented while rehearsals went on in Camden Street. Annie would sit by the stove, quietly sewing, friendly to all and greatly interested in the Irish style of acting which was entirely their own. They moved only when the action demanded, otherwise they stood still and listened. They spoke clearly and in their natural Celtic rhythms. Yeats's philosophy was that by cutting out all unnecessary movements proper attention could be given to the language. He had once suggested to a group of actors that they should rehearse in barrels, so that they could not move their arms and bodies freely, and then he thought that the barrels could be on castors so that he could shove them about the stage with a pole when action was required. He did not record the actors' reactions to his ingenious idea, but certainly the Irish players knew how to stand still and the effect was simple and beautiful.

Marie Nic Shiublaigh, who was to play the poet-hero's sweetheart in *The King's Threshold*, remembered Miss Horniman as a likeable person with a quiet wit who 'never tired advising us on stage matters'. Annie was certainly greatly experienced from a playgoer's point of view. She had seen more plays than any of the company and could talk to them about Ibsen and Wagner. She not only went to all the new plays but she read their texts and had the advantage of being able to read German, French and Italian. She had never been on stage but this was no particular disadvantage among the Irish players, nearly all of whom were amateurs.

The only one with any professional experience was the stage manager, William Fay. He had left home at the age of eighteen to join a touring company as advance publicity agent, which in simple terms meant persuading shopkeepers to stick a poster in their shop window. They toured the towns and villages of Ireland and by the time they moved to Scotland he was playing small parts. For a few years he moved from one company to another and toured Wales and England, picking up useful tips on every aspect of staging a play, before he landed back home in Dublin. Meanwhile his elder brother Frank had opted for a safe secretarial job and made acting his hobby. When Willie came home, Frank persuaded him to take a job in electrical engineering. They both spent all their free time in the Ormond Dramatic Society.

Without the Fay brothers the Irish dramatic movement would

probably never have got off the ground. They were not interested in literature or politics but only in the art of acting, and their dream was a theatre of their own. Meanwhile they got on with their acting as best they could, using their ingenuity to eke out their meagre resources. They had been inspired by stories of Antoine, who had started his Théâtre Libre in Paris in 1887. Willie Fay recalled that 'he was not a man of the theatre when he began, but a man engaged in business, and he had to try his experiment without capital. He and his company did all the work of production themselves, both clerical and acting, without payment of any kind. They even delivered the tickets by hand.' Willie painted the scenery and brother Frank coached the actors in their lines. Wigs were a luxury quite beyond them and one red-haired actor was shown how to dust his head liberally with cornflour. But he was not shown how to remove it afterwards and his effort to wash it out with hot water was 'an error of judgement that obliged him to go to bed with a head like an apple-dumpling'.[7]

They called their band of players W. G. Fay's Irish National Dramatic Company and for their first performance George Russell gave them his play *Deirdre*. Russell was a great friend of Yeats, a poet and mystic who was loved by everyone for his saint-like honesty. He had taken the name of an eternal spirit for a pseudonym but AEON became AE through a printing error, and thus he was known. Yeats gave his *Kathleen Ni Houlihan* to fill out the evening and he persuaded Maud Gonne to play the title part. She was president of the women's section of the Irish National Society, known by their Celtic name Inginide na hEireann (Daughters of Erin), and they gave their full support and made all the costumes. The three performances in April 1902 at St Theresa's Hall in Clarendon Street were an instantaneous success, particularly due to Maud Gonne, who was described by Willie Fay as 'a beautiful tall woman with her great masses of golden hair and her voice that would charm the birds off the bough'.[8] The hall was filled with ordinary working people, not the usual sort of theatre audience. They could have gone on playing to full houses for at least another week if money and time had allowed. On the strength of these performances the Irish National Theatre Society had been formed and Yeats had agreed to be president because AE did not want the position.

There was another play being rehearsed in the Camden Street rooms alongside *The King's Threshold*. It was the first dramatic effort from an Irishman whom Yeats had met in Paris in December 1896. John Millington Synge was scraping a living in France by reviewing and occasionally playing in an orchestra and Yeats had persuaded him that Ireland had need of him; he must return to his native country to absorb his own language and folklore. For the past four years Synge had spent much of his time in the Aran Islands and the Irish countryside, and by 1903 he had written one book and had two plays in manuscript. From January to March he had been staying with Yeats and Lady Gregory in their London flats, giving readings of his plays *Riders to the Sea* and *In the Shadow of the Glen* to the leading literati. In June he had read the second play to the Irish players and this was voted for performance. The Society was run on democratic lines, every member having an equal voice in the choice of play.

Opening night at the Molesworth Hall was on 8 October 1903. The plays ran for three nights to a mixed reception. *In the Shadow of the Glen* raised a storm of abuse from press and public, for Synge had taken two of Ireland's most sacred myths, the purity of womanhood and the sanctity of marriage, and smashed them into pieces. Oscar Wilde described the furore as 'the rage of Caliban at seeing his own face in the glass'.[9] *The King's Threshold* passed with little comment but Annie's costumes came in for many favourable notices, and she pasted the one from the *Freeman's Journal* in her scrapbook:

> The talented lady who has acted as Mr Yeats' creative
> scenic artist has produced for the setting for *The King's*
> *Threshold* a form as complicated and as beautiful as that
> which dominates a string quartet of Mozart . . . form is
> certainly the secret of these costumes and this scenery –
> form and a delicate perception of the beauty and value
> of colour tones. The costumes are classic in the dignity
> and beauty of the lines of the draperies, the restraint
> and harmony of the colours, but the Celtic and romantic
> influence comes out in the elaborate detail of the rich
> ornament – the jewelled devices, the embroideries, the
> designs in precious stones . . . Even the properties are

made to harmonise with the central idea . . . the effect
is . . . of a perfectly homogeneous composition inspired
by rare intelligence and a poetic imagination.[10]

The players counted themselves fortunate to have Annie. Marie
Nic Shiublaigh remembered the patient way she had sewn countless
numbers of pearls on to the royal costumes; 'she gave wholeheartedly and with an almost embarrassing readiness.'[11] Over the
years, however, there has been a reversal of the favourable opinion
of Annie's artistic contribution. In 1961 Elizabeth Coxhead in her
biography of Lady Gregory wrote dismissively that 'unfortunately,
her designing talent was meagre'. In 1970 James Flannery in his
book on Annie's relationship with the Irish, described her costumes
– judging from only a picture – as 'stiff, graceless, ill fitting and
lacking in any sense of unity or style'. From this time nearly all the
commentators on Irish drama (most of whom have been Irish) have
followed the same line, transferring criticisms of the costumes into
comments on Miss Horniman herself. In 1985 Mary Lou Kohfeldt
in another biography of Lady Gregory described Miss Horniman
as 'neither graceless nor ugly, but often appeared so'. Can it be
that some of the Irish could never forgive Miss Horniman not for
her wealth but for being English? Perhaps inevitably they would
find it very difficult to be on the receiving end of generosity from
an unwelcome source, to be under an obligation with no hope of
redeeming it.

Unlike Annie, Lady Gregory was comfortable playing the role of
Lady Bountiful. She could handle servants and the aristocracy,
although she was uneasy with the people in between. She never
regarded the actors as her equals, and would patronise them or
nanny them. Characteristically, she would provide an enormous
home-made cake, known as Lady Gregory's 'barm brack' for dress
rehearsal parties; crammed with raisins, currants and lemon peel
laced with porter, one slice was a meal in itself. At first Lady
Gregory was unsure how she should respond towards Miss Horniman, who was wealthy and her money needed in the society but
who came from trade. Lady Gregory resigned herself to being
welcoming. Annie's approach was very different. She treated
everyone in the same straightforward way so that the players
warmed towards her. She was very much enjoying using her

creative talents which had lain dormant since her days at the Slade, and putting her money to what she felt strongly, echoing her father's example, was its rightful use – for the entertainment, enjoyment and education of the general public.

When she had cut out the costumes in London, Yeats had thought they were beautiful and would help his play to make 'something of a stir'. After the opening night Annie was riding high on the crest of the wave, buoyed up by the joy of achievement. She wrote excitedly and gratefully to her Demon friend, 'Do you realise that you have now given me the right to call myself "artist"? How I thank you.'[12] She was already working on her new assignment, designing the costumes for his next play, *The Shadowy Waters*. She knew the play intimately for she had shared in its growing over the past ten years. One Bank Holiday he had read the first sketch to her in an ABC Cafe, and she had been aware how much the rituals and symbolism from their Celtic mysteries were embedded in it. It was a mood-play of mystery and romance, and the stage design and costumes were to echo and reinforce the sense of mystery, giving it a kind of Wagnerian unity. No one in the Irish company knew more than she did about this. Together they worked on ideas for scenery and costumes, striving for a monochrome effect that would give the sea and sky as much presence on stage as the characters. Annie hoped that her costumes would be a better fit this time, now that she had the advantage of knowing the actors who would wear them.

While rehearsals were in progress Yeats was in America on a lecture tour, giving valuable publicity to the Irish National Theatre Society, but he was very anxious that everyone back in Dublin should get his play right. 'It is almost religious, it is more a ritual than a human story. It is deliberately without human characters,' he explained from the other side of the Atlantic Ocean to Frank Fay, who was to play the leading part of the ancient Celtic Sea-King, Forgael.[13] The verse drama was quite an experiment for both actors and audience. The poetic language was beautifully spoken, and appreciated as fine singing or music, but the meaning was beyond them. In Willie Fay's opinion, 'The majority detested the whole thing and said so. When they didn't abuse Mr Yeats they abused us.'[14] Miss Horniman's costumes were seized upon as something in the whole affair that could be understood. Again the

Freeman's Journal gave her high praise: 'The costumes were a remarkable feature of the performance, and the entire mounting of the piece, set in the dim colours of a subdued green, harmonised beautifully with the motif drama, the action of which takes place on the dark waves of a cold Northern sea.'[15] Into her scrapbook went this notice and Annie marked it prominently with bold lines on either side.

Annie was to work on one more production for the Irish players but this was not due to be seen until the end of December 1904, which was eleven months away. However, far from being quiet, the year developed into one of the most exciting and most eventful in Annie's life. During this time the Abbey Theatre was planned, built, decorated, furnished and at long last opened. Annie always maintained that it was her idea to found a permanent home for Yeats' plays and for other plays that she felt could not get a fair hearing in the commercial theatre. She believed that the idea had first come to her while she was sewing the costumes for *The King's Threshold* in her London flat. She had written straightaway to Yeats but he had not at that time been enthusiastic. Yeats preferred to remember that she had been so carried away by his rhetoric one evening in May 1903 at the Queen's Gate Hall, when he was calling for freedom for the artist in Britain to perform masterpieces, that she had immediately offered him a theatre. Perhaps both are right, though it would be in character for Yeats to claim the credit for his powers of persuasion and to dismiss Annie's ideas at the time as of little merit.

Wherever the idea first germinated, it grew strongly within Annie's mind and heart during 1903. It was reinforced by the success of the Irish players in London, by Yeats' publication of his principles in the press and in an autumn magazine called *Samhain* that came out to coincide with the performances of the Irish Literary Theatre. Before *Samhain* there had been *Beltain*, the name for the ancient Irish spring festival. Both magazines publicised the work of the Irish theatre and corresponded to the theatrical seasons. In the September 1903 issue of *Samhain* Yeats called for the reform of the theatre so that it should become 'a place of intellectual excitement. A place where the mind goes to be liberated, as it was liberated by the theatres of Greece and England and France at certain great moments of their history, and as it is liberated in

Scandinavia today.' He believed that Ireland with her national struggle, her old literature, her folk imagination, would follow the dramatic path of Norway. England had nothing to offer to artistic effort.

On 1 January 1904 Annie took the first step to turn the idea of a theatre into a reality. From her London home she wrote to George Roberts, secretary of the Irish National Theatre Society, with the news that she had unexpectedly received a sum of money which she had determined to spend on a theatre for them. At the end of the month, when she was about to return home from Dublin after her success with *The Shadowy Waters*, she confided in Willie Fay that she was putting some spare money into Hudson Bay shares and, if she made enough profit, she would do something for the actors. The news put Willie Fay into a state of suspended longing, and he took to studying the stock market as a punter studies the field. This confidence shared with Willie Fay shows a mischievous side to Annie's nature. She had already decided to fund a theatre and she had the money to do so. That she should put her gains from the stock market into a theatre made a delightful story which Annie loved to tell, perhaps relishing the imagined outraged reactions of her Quaker grandfather and her father.

Annie dismissed her wealth as not very great, in which she was quite sincere, although 'wealthy' is of course a vague term and one man's poverty is another man's riches. Willie Fay observed that 'the common notion that Miss Horniman was an extremely wealthy woman, to whom the venture was a mere bagatelle, is a commonplace error. I have reason to know that her income at that time barely touched four figures.'[16] On her grandfather's death in 1893 Annie had inherited about £40,000 which had been invested to give her a steady income and she had benefited on the deaths of her mother in 1895, her maiden Aunt Elizabeth on her mother's side in 1897, her Uncle Henry on her father's side in 1900 and her grandmother in 1900. An income of over £700 per annum at this time would put her in the top three per cent of the population. Annie, however, had been brought up to use her money wisely and well. She did not have money to waste. Her well-placed hint to Willie Fay sent him scouring Dublin for an empty theatre, hall or any building that would suit his players and Miss Horniman's pocket.

6

The Abbey Theatre

In 1904 local authorities started to tighten up their fire regulations in theatres, following a serious fire in a theatre in England and an even worse one in Chicago where people lost their lives. Some small back-street theatres were forced to close, among them the Hibernian Theatre of Varieties in Abbey Street in Dublin, which had been unable to make the alterations required by the Corporation's Fire Department. It had once been the National Theatre but had become commonly known as 'The Mechanics' because it was attached to the Mechanics Institute which had been built on the razed site of the old Theatre Royal Opera House. Just next door and round the corner in Marlborough Street was an empty building which had served a variety of uses, from a savings bank to the city morgue.

In London, Annie heard these particulars from Willie Fay and replied that their luck was in, for her Hudson Bay shares had done well. He came over in person in March with the Irish players for their much acclaimed West End appearance at the Royalty Theatre and she sent him back with the longed-for news that she would follow him shortly to sign the contracts to lease the Abbey Street and Marlborough Street buildings. By 10 April Annie was back at her usual hotel in Dublin where she had grown accustomed to its quaint ways. On her first visit, her rickety breakfast table had been balanced by a slice of bread slipped under the short leg by the waitress and when Willie Fay welcomed her back he asked her if it were still under the table leg. 'Yes,' said Annie, 'but they have toasted it now.' It would seem that she had the measure of her Irish friends.

Her first appointment was with Joseph Holloway, the architect who was going to convert the buildings to provide a new stage and dressing-rooms. Annie asked if he would mind joining her in the Smoking Room for she could not do business without a cigarette. The startled architect may have wondered what he was letting himself in for in doing business with a woman who smoked in public, but he was soon disarmed by her quiet manner and her honest, direct approach. Next morning they went to inspect the properties together, only to be shooed out of the Mechanics Institute by an indignant manager who demanded that an appointment be made. After going through the necessary protocol, they returned a few hours later, this time with Willie Fay and Yeats, who met the architect for the first time (although he had heard a great deal about this fanatical theatregoer who turned up to rehearsals and never missed a first night).

Holloway's estimate for turning the buildings into a theatre that would comply with safety regulations came to £1,300, and Annie accepted on the spot. That night he wrote up the day's events in his diary, describing how the theatre manager had told them they had a cheek to wander on to the stage, calling them 'land grabbers!' and shouting as his parting shot, 'May you and your morgue have luck!' Holloway added, 'I am just thinking how I can face him to survey the place tomorrow or the next day.'[1]

Annie returned to London and from her flat wrote a formal letter to the President of the Irish National Theatre Society, which began:

> Dear Mr Yeats,
>
> I have a great sympathy with the artistic and dramatic
> aims of the Irish National Theatre Company, as publicly
> explained by you on various occasions. I am glad to be
> able to offer you my assistance in your endeavours to
> establish a permanent Theatre in Dublin.[2]

The letter was long and business-like, detailing conditions and arrangements, her responsibilities and theirs. She gave notice of her intention of letting the theatre, when it was not being used by the Society for rehearsals or performances, for other suitable lectures, concerts, etc. To this end, she made it clear that the seat prices could be raised but not lowered, which, as she explained, might lead to cheap entertainments and to a lowering of the value of her building. Annie thought that this was all fair and reasonable. She was going into a business arrangement, although her gesture seemed one of unbounded generosity in many Irish eyes.

'I can only afford to make a very little theatre, and it must be quite simple,' she told the company. 'You all must do the rest to make a powerful and prosperous theatre, with a high artistic ideal.' For Annie the riches would lie in the plays and productions. It was exactly ten years since her last theatrical venture at the Avenue Theatre and she was involved once again with providing a theatre for plays by W. B. Yeats in particular.

On 11 May her offer was accepted, signed by twenty-two members of the Society. They undertook to abide by all the conditions laid down in her letter and to do their utmost for the Society. Later Annie would have cause to remind them of their promise but now she set about fulfilling her side of the contract. She had definite ideas of the effect she wanted to create in her theatre and how she would achieve it. She commissioned Irish workmen to construct the building, Irish craftsmen to furnish it and Irish artists to decorate it. This was good for Irish industry but it also made the subject of Miss Horniman and her new theatre a talking point in every Dublin home.

Someone was needed to keep an eye on the construction work and see that Annie's instructions were being carried out. Willie Fay decided to abandon his secure trade as an electrician in order to take on the job of overseer, for which it was agreed that Annie would pay him a wage of thirty shillings a week. He was thought senseless to go back full-time to the precarious life of the theatre, just as an English woman was to finance an Irish theatre. It would not have been understood if Annie had tried to explain, as she did a few years later to the Reverend James O. Hannay (who wrote under the name of George Birmingham): 'In my soul I felt that I was doing something in Ireland that had to be done by an outsider, by someone with no axe of her own to grind, something far wider than any artistic effort.'[3]

She knew that she was taking on an enormous task, but nothing appealed to her more than a challenge. The extent of the challenge was something she could not have been expected to appreciate fully, given the numerous currents running under the surface of Irish life. When William Yeats' artist father, J. B. Yeats' was working on her portrait in January of that year, he already sensed an uneasiness between her and some of the company (without mentioning anything specific) and he made the observation that 'one never knows what may result'. As a result of her involvement with his son, he had made a drawing of Annie when she had first come over to Dublin to sew the costumes for *The King's Threshold* and this new painting was destined to hang in the new theatre foyer. It is a romantic study of a pale and resolute woman with large wistful eyes, wearing a richly patterned dress that encloses her small neck in a dark pleated frill, the long sleeves buttoned closely round her tiny wrists. Her long bony fingers are softened by decorative gold rings and she sits stiffly on a firm upholstered chair, her head resting almost wearily on its back.

Annie got on well with Yeats' father, although sister Lily Yeats said that she found Miss Horniman 'fatiguing'. Nevertheless Annie was giving the Yeats' family income a great boost by commissioning J. B. Yeats to paint all the leading figures in the Society so that the portraits could hang in her new theatre, an act which was bound to help his reputation as a portrait painter. Yeats senior was always short of ready money and on the look-out for likely sitters. He only asked about £20 for a head portrait, with a further £10 if the hands were included. He was a most unbusiness-like man, full of good intentions which melted away at the first social invitation or a chance meeting with a crony, when a few hours could be whiled away in gossip. He hated routine and once remarked that if you wanted it, you could find it in a lunatic asylum.

In June 1904 there was an exhibition of Irish paintings at the Guildhall in London that included six paintings by Yeats senior. At the same time his son had one of his plays being performed for three nights at the Royal Court Theatre. Annie generously invited the artist to use her flat and gave him her ticket for the play; 'the best seat in the house', he wrote to Lily. The Stage Society, the subscription society which Annie had joined in its opening year of 1889, was putting on *Where There Is Nothing*, directed by Granville Barker. Lewis Casson, at the very beginning of his career, had two small parts. The play had originally been planned between Yeats and George Moore in 1901 but Moore had backed out when Yeats joined forces with the Fay brothers. Both wanted to hang on to the plot, Moore saying he would turn it into a novel, but Yeats beat him to publication with help on the dialogue from Lady Gregory and Douglas Hyde, founder and first president of the Gaelic League and writer of Gaelic plays. Moore was furious and when he met Yeats in London at the time of the performance he refused to shake hands and turned on his heel without a word. They were never friends again and seemed to delight in hurling insults at each other. 'I tell you he knows no more about managing a theatre than a turbot from the North Pole,' wrote Yeats,[4] while Moore declared, 'What a damned fool a clever man like Yeats can be when he is in the mood to be a fool.'[5]

Before the performance there was a celebratory dinner at a nearby restaurant for father and son Yeats, with Annie and Florence Farr, who was leading the chorus in the play, Irish artists Charles Shannon and Charles Ricketts, and Lady Gregory's son Robert who was studying at the Slade School of Art while finding time to work on stage designs for Yeats. At the theatre Annie sat in Yeats' box with the poet and literary critic Arthur Symons and his wife. Annie and her Demon-playwright were obviously very good friends at this time. He had just had his thirty-ninth birthday and she was forty-three. There have been speculations about Annie being madly in love with the handsome Irish poet, but there is no evidence of it. None of her letters speaks of love, although many of them reveal a deep and committed friendship. Later there would be a coldness between them and Yeats would certainly make hurtful and sneering remarks about her.

While Yeats senior was staying in Annie's London flat he wrote gossipy letters to daughter Lily and he passed on a story Annie had told him that 'a witch' had foretold that she was going to marry a man 'from overseas, tall, dark, and very thin, with some decorations' – a description that fitted his son remarkably well. When Annie asked why she should marry him, the answer came, 'to make him a comfortable home'.[6] Her playwright was indeed notoriously lazy, undomesticated and absent-minded. St John Ervine described how 'he could not cope with the most familiar facts of life. He began letters but forgot to answer them. If they were finished they were folded in wrong envelopes. A letter would lie on his desk for several days because he had no stamps, and seemed not to know where they could be bought. If he went out to post a letter, he was more likely to put it in his pocket than the pillar-box, and it would lie there for days.'[7] Annie had been indispensable to him as a secretary and took on many personal favours for him, fetching and carrying and running errands, clearing up his rooms when he was away and tidying his drawers, complaining at the state they were in. It would not have been much different if she were his wife! But did she want the job?

The story of the letter has often been seized on as evidence that Annie was 'after' Yeats. It has been taken at face value, like many of Annie's comments, completely overlooking her wit. It would be characteristic of Annie to talk about the fortune-telling with tongue in cheek and speak of a 'witch' with light-hearted, self-deprecating humour. Maybe J. B. Yeats appreciated the tone in which she told the story but did Lily? A few years later Gerald Cumberland, a Manchester drama critic, made a shrewd assessment of Annie: 'she affects a blase pose, and turns most things to charming ridicule . . . She has something more than a pretty wit, and delights to snub the affected and conceited. She finds the respectabilities of life intensely disagreeable . . . above all she detests what is ordinary and commonplace in life and thought.'[8] Yeats was always in need of money and he knew that his one hope of a theatre lay in Annie's generosity, but marriage between them was not a requirement for either. She could serve his genius without a wedding ring and he could find all the care and comfort he needed at Coole Park. Annie gave money to guarantee publication of his writing and plays, while Lady Gregory gave him pocket money and pampered him with little luxuries.

At the end of the summer of 1904 Annie was back in Dublin occupied with the need to obtain a licence for her theatre. She engaged a firm of Dublin solicitors who applied to the Castle for the required Royal Letters Patent. She learnt that the petitioner must be domiciled in Ireland and, as there was no question of her giving up her London home, a substitute had to be found. The first idea was to ask Yeats senior to act on her behalf, but he was not eligible as he was living with his daughters in Dublin at the time. The next person who came to mind was Lady Augusta Gregory, who agreed to stand in for Miss Horniman as long as she would incur no financial burden. In some ways it was an unfortunate choice as, right from the start, it created an illusion of ownership that Lady Gregory later accepted as her right.

Annie was invited to stay for a weekend at Coole Park while the legal negotiations were in progress. It was an invitation that was extended to very few women, and it is doubtful that Annie fully appreciated the compliment. Lady Gregory liked to organise her guests rather than entertain them, which made Yeats' father feel uncomfortable and unrelaxed in her home, though Yeats himself lapped up the luxury that was offered to him. It was Annie's only invitation and the next year, when Yeats and Synge were there and she was not, she seemed glad to be out of it. 'I would establish myself on a sofa in curling pins and an old dressing-gown and refuse to move, only moan and drop ashes on the carpet,' she wrote to Yeats.[9]

There were complications over the theatre licence. The bigger Dublin theatres were opposed to a licence being granted to yet another theatre that would overlap their own dramatic territory. The matter went to the courts, where Annie much enjoyed the legal tussle. Yeats went round the town collecting witnesses to speak on their behalf, while she, as he wrote to Lady Gregory, 'gave her evidence first and was entirely admirable. She was complimented by the Solicitor General and is as proud as punch. Excitement always seems to give her the simplicity which she sometimes lacks. She was really most impressive.'[10] He added with unusual modesty, 'I think I was a bad witness . . . I was disappointed at being hardly cross-examined at all – by that time I got excited and was thirsting for everybody's blood.'

The barristers were not interested in the literary debate but in drawing up a legal document that would prevent Miss Horniman from letting her theatre to commercial travelling companies, which would lower the tone of the neighbourhood and the rental value of the buildings. Annie made it clear that she had no desire to make any money from her theatre but, at the same time, she did not want to waste money. She wanted a patent that would run for twenty-one years and she undertook to give the theatre free to the Irish National Theatre Society and for performances by the Elizabethan Stage Society which produced plays not ordinarily performed in theatres. She did not want to take any part herself. 'I simply want to make them a present of it.'

At last, on 20 August 1904 a patent for six years was granted to 'Dame Augusta Gregory', with Miss Horniman meeting the cost of £455 2s 10d. The patent would cease if the Irish National Theatre Society were dissolved. They were now free to put on plays in the Irish or English language written by Irish writers on Irish subjects, or such dramatic works of foreign authors as would tend to interest the public in the higher works of dramatic art. The plays were to be chosen by a reading committee. 'Dame Augusta ' was commanded, among numerous requirements, not to stage 'any exhibition of wild beasts or dangerous performances or to allow women or children to be hung from the flies or fixed in positions from which they cannot release themselves . . . It being our Royal will and pleasure that for the future our said theatre may be instrumental to the promotion of virtue and instruction of human life.'[11] Lady Gregory has been aptly described by William Murphy as being 'like the owner of the only football among a group of boys eager to play.' The ball would ostensibly remain hers for the next six years with many a squabble over the rules. But for now Annie owned the football pitch and held the whistle.

While the patent drama was being played out in the courts, the new Abbey Theatre was taking shape. On 4 August Yeats wrote to Lady Gregory:

> I have just been down to see the work on the Abbey
> Theatre. It is all going on very quickly and the company
> should be able to rehearse there in a month. The other
> day while digging up some old rubbish in the morgue
> which is being used for dressing rooms, they found
> human bones. The workmen thought they [had] lit on a
> murder at least but the caretaker said, 'Oh I remember
> we lost a body about 7 years ago. When the time for the
> inquest came it couldn't be found.'[12]

The newspapers had a great time with their headlines. 'The Muse at the Morgue' was how Dublin's *Evening Mail* opened their story on the theatre patent.

Meanwhile Annie was pursuing her policy of buying Irish. From Lily Yeats she ordered embroideries from the Dun Emer workshops to hang on the theatre walls. She commissioned Sarah Purser to design stained glass windows in her Dublin workshops, opened the previous year with the Gaelic name of 'An Tur Gloine' – The Tower of Glass. Miss Purser contracted to make two windows and three lunettes for £24, which Annie thought was wonderfully cheap. 'I do not wish to have any symbols of any sort which are not already perfectly well known to the general public or which could be called either religious, occult or pagan,' she instructed.[13] The chosen image was a tree in leaf against a blue sky, which could mean all things to all people.

Annie described stained glass as 'the delight of my eyes' and she had already installed two glorious windows in her London flat. They depicted full-size Wagnerian figures and had been designed by Sylvester Sparrow, an artist who had collaborated with Walter Crane on some religious stained glass windows as well as working on his own in a distinctively dark and dramatic way. Annie had approached him with the idea of a Wagnerian window depicting Wotan calling up Erda, from Act 3 of *Siegfried*. It had been so successful that her next idea had been for a window depicting Klingsor calling up Kundry, from Act 2 of *Parsifal*. Both subjects had seemed at first impossible to execute, until Annie threw down the challenge, 'Is it worthwhile doing anything but the impossible?'[14] She seemed to know before the artist that the shades of light and colour in the stained glass would give a mysterious element and dramatic quality to the supernatural scenes of magician, goddess and temptress that would speak more eloquently than any painting.

The final touches in the Abbey Theatre were large copper-framed mirrors from another Irish workshop, the metalworks at Youghall, and a woodcut by Elinor Monsell. This last work gave to the Society the motif of the Irish legendary Queen Maeve holding in leash the Irish wolfhound. It was reproduced on all their posters and programmes and became a famous emblem.

Impatient to test their powers in the new theatre, the actors began to rehearse there on 31 October among the half-finished work of electricians, painters and carpenters. By mid-December the theatre was finished. The press had been given a preview and wrote glowing accounts of how the old unsightly buildings had been transformed into 'a stylish new theatre, capable of seating 562 persons', richly carpeted, patriotically furnished, lit throughout by electricity. Annie had achieved her ambition, to provide a comfortable theatre with every seat having a perfect view of the stage. She gave a tea party and took her guests on a conducted tour; she gave presents to all her workmen and thanked Joseph Holloway for his skill and effort. He responded that she was 'the most capable business-woman I ever had to deal with'.

Opening night was set for Tuesday, 27 December 1904. The Irish National Theatre Society were presenting four one-act plays. Two were new plays – *On Baile's Strand* by Yeats and a comedy by Lady Gregory, *Spreading the News* – followed by two revivals – Yeats' *Cathleen Ni Houlihan* and Synge's *In the Shadow of the Glen*. The plays, however, were overshadowed by the event itself. This was the night when the Abbey Theatre was born, the first endowed theatre in Britain and the beginning of the repertory movement, and it was Annie Horniman who had made it possible. Trouble, however, lay ahead. Yeats' words to Frank Fay in August 1903, before Annie first crossed the Irish Sea, would prove prophetically true: 'All theatrical companies make rows but ours seems to have more than the usual gift that way.'[15]

7

Opening Night and the Tarot Cards

On Tuesday night, 27 December 1904, the leaders of Dublin life made their way down Marlborough Street to the smart entrance of the new, much-talked-of little theatre. Dubliners had thought the Abbey Theatre would never be ready for launching on its voyage of artistic experiment, made possible by Miss Horniman who had paid all the bills, leaving a small balance of forty pounds in hand. The Irish National Theatre Society were facing the future with confidence and the night was for celebration. It was a fashionable occasion but also a serious theatrical event that had sent ripples across to England and even over the Atlantic to America and Canada. New York's *Daily News* and Toronto's *Globe* were covering the story and the *Manchester Guardian* had sent over its most promising young correspondent, John Masefield, who described the experience as 'strangely new and strangely beautiful'.

While the foyer filled up with distinguished people 'scrutinizing the fittings and discussing the history of the theatre, standing in little knots on the stairs', last-minute adjustments were being made backstage to props and lighting. Willie Fay, dressed for his part of Barach the Fool in Yeats' new play, with 'a wild wig slipping sideways over his elfin face', scrambled high overhead among the lighting.[1] Beneath him figures hurried to and fro with ladders, canvas screens and Miss Horniman's fantastic costumes. Those members who were not in that night's plays tried to keep out of the way, fortifying themselves with bread and cocoa. Everyone had been at the theatre from the moment they could get away from work. In a dark corner on an upturned property basket Synge sat rolling a cigarette, delighted that one of his plays had been chosen for the opening.

Yeats was feeling very confident about his new play, for last night his horoscope had showed that the stars were quiet and fairly favourable. He cut a dashing figure in his evening suit as he divided himself between backstage and the front of the house where Arthur Daley, the Society's one musician, was entertaining the audience, standing at the edge of the stage playing plaintive Celtic airs. He had once played in the same Parisian orchestra as Synge.

The audience moved slowly to take their seats, trying to take in all the features of the stylish little theatre, including the many portraits of the Society, among them a splendid one of Miss Horniman. Heads twisted and turned in an effort to catch a glimpse of the famous English proprietress but people were distracted by the rich carpeting, the triple electric lamps, the red leather seats individually divided by polished brass fittings and the eye-catching programmes – printed in red and black with Elinor Monsell's emblem on the brown paper cover. The house was full as the curtain rose on the first of four Irish one-act plays.

Spontaneous applause greeted the opening set of *On Baile's Strand*. Robert Gregory's simple and imaginative designs bathed in beautiful light suggested the remote epic world of Ireland's ancient heroes. Yeats' verse play told the tale of Cuchulain, who kills a young warrior whom he discovers is his son. He goes mad with grief and plunges into the sea, lashing out at the waves with his sword until he falls, overcome with remorse. Frank Fay as Cuchulain surpassed all his other performances and Willie Fay as the Fool created 'a beautiful phantasy' but Yeats' next play, *Cathleen Ni Houlihan*, with Marie Nic Shibulaigh in the title-role received more general acclaim. In a swift change of mood, Lady Gregory's *Spreading the News* was played at a great rate. Finally the curtain rose on Synge's *In the Shadow of the Glen*, which had caused such an uproar at its first performances the previous year. This time the audience were not in the mood to complain and the night ended with tremendous applause.

Yeats bounded on to the stage, buoyed up by the tension and excitement. Always ready with a few hundred words, that night he was inspired. He paid tribute to Miss Horniman whose 'spirit and generosity' had caused a worthy home to be built for the Society. 'We shall take as our motto these words written over the three gates of the City of Love by Edmund Spenser,' he proclaimed. 'Over the first gate was, "Be bold!", over the second, "Be bold, be bold! And evermore be bold!" and over the third, "Yet be not too bold!"'[2] The audience went out into the night, wishing for more.

Joseph Holloway wrote in his diary that 'the opening night of the Abbey must be written down a great success. Long life to it, and to the Society which gave it birth through the generous impulse of Miss Horniman.'[3]

Annie, however, had not been present to receive her share of the limelight and applause. She had returned to England. Not only had she missed the realisation of her dream of owning her own theatre, but also her due for the costumes in Yeats' play, for which she held artistic responsibility. Her absence was so inexplicable that it has often been assumed that she was there. Some contemporary newspapers – the *Glasgow Evening News*, the *United Irishman*, the *London World* – indeed reported her presence, relating that she was in the front row with other VIPs. Yet no one described her appearance, and if Annie had been there, her arrival in the theatre entrance would have created a buzz and every detail of her distinctive dress would have been noted, for Annie certainly knew how to dress for the occasion and she cut a striking figure with her cultivated medieval romantic air. Her erect carriage made her seem taller than she actually was, and her dress style emphasised her slimness and height. She loved the rich colours of stained glass and richly textured materials, often buying furnishing material at Liberty's in Regent Street and having it made into gowns in her favourite style, with a high neckline and sleeves that folded generously from shoulder to elbow and fitted tightly round her slim wrists. Sybil Thorndike, who met her a few years later, described her dress material as 'beautiful stuff that you would only think of for curtains, and are surprised to see how well it furnishes the human body.' She told her brother that Miss Horniman made a real picture: 'I like seeing people as if they'd been painted by someone – Miss Horniman looks like that.'[4]

It is not known where Annie was on the opening night of the Abbey Theatre. All that William Fay recorded is that she had to return to England. He was genuinely sorry that she missed the excitement, regarding her as he did as 'the real sage-femme of the Abbey Theatre, without whose aid it would have been still-born'.[5] Neither was Lady Gregory present for the grand opening, for she was ill at home at Coole Park. Yeats tried to persuade her that she was well enough to attend by telling her how much her presence would be missed by the actors. He seems to have made no such plea to Annie, but by this time their relationship was uneasy and there had been stormy scenes between them at rehearsals.

Yeats' behaviour at rehearsals had been a test of everyone's patience. Joseph Holloway said that he was 'a strange odd fish with little or no idea of acting, and the way he stares at the players from within a yard or two of them, as they act, would distract most people. You would think he had a subject under a microscope he stares so intently at them.'[6] He had taken to carrying a black stick which he swung to and fro as he pondered over a knotty problem. And there seemed to be a number of these in staging his new play, from Frank Fay's inability to understand his part to Florence Farr's musical settings for the two lyrics. At last the swinging stick rasped on Annie's fraught nerves and she exclaimed, 'For goodness sake, Willie! Stop swinging that stick, or leave the rehearsal!'[7] Udolphus (Dossy) Wright, one of the actors, said it was the only time that he saw Miss Horniman lose her temper.

The particular trouble between Annie and Yeats was over the king's costumes for *On Baile's Strand*, which he was not happy with. In January, when ideas for costumes and stage design were first being thrashed out, he had reminded Frank Fay that 'Miss Horniman has to learn her work and must have freedom to experiment.'[8] The costumes she had designed for the kings were in red or green, with fur-trimmed cloaks which billowed out from their shoulders. Yeats likened them to 'extinguishers', and to 'Father Christmas'. The actors stood around like tailors' dummies while cloaks were taken off and put on and taken off again. After Annie and Yeats had indulged in much plain speaking, a compromise was eventually reached by which the red-robed kings carried their cloaks. Annie thought that the outcome was not as archaeologically correct as she had intended. 'Hang archaeology,' said Yeats. 'It's effect we want on the stage.' Annie gave way. Certainly the effect on opening night was tremendous and there was prolonged applause at the exit of the kings.

It seems that her experience over the costumes, her last attempt at costume design, helped Annie decide to turn to the business side of the theatre and not 'interfere' (as she saw it) on the artistic side of productions. She realised that constant squabbles at rehearsals were not helping and from this time she bowed out of the creative side to concentrate on management. This did not require her presence constantly at the theatre; her work would be much more in London and the English provinces where contacts and publicity were needed. Thus right from the start of the Abbey Theatre, Annie's responsibilities took her away from the centre of activities. It has often been wondered why Annie put her money into an Irish theatre in the first place, and her involvement has been considered simply as the impetuous act of an eccentric woman, decided upon almost incredibly by tarot-card reading. Yet though she was certainly mindful of the messages which she read from her cards, it is more that they mirror-like, revealed intuitively held ideas and half-submerged feelings. Ever since she had been expelled from the Golden Dawn in December 1896 her search for perfection had become increasingly identified with the theatre. Yeats' Castle of Heroes envisaged in his Celtic mysteries had been transformed into the reality of the Abbey Theatre.

Early in 1902 Annie had advised her Demon: 'Work on as best you can for a year, let us say, you should be able to persuade people during that time that you are something of a dramatist and Mr Fay should be able to have got a little practice for his company.'[9] They had been turning to their tarot cards for guidance. In June Yeats had discussed with Gordon Craig the possibility of staging some of his work in London. 'But for divination I should believe that something will come of it,' he wrote to Lady Gregory.[10] It did not need divination to predict that Gordon Craig's vague promises would not result in anything in London that year, while in Dublin the play that the Irish players were putting on was *Sold* by James Cousins, which Yeats thought was 'rubbish and vulgar rubbish'. The tarot cards were telling them what they knew in their hearts: that the time was not ripe for the kind of theatre they wished to build.

In her early days in the Golden Dawn, Annie had received instruction from Mathers in astrology, fortune-telling and the occult significance of the tarot cards. She probably used the Marseilles pack of cards, as did Yeats whose well-thumbed pack still survives. She had a reputation among friends for accurate divination and in 1895 had been asked to predict the most favourable time to publish a book called *Boconnoc,* subtitled 'A

Romance of Wild Oat-Cake', a weird piece of fiction by Herbert
Vivian. Annie had drawn up a horary figure, mathematically
plotting the heavens at the exact moment of posing a question, and
from the calculations she had made a forecast. It was painstaking
and precise work which Yeats had never mastered like Annie had.
He once moaned to Florence Far, 'I am trying to work at primary
directions, but my head reels with all the queer mathematical
terms.'[11]

On 1 March 1903 Annie had made the first of the four tarot
readings that were to influence the Abbey Theatre decision. She
began: 'D. [Demon] and I spoke today of a current and plans of
working in it.'[12] This suggests that she and Yeats felt that the time
was right to take the first step towards achieving their dreams of a
new kind of theatre. February had been an eventful month. Annie
had resigned from her office of Scribe in the Golden Dawn and was
looking for an involvement. Yeats had been devastated by the news
that Maud Gonne, his one true love, had married in Paris Major
John MacBride, veteran of the Boer War, Irish republican and
Catholic, and symbol for Maud of all that was best in Irish
manhood. She had kept Yeats trailing along for years, using him in
her political ambitions, and now had committed an act of misplaced
patriotism and of defiance against her former French lover, the
father of her daughter. 'Who would have thought it all, and more
than it all, would come to naught' Yeats wrote in a poem shortly
afterwards.[13] He needed his friends very much at this time and
turned to Augusta Gregory for comfort in the peace of Coole Park
before again seeking consolation in his work.

Perhaps Annie felt that this was the time to pluck him out of the
political arena which she abhorred. The tarot cards would provide
the advice, with the Prince and the Queen of Swords the represen-
tatives of Yeats and Annie. She was using centuries-old symbols.
The four suits of Wand, Cup, Sword and Pentacle relate to the
four sacred objects of Arthurian legend, the four images of the
Grail; they appear in Celtic literature as the four treasures of
Ireland – the Spear of Lug, the Cauldron, the Sword and the
Stone. The twenty-two trumps correspond to the twenty-two
Hebrew letters and to the twenty-two lines in the symbolic Tree of
Life. The four letters Y H V H of the Hebrew name of God are the
means of cutting the cards. The four elements of fire, water, earth

and air are contained in the four suits. Through these interrelated, interdependent correspondences truth would be revealed.

Annie cut the pack of cards twice to make four piles, which she turned upwards to reveal the four bottom cards that give a general indication. One of them was the Prince of Swords, the significator for Yeats, which she interpreted to mean that he would 'intellectualise the whole'. The general indications were positive and cautiously optimistic. Then she spread out in a horseshoe shape the pile of cards that held her significator, the Queen of Swords. The Queen's position showed good fortune and gain, and, when Annie came to pairing the cards, the same message was there. Success would have to be earned, there were signs of a little unease, but Annie read that 'a passing way has come through a radical change in her hopes – this will give her authority . . . work for love will be completed under a Divine Force'. In the pairing there was the same message that 'work for love will bring Divine Wisdom'. She saw signs of 'complete change from Death to Life affecting all planes – passing away of a brown-haired woman on one plane, on others a spiritual happiness will come'. The removal of Maud Gonne by marriage was going to make the all the difference in her relationship with Willie Yeats. She could have confidence that his talents would no longer be 'plebeianised' through party politics.

Two months later Annie was anxious about Yeats and turned to her cards again. The Irish players had come to London to perform three of Yeats' plays, *The Hour Glass*, *Kathleen Ni.Houlihan* and *The Pot of Broth*, as well as *Twenty-Five* by Lady Gregory and *The Laying of the Foundations* by Fred Ryan, a member of the Irish National Dramatic Society. There were to be two performances at Queen's Gate Hall in Kensington. Annie consulted her cards: 'How will the result of tomorrow's performances affect the Prince of S.?' She found a mixed bag of predictions with good news predominating. The cards forecast 'a gain of authority' for Yeats in his dramatic affairs and that 'the matter in hand is profitable swiftly . . . and leads to further inspiration . . . friendship and affection join together – Success comes with the smooth happy current.' The main source of friction seemed to lie in Yeats' relationship with Willie Fay and Annie noted, 'Fay and Prince S. work together though they are not harmonious characters.'

The cards were giving out healthy signals and the Irish players were a huge success. A. B. Walkley, *The Times* critic, was enchanted by the way the actors spoke their lines. 'We had never realised the musical possibilities of our language until we had heard these Irish people speak it.' Their very amateurishness was considered a virtue. They moved 'with a little natural clumsiness, as of people who are not conscious of being stared at in public. Hence a delightful spontaneity . . . they have something of the self-importance of children surpliced for service at the altar, or dressed-up for a grand occasion.' Yeats seemed well set on his path to 'a drama of energy, of extravagance, of fantasy, of musical and noble speech'. He liked to remember that it was after one of these London performances that Annie had been so impressed by his speech from the stage that she offered to find him a theatre.

However, the tarot cards were not only giving messages of sweetness and light. They warned that there was 'some opposition to be overcome in further carrying out the ideas materially' and Annie noted 'determined opposition'. She was not wrong. Over in Dublin the Irish nationals were smarting at the London success of their National Dramatic Company and their jealousies would fuel later grudges. On 13 September Annie once more turned to her cards for guidance on 'D's affairs in connection with the theatre'. All the messages were read to relate to her Demon and her cryptic notes reveal little to the uninitiated apart from an overall picture, which is a mixture of good and bad news. The good news was that Yeats was leaving anxiety behind and moving into a good material current – 'New energy leading to Fame and gain of power'. The bad news was that 'worries are great', 'irresolution stirs up fresh anger and malice' and finally 'disappointment in friendship crowns all'. This last pronouncement has been taken as a warning that Annie should have heeded. Annie, however, was not asking for guidance for herself this time and she had no reason to be worried about her friendship with her Demon. The cards spoke of a fair young woman who 'is very angry but prudently restrains herself – she makes some final decision which will alter the mind and work of Prince S'. Maud Gonne MacBride, still very much involved with Irish politics, wanted the theatre to be a propaganda tool. Yeats had called for freedom for the theatre and in reply to his call Maud had written to the Irish papers: 'Mr Yeats asks for freedom for the theatre, freedom even from patriotic captivity. I would ask for freedom from the insidious and destructive tyranny of foreign influence.'[14] Annie thought that she could plainly see who was her enemy.

On 9 October 1903, the day after the first performance of *The King's Threshold* in the Molesworth Hall, Dublin, she made her fourth tarot card reading. Yeats' play had expressed his belief in the essential freedom of the creative spirit, bound to no political persuasion or social creed. This time she asked her cards for personal guidance. 'What is the right thing for me to do in regard to the I.N.Th. Now?' When she had played out the cards in the familiar horseshoe shape, she studied them earnestly. 'I am in a happy friendly successful current, which will carry me on if I decide with a certain amount of self-assertion.' She had indeed made friends with the Irish players, who had made her welcome among them; her costumes had been a successful first attempt. 'Some gift will cause quarrels and anger but it will bring good fortune and gain whilst away from home – self-assertion is absolutely necessary.' Again the emphasis was on her self-assertion; she must speak up for herself, an English woman in an alien land. It was a strangely accurate prediction that would be played out in the next few years. Annie had now made up her mind and she sent the reading to Yeats with a letter telling him that it seemed 'as if it were already ordained'.

It took fourteen months of practical decisions for Annie and Yeats to turn their hopes and dreams into the reality of opening night, 27 December 1904. Yet on that night, Annie chose to be back in London. She mysteriously disappeared not quite back to the anonymity of the Avenue Theatre venue of ten years ago but certainly into the shadows, and no one seemed to notice or to think it strange. Annie had been moving among the Irish people in Dublin for a year and she always felt herself to be an outsider however kindly she was treated. Before she had signed the draft agreement for the theatre, she had been particularly upset by the decision over George Moore, whom she saw as her enemy. He and Yeats had a jealous relationship, sometimes creatively joined together, other times not even acknowledging the other's existence. Although Moore had scorned and ridiculed the efforts of the Irish National Theatre Society, he now wanted to join and Annie was amazed that the Irish players wanted him back again, and as their vice-president. 'Never,' she declared. Once an enemy always an enemy in her book. If he returned to the fold, then she would go; they would have to choose. They discussed the desirability of having his undoubted talents working for them and paid scant attention to her feelings.

The truth was that Yeats wanted Moore on his side again because he wanted to do a deal with him over a play which they had jointly written, and Moore probably had equally devious reasons for wanting to join forces with the Society. Annie could not understand these subtleties. She wanted everyone to behave openly and honourably, to speak out if there was disagreement and to take the consequences. She did not appreciate what Yeats meant when he told her that she acted 'by the book'. She could not make compromises because she felt that her 'self-respect' would be damaged. Others with whom she would not compromise or meet socially were the patriots. She had made plain her revulsion to national feeling from whatever direction it came and although she allowed that others felt differently she expected the same tolerance and respect for herself. Patriotism and politics, she felt strongly, did not belong in a theatre and she would have none of them in hers. Yeats had written that 'art is tribeless, nationless, a blossom gathered in No Man's Land'[15] and Annie believed that he meant it.

Behind Annie's decision to be in London for the Abbey Theatre's opening night lay the recognition that it would be more comfortable for the Irish to acknowledge their obligation to her if they could do it in her absence. She had given her own 'At Home' at the new theatre a week before opening. It was now time for her to return to England to find her real friends, other interests and different responsibilities. Since her Slade School days, when she had first helped Bergie and Mathers with regular sums of money, she had always responded to calls for help, especially from young people with talent. She gave money without moralising. She did not pass judgement on their behaviour, only assessed their need in ways that many would have thought very odd. One young girl sought Annie's help to launch her into society so that she could make a good marriage. 'How can I capture a man in these rags?' she sweetly asked. Annie, amused by her impudence, gave her thirty pounds and made no fuss when the money was spent on one set of elaborate evening clothes. Yeats once explained that to people of her mystical persuasions 'conventional errors seem to them trivial, and all defiance meritorious'.[16] When regret was expressed at not being able to repay her generosity, Annie replied, 'I am merely a custodian of the money I control. All I ask is that should you ever be in a position to help anyone, pass it on.'[17] Annie's young protégées were her friends and some remained loyal to her all her life. Her personal life was private territory where few presumed to trespass. Yeats was one of the few who was given special dispensation but that was because they shared each other's dreams and because his talent, which it was her privilege to serve, towered over anyone else's.

8

From Democracy to Professionalism, 1905–7

Within a very short time Annie was made uncomfortably aware of the size of the Dublin challenge. The Irish National Theatre Society was aiming for performances every month instead of three times a year as of old. This could only be achieved by a company of full-time professional actors able to give all their time and energy to the theatre and this meant an injection of money to pay salaries. The Abbey Theatre's profit after the opening production had been £90, a good start, but the next production made only £30, even without expenses for acting. At this rate it would be impossible to build up a reserve fund for touring the provinces, and they could not become a truly national company without this. Their only hope of extra money lay with Miss Horniman.

The play in February 1905 was Synge's *The Well of the Saints* which produced an uproar and abuse of everyone involved. Synge's characters were grounded in reality, which meant, so Willie Fay thought, that they were all bad-tempered and inevitably infected the audience. The theatre critics refused to see these characters as Irish in their unloveliness, and denounced them as caricatures. Joseph Holloway wrote in his diary that the play was 'Billingsgate' and 'quite intolerable to an Irish audience'. Dubliners were suspicious of the controversial playwright who had returned to live among them, and they showed their hostility by staying away from the theatre.

While the company was being bombarded by attacks from outside, it was reeling from body blows from within. The leaders were aspiring towards professional status, and to many of the rank and file members this meant commercialism and a sell-out of the national cooperative spirit in which the company had been formed. The actors divided into two camps, for and against professionalism.

There was a lot of double-talk and double-dealing as those who were considered dispensable were pushed to the side while the star players were offered bribes to stay, perhaps in the form of a few extra shillings a week or a promise of future support.

Annie did not belong to these rival and shifting groups. She was outside the manoeuvrings on three counts – she was English, she did not belong to the Society and she was only a visitor to Dublin. In any case she did not have the necessary temperament for playing politics and she was incapable of appreciating the battles that were being fought behind closed doors. She wanted to progress to bigger and better things and she thought the Irish players would want this too. Maybe they did, but their priorities were not in the order of Miss Horniman's. She was prepared to subsidise them with more money. She wanted the company to adopt professional attitudes and the only way forward was for the principal actors to be free to rehearse during the day and to be able to give a fresh, wholehearted performance in the evening. In June 1905 she made a formal offer of £500 for salaries and guaranteed to finance a London trip which, she felt sure, would enhance their reputation and make money to go into a touring fund. She also hinted to Yeats that she was prepared to extend the theatre to provide workshops where they could make their own scenery.

It is difficult to know whose ambitions were the greater at this time, Annie's or W. B. Yeats'. They both had their eyes on a European reputation. Yeats had thoughts of making the Abbey Theatre a centre for verse-speaking and verse-productions, using his own poetic drams as the pivot of their activities. He was already engaged in experiments in musical chanting with Florence Farr, and they had given a number of performances in England. He knew that in Florence and Frank Fay he had two very beautiful verse-speakers. Annie's thoughts were turned towards building a municipal theatre of the kind that she knew so well in Germany. She believed that Synge's plays were the key to European recognition while Yeats' plays built up a home audience that would learn to appreciate his talent. She had cast Synge's horoscope last year, accurately outlining his character and talents. She had told him that he had an imaginative faculty of a disturbing nature to others and went on: 'Comparing your planets with those in Mr Yeats' nativity I find it clear that his influence has been excellent for both of you . . . and you will add to the prosperity of his theatrical schemes.'[1] In 1906 Synge's plays broke into Europe. *The Well of the Saints* was performed in German at the Deutsches Theater in Berlin, and *In the Shadow of the Glen* was translated into Bohemian and acted at the Inchover Theatre in Prague.

Meanwhile in Dublin in September and October 1905, there were meetings to resolve the vexed question of professionalism that had occupied them all summer long. On 6 October Yeats revealed his hand in a letter to Florence Farr: 'We are turning into a private Limited Liability Co. in order to get control into a few hands. If all goes well Lady Gregory, Synge and myself will be the Directors in a few days and will appoint all committees and have more votes between us than all the other Shareholders . . . We have all the really competent people with us certainly.'[2] The new board was to be a triumvirate. Miss Horniman, who had already spent £4,000 on facilities for the Irish National Theatre Society, was barely mentioned throughout all the discussions, or in the notes and letters that passed to and fro between the three primary schemers. She had written to Yeats in September that she was most willing for the Society to become a limited company, 'but I consider that the value of the shares should bear an exact proportion to the voting power.'[3] Annie was obviously thinking along normal business lines: the people with the most money at stake should have the greatest voting power. This, however, was not what the three prospective directors had in mind.

In September Willie Fay mentioned that Yeats had broached the subject of a limited company to him with a possible board that included Miss Horniman, and he was all in favour. Yeats had obviously sold the idea well. But by 24 October, when the new title of National Theatre Society Ltd was registered, the name of Miss Horniman had disappeared along with the word Irish. Her name was not on the theatre patent, not on the board of directors of the society; officially she belonged neither to theatre nor company. There was talk of a business committee being formed where presumably her voice would carry weight but, along with other committees that were vaguely in the air, it did not materialise. She had allowed herself to be put into the position of paying the bills and having no authority. She would learn that it was a very painful seat to occupy.

There is plenty of correspondence still in existence between the three new directors as each worked to protect his or her own back. Each one was writing material for the Abbey Theatre stage and each, naturally enough, pushed his or her own work, but at the same time each author realised that there was safety and power in the three of them speaking as one voice over the management of the Society and the theatre. Annie was willing at this time to give Yeats the freedom to put forward her point of view and to act in her interests. At first her trust in Synge and Lady Gregory was complete, since she took it that they were all working to a common purpose. However, making Yeats her spokesman damaged the credibility of both. His opinions were taken as hers and vice-versa, and it was not long before Synge and Lady Gregory were keeping thoughts and information from Yeats when he was in London with Annie. Synge excused his behaviour on the lines that Yeats could be 'so careless about his letters'.

Annie may have thought that the Irish folk were making a lot of fuss over trivialities while she got on with the real work. She was busy arranging advance publicity and organising accommodation for the players who would be coming over for the English tour. She had been incensed when Willie Fay had told her that the manager of the Oxford theatre had turned them down, saying that he wanted no Irish plays. She decided to show that her company was not to be trifled with and went to both Oxford and Cambridge, met the mayors, the vice-chancellors and the local ticket agents, circularised 'everybody that mattered and some that didn't', and booked the Corn Exchange Hall in Oxford and the Victoria Assembly Rooms in Cambridge. When Robert Bridges was asked a few years later what it was like to negotiate with Miss Horniman, all he could say was 'Lions and tigers. Lions and tigers.'[4] She found rooms in colleges for the actors who, before they left Dublin, had signed their new contracts with the limited company. Then she went on to London and booked St George's Hall, Langham Place, which was owned by a Mr Maskelyne who was not often persuaded to let his stage to outsiders; Willie Fay thought she had been particularly astute in getting it for them.

The English tour was a great success. Willie Fay described the Oxford scene: 'Down to the Corn Exchange came everyone of note in Oxford from all the colleges. It was the first time we had played to a cultured audience of this kind, who could see that our authors were far in advance of what the ordinary theatre was supplying.'[5] After the performance 'we were shown the principal sights, and tasted the very best from college cellars'. The next stop was Cambridge where they played to full houses which were followed by lively discussions in college rooms into the early hours. Their reception at the university towns carried them to London with heads held high, and here Yeats' poetic splendour and Synge's dramatic genius were fully appreciated by distinguished audiences and the leading London critics.

The National Theatre Society Ltd went home to Dublin with the English praises ringing in their ears, to be met by a bombardment of criticism and complaints from their own people. First the nationalists objected to the word Irish being dropped from their title, secondly they objected to the tour in England in order to collect English money to fund a tour of the Irish provinces, thirdly they objected to a new play in the repertoire, *The Land* by their own playwright Padraic Colum, having only one London performance and that a matinee, and finally they objected to the one shilling seats at the Abbey Theatre, which they said were too expensive and prohibited the ordinary people of Dublin from attending their own theatre. Arthur Griffith, editor of the *United Irishman*, summed it up: 'Everybody will be sorry for the conversion of our best lyric poet into a limited liability company.'[6]

Now was the time chosen by the actors who had fought against losing their amateur status to walk out. They felt that their Society had been hijacked for literary purposes. They wanted to perform plays of their people by their people; they wanted a say in the choice of plays and in the way the parts were shared out. They had been one big happy family, bonded together by poverty and hardship, and they did not want to change. They took with them their leading lady, their own playwright and their two former secretaries and set up a new group, calling themselves by the name that had just been discarded by the original company – the Irish National Theatre Society.

Utter confusion followed and never completely cleared. If Annie had given a common identity to the theatre and the players, the Abbey Theatre Company could have been formed, for she was the one who could have insisted on this because she was funding both.

There would have been less opportunity for the nationalists to imagine that they could hitch their particular bandwagon to Miss Horniman's purse strings. It would have prevented such comments from the press as 'Why should an English lady (however estimable) have so administrative a connection with the Irish National Theatre Society? Is not the society able to manage its own affairs?'[7] Loyalties were broken and could not be retied in a common cause. Yeats was exulting in the battle. He liked to think of himself as 'distinctly dangerous'. 'Somebody must be a devil', he declared, and he evidently wanted the role. Synge, fighting ill health and preoccupied with his own plays, hoped that tempers would cool. Lady Gregory, privately arrogant and aristocratic in her attitude to the actors – 'Maire is such a goose one should not hold her responsible as one would do another,' she wrote to Yeats[8] – publicly tried to pour oil on troubled waters. She was afraid that if they lost their actors, 'we wouldn't know what class would be coming in.'[9]

The year of 1905 passed away in recriminations and restructurings. The new year began with a firm resolution to get on with the job of running the theatre and no nonsense from anyone. Annie's money was with the directors and she reminded them that it had been given to build a theatre in the service of art and it was never to be used for propaganda purposes. She could be excused for being suspicious, especially of the newly formed group who were hoping to use the Abbey Theatre, but her single-minded vision of theatre was inconvenient and exasperating to the Irish. Lady Gregory wrote to Synge on the subject: 'I myself think a propagandist theatre would be very useful, but it is not what she spent her money for. But I wish she would let them act what they will, and show their weakness, and fizzle themselves out.'[10]

During the winter of 1905 and spring of 1906 Annie was often away from Dublin for long stretches, in London, Paris, Prague, Bayreuth, Dresden, always attending theatres and operas, museums and art galleries. She had decided that divided interests at the Abbey were damaging and that it would be better if she left the running of the theatre to Willie Fay and the directors. She had resolved to interfere less. But when the breakaway group, now calling themselves the Theatre of Ireland, sought to use the Abbey for a performance of *The Land*, she indignantly refused. She reminded everyone that when she first offered them a theatre, they had all signed an agreement. Those actors who had left had broken that agreement and had not given her personally any reason for their actions. Annie was smarting from neglect. The members were too busy fighting among themselves to have considered the woman who had given them their theatre. She deserved to be consulted before decisions were made. From Paris in January she wrote to Synge, 'If anyone thinks that "Irish" or "National" are anything to me beyond empty words used to distinguish a society, merely a trifle for convenience, they are much mistaken.'[11] This was foolish talk. The Irish would not thank her for belittling them.

In April 1906 Annie booked the Midland Theatre in Manchester, the St George's Hall in Liverpool and the Albert Hall in Leeds for the Irish players. They were a success and a second, more extensive tour followed closely on the heels of the first. From May to July, the National Theatre Society Ltd played in Cardiff, Glasgow, Aberdeen, Newcastle-on-Tyne, Edinburgh and Hull. They were welcomed everywhere. Annie travelled on the tour with them and it is not surprising that they were often known as Miss Horniman's Company. It tripped off the tongue more easily than their true name, which the press often got wrong although their Irishness was never in doubt. Annie had secured Alfred Waering, business manager to Mr Herbert Beerbohm Tree, to organise the tour, on the promptings of Willie Fay who had met Mr Waering in April and had been led to believe that he would be between seasons and able to join them. Armed with a repertoire of seven plays, scenery and understudies, the company were on professional contracts in first-class theatres. It was an exciting time that stretched everyone's resources to the limit, revealing flaws and weaknesses.

By the tour's end, everyone had a different tale to tell and each tale was enriched by the telling. Willie Fay's view was that just when the tour came to an end, 'we were beginning to enjoy it and everything was running smoothly. Artistically it was an unqualified success.'[12] But he was head over heels in love with Brigit O'Dempsey, one of their new actresses, who, Synge said, was 'one of the most silly and vulgar girls I have ever met.'[13] Perhaps this was a case of sour grapes. Fay and Synge were of a similar age, mid-thirties, and Synge may have wished that he could have swept his twenty-year-old Molly, the reason for Synge being on the tour, off her feet in the same way. Whatever the directors thought of Brigit, they agreed that Willie Fay would be little use to the company until he married her and they turned a blind eye to the fact that, under Irish law, Brigit was under marriageable age. They breathed a sigh of relief when Fay dashed off to Scotland for a weekend in October to marry his sweetheart. Synge grouched at having to do some of the donkey work on publicity. Trailing round shops and press offices with bills and posters was not his idea of proper work for a dramatist, and he was worrying about what Molly was up to while he was away from her side. Mr Waering's recollection of the tour, however, was that Synge's help as company anchor had been invaluable, keeping them on a steady keel and smoothing the waters after sudden squalls.

It was Annie who was largely responsible for these stormy patches. She was very anxious that the tour should be a success, artistically and financially. One without the other would not do. And emotionally she was at a low ebb. In March her father had died rather suddenly. She had never made up the quarrel with her family after her father's remarriage nine years before and her reply to brother Emslie's affectionate letter telling her of their father's death was brisk and business-like. She wrote as to a stranger, thanking him for his 'courtesy in sending the telegram and letter'. She accepted the legacy of £25,000 conditionally, saying that if it were 'unburdened by such conditions as would prevent me from accepting it, I shall eventually give it to some public object. I wish this to be known.'[14] Annie's chance to mend a few family fences was beyond her. She was unable to forget past hurts, she placed such a high premium on what she called her 'self-respect'.

On the tour Annie despaired of Willie Fay's management. When she tried to take over some of the decision-making, she felt that she was not being taken seriously because of her lack of an official position in the company. They almost came to blows at one point, when she described him driving her out of his room like 'a stray cat driven out of a kitchen'. She was also appalled by the behaviour of some of the young actresses who would chat up strangers on railway platforms, and laugh and talk in a loud boisterous manner. The noisy late-night parties at their hotels distressed her too, and by the time they reached Edinburgh, she had had more than enough of Willie Fay's management, which even Synge admitted was deplorably careless. She was mortified by the falling of standards on and off the stage. 'It may be commercial to want Frank Fay to have his wig on right, if so, I glory in being commercial,' she snapped defiantly.[15]

She wrote a list of proposed plans for the future of the Abbey which gave complete control to the directors, including the right to lower the price of the shilling seats for the Society productions but not for any visiting companies. Her concessions were described as Home Rule for the Abbey. She undertook to pay quarterly in advance £500 a year for salaries and £100 to cover administration of the tenancies in her buildings. The money that came in from rents would be used towards the rent, rates and taxes of the theatre. She would meet any bills for repairs and would pay half of scenery costs. It was a most generous and selfless settlement. The only controls that she sought were over the right to refuse publication of plays in the Abbey Theatre Series, published by Maunsell & Co, which had not been performed by the Society and which she did not think fit, and over alterations and additions to the theatre building. She ended by declining to have anything further to do with the company until they proved worthy of her trouble. It had been an arduous tour and everyone's tempers were ragged as they parted company, Miss Horniman to London and the actors home to Ireland.

As she reflected on individual behaviour, Annie decided that Willie Fay had deliberately sabotaged the tour because he had wanted to stay in Dublin where he had more authority than on the road. It seems unlikely, but her thinking reveals how biased she had become towards the Irish players. The tour had been such an unhappy experience for her that she now moved Willie Fay and Synge over to the side of the enemy, like chessboard figures ranged against her queen. The only people she felt were still on her side were the two who had not been on the tour, Lady Gregory and Yeats. She resolved that she must rescue Yeats from wasting his life on administrative matters and, to this end, she added a further £200 quarterly to her Abbey subsidies to pay for a business manager. W. A. Henderson, secretary of the National Literary Society, was duly appointed in October. By doing this, she felt that she had removed the grievances that had built up between her and her Demon over the last months. She felt able to go off to the Continent with a clear conscience.

1. Frederick and Rebekah Horniman with Annie and Emslie.

2. The rear view of Surrey Mount. On 1 June 1895 the gardens were opened to the people of London.

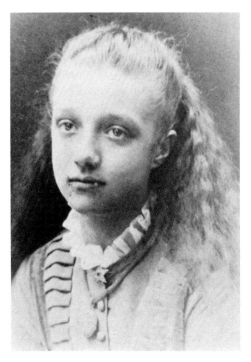

3. and 4. Annie in her growing years, from a golden-haired girl to a rebellious young woman.

5. The Zoological Rooms at Surrey House Museum.

6. Annie's involvement in the Avenue Theatre venture was a closely guarded secret. Later she liked to refer to it as a 'fruitful failure'.

7. Pencil drawing of Annie by J.B. Yeats, 12 April 1905.

8. Pastel drawing of Annie by Laura Anning Bell.

AJAX YEATS DEFIES THE CENSOR.

Much excitement has been caused in Dublin owing to the determination on the part of the Abbey Theatre, of "Playboy of the West" notoriety, to produce a play of Bernard Shaw's in defiance of the warning of the Viceroy.

9. W.B. Yeats poses in his study at 18 Woburn Buildings for the *Tatler*, June 1904.

10. This was one of over two hundred pages of press cuttings that Annie pasted into her Irish scrapbooks.

11. Lewis Casson and Sybil Thorndike met and married while they were at the Gaiety Theatre.

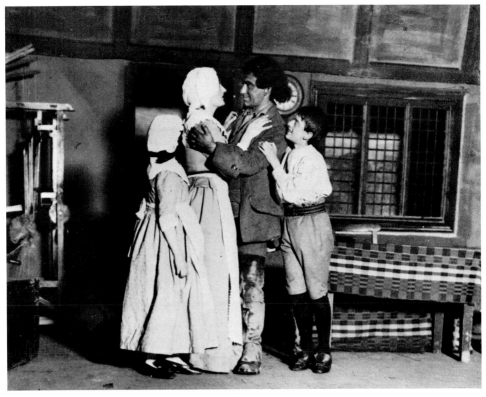

12. A scene from *The Whispering Well* that had its first performance at the Gaiety Theatre in March 1913. Sybil Thorndike is second left.

13. A scene from *Hindle Wakes*.

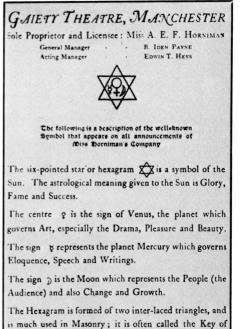

14. Annie asked Silvester Sparrow to design a stained-glass window for her London flat, depicting Klingsor calling up Kundry from *Parsifal*, Act II.

15. Annie carried her astrological beliefs into every part of her life.

16. Annie and Edwin Heys return from a triumphant tour of Canada and the United States in March 1913.

17. Annie is wearing her famous dragon pendant, five inches long and emblazoned with over three hundred opals.

18. Miss Horniman unveils a memorial tablet to Stanley Houghton, 10 February 1915. The inscription reads: 'The Younger Generation is bound to win. That's how the world goes on.'

19. The stage of the Gaiety Theatre redesigned in 1908 by Frank Matcham.

20. Ben Iden Payne is seated in the centre of the Gaiety actors whom he engaged for the first full season in 1908.

21. Annie in one of her fabulous dresses.

From July 1906 to January 1907 Annie travelled around Europe with brief returns to London to attend to business, catch up with her mail and renew her wardrobe. She always travelled simply and stayed at the same quiet hotels and lodging rooms, sometimes alone and sometimes accompanied by one of her young protégées. She behaved like an indulgent aunt, entering into their adventures and enjoying seeing her favourite places through their inexperienced eyes. Helen Pullen-Burry was one of these special friends, a generation younger than Annie. They had first met when Annie had arrived hot and dusty in her cycling gear at Helen's family home in Hampshire, where she had come for an evening of astral exploration. Helen remembered a holiday in Austria where Annie, who detested heights, nevertheless took her on the cable cars, flinching and holding on tightly as the young girl peered down excitedly at the chasms over which they swung.

Throughout these holiday months, Annie carried on a constant correspondence with her 'dear Demon'. He was her eyes and ears at the Abbey Theatre and they discussed details of everyone's behaviour. She sent forwarding addresses and complained when there was no letter awaiting her. 'What is the use of my sending you my address I wonder! I shall be here until the 21st.' This was in August from Bayreuth, where she had obviously travelled by bicycle for she wrote that she had arrived 'a terrible spectacle with *both* eyes damaged and a swollen cheek as well.' There is a gaiety to her writing as she tells him, 'I'm getting fat, the heat and the beer agree with me and there are no mosquitoes.' Each year she met old friends and new at the summer festival. That year Miss Jessie Weston was staying at 51 Richard Wagner Strasse. 'Have you taken any notice of her new book which she sent you?' she scolded. Her old friend Helen Rand had called on her and they were putting behind them 'the reasons which have kept us apart for so long'. Her demon would know all about the reasons, connected with Annie leaving the Golden Dawn in 1903 and Helen Rand joining up with the rival group. The incidents still rankled with Annie and she wrote, 'I've done with transcendental minds and I am thankful . . . They may be on a higher plane, but I had rather a lower plane where a sense of humour and self-respect find a home.' She wrote that she intended to treat Helen Rand as if she had been out of the country for many years.[16]

She had a continuing supply of vivid yellow notepaper, printed with her London address and her personal astrological symbol of an orange eight-pointed star inside of which was the wand of Mercury that would attract beneficial currents to her literary and business enterprises. Her telegraphic address was 'Tintenfisch', the German word for cuttle-fish, which emits a black inky fluid that makes a useful protective screen. It was well chosen by Annie in her typically witty way. (She translated it to Bernard Shaw as octopus, telling him in 1910 when he was offering her two new plays for production that he had behaved rather well towards the Octopus.) On her demandingly bright paper she wrote to Yeats with affection and frankness; she criticised, carped and cajoled, always at great pains to clear away any misunderstanding. There seems to have been a great deal of talk if not outright planning between them about his plays. He could be confident that her money would be used to further his ambitions in the best possible way and if part of the price that he had to pay was scoldings and naggings, he could let them flow unheeded. Annie wrote to him as though he were her irresponsible brother; 'simply ignoring what is said or written' only made her think all the more about what he had ignored. She was forty-six and her wayward Demon was forty-one. No wonder he unburdened himself from time to time to other sympathetic ears. In September he wrote to Florence Farr that he had endured a bad time with Miss Horniman 'whose moon is always in the full of late, but hope a letter yesterday has quieted her.'[17]

The letters from Yeats to Annie have not survived so how much he agreed with her criticisms and how much he went along with her dreams and schemes can only be guessed from her replies. It is certain that they both wanted an artistic theatre capable of performing great plays of all kinds and they both wanted to widen the scope of the Abbey to include other than the peasant plays that were so popular with the Dubliners. Annie very much wanted his work to reach a wider audience and tried hard to persuade him to give his new play, *Deirdre*, to Mrs Patrick Campbell to tour England, or failing that, to ask her over to Dublin. Yeats preferred another actress, Miss Darragh, whose performance in Oscar Wilde's *Salome* in London he had thought magnificent:

> I am inclined to think, though I have not seen enough
> of her yet to be quite certain, that she is the finest

tragedian on the English stage . . . Mrs Campbell and
her generation were trained in plays like *Mrs Tanqueray*
. . . This school reduces everything to an emotional
least common denominator . . . A new school of acting
is now growing up under the influence of the various
attempts to create an intellectual drama, and of changes
deeper than that. The new school seizes upon what is
distinguished, solitary, proud even. One always got a
little of this in Mrs Emery (Florence Farr) when she was
good, and one gets a great deal of it in Miss Darragh.[18]

In November Miss Darragh played the lead in two of Yeats'
plays at the Abbey. She proved a mixed blessing. She was a strong
dramatic actress and made Yeats' poetic plays a great success but
her sophisticated style of acting jarred against the natural simplicity
of the Irish players. 'It was like putting a Rolls Royce to run in a
race against a lot of hill ponies, knowing each inch of the Mountains
of Mourne, bogs and all,' reminisced Willie Fay.[19] Miss Darragh
had been imported from London and was a friend of Miss
Horniman's, which made her an object of suspicion from the start.
Annie had warned her to speak of her 'as a person of no weight'
and to act as if she disapproved of her in every way. 'This should
make things better for your efforts.' Miss Darragh indeed spoke
disparagingly of Miss Horniman but she acted as though she were
her special envoy, causing her to be disliked and resented by
everyone. Miss Horniman was blamed for influencing Yeats to
engage her, when in fact he had chosen her in preference to Annie's
suggestion of Mrs Campbell. He had even suggested to Synge that
if he could get better performances in England, they could make
enough money to dispense with Miss Horniman's subsidies and get
her off their back – a fine example of what James Joyce has called
his 'treacherous instinct of adaptability'.

Annie seems to have been oblivious of his disloyalty, although
perhaps she did suspect him and sought to hold him by presents as
well as promises of financial support. In Bayreuth she bought him
a toothbrush box and soap envelope and a pair of eighteenth-
century brass candlesticks. 'Own up that I treat you better than
you deserve,' she wrote. In Dresden she found him a steel cigarette
case, 'not the most valuable now but I have got one as I know that

you like them better than silver'. In Pont-Aven she wrote that she would like to bring him here, 'only you would object that there is so little water in the Loire and that it has not the "healthy" characteristic in particular of the Liffey'. This time she bought him an old French ring which bore the motto of King Francis I – 'Tout est perdu fors l'honneur' – all is lost save honour.[20]

Her differences with her Demon, she thought, were insignificant. She wrote to him in December, 'our interests are like Tweedledee and Tweedledum who fought a renowned battle' – these were the names given to two quarrelling groups of musicians between whom there was little difference.[21] But her quarrels with the National Theatre Society Ltd were of a different magnitude. She was determined to find a formula for success which in her opinion meant finding someone to relieve Willie Fay of much of his present responsibility. She now put no trust in Synge, whom she thought only cared about his own plays and was unwilling to fight for the theatre in general. Unfairly, she overlooked that Synge was a sick man. Annie only remembered that he had spoken against her behind her back during their Scottish tour instead of arguing it out with her face to face. And he wanted nothing to do with London or English professionals, but to hold the Abbey for Irish plays and the Irish people.

Annie recognised that the way forward was to find a good managing director, and not someone who could be manipulated by Willie Fay. She felt that it was time to broaden the base of the Abbey, to attract outside players, perform more than Irish plays and appeal to a wider audience by undertaking English and later American tours. She made an offer of £500 as a salary for a managing director, leaving Willie Fay to manage the peasant plays, and she spelled out the kind of man she wanted – 'He should be fairly young, of good manners and such a temper as will make the position possible for him. He must have practical stage experience as well as experience in stage management of all classes of plays. He would need to be able to stage manage anything and be competent to produce all plays except those treating of Irish peasant life.'[22] Annie's ideas made good sense in every way, not just good business sense, but such a man would undoubtedly be English and by broadening the base of the Abbey it would undoubtedly become less Irish.

On the last day of 1906, from the Hotel Oriental, Algiers, she wrote to 'My dear Demon' and marked it *Private*. She knew that Synge was against bringing in a new man and this was her last attempt to try to persuade Yeats into a decision. She began: 'Mr Synge wants Fay to run the show, he is too lazy to care about anything except his own plays and too cowardly to fight for the whole. Unless Lady Gregory will decide you will be obliged to give in and Fay will only permit a cheap man whom he can virtually dismiss to be engaged . . . I cannot and will not strengthen the present state of things; it would (to put it baldly) be sheer waste of money.' She went on to urge him to put his talent first, to put his literary and poetical work before the work of the Abbey Theatre, to go on writing plays and to get them produced wherever he could. 'Your work is too valuable to the World, my dear friend, for me to allow any loyalty to the theatre on *my* behalf to cramp it . . . Life is short and you are only just coming into your full powers.'[23]

Over the previous two years Annie had many times seen the road ahead fork, with one way pointing to Yeats' interests and growing international recognition and the other to the Irish national interests that Fay represented. If she really thought that Yeats was keeping his work for the Abbey out of any sense of loyalty to her, she was, however, sorely misguided. He may have led her to believe this and at the same time hinted that when her patent at the Abbey expired in 1910 she could take his plays elsewhere. She ended her letter by telling him either to engage a first-class managing director or to put her offer and all that it implied out of '*our*' mind. They were acting as one. Annie wanted great things for her Demon's plays. Did he want as much? The next year would play out the warnings that the tarot cards had given. Now she asked him to remember that her effort was on his behalf and for his work. She wished him 'A happy New Year' and signed herself 'Yours, Annie'.

9

The Playboy and the English MD

In January 1907, while Annie was still escaping from London's winter chills and fogs, Yeats travelled from Dublin to Waterford to make the acquaintance of Ben Iden Payne who was on tour with Cyril Keightley's company. Annie had left the Abbey directors to make the decision over her offer to pay for a professional managing director. Lady Gregory had reluctantly accepted that it was an expedient move. She had been worn down by Yeats, who dreaded 'more and more the scheme of letting Fay practise on classics and so to make us ridiculous in the eyes of the few who matter. It comes to this – why am I to be sacrificed to Fay's vanity and Mr Synge's egotism?'[1] She suspected that if she did not agree, Yeats would take himself and his plays to England and she would be left with the Irish. Synge did not like it but he could not prevent it. A compromise was reached in that a new man would be engaged for a six-month trial, and the three directors agreed among themselves that once they had built up their home audience they could afford to be free of Miss Horniman; it was just a question between them of the best way to do this. But though Yeats went along with his fellow directors while he was with them, he sang a different tune to Annie. He allowed her to believe that her money and his genius could forge a working partnership.

When he arrived at the Waterford theatre he went backstage and between scenes introduced himself to the twenty-five-year-old Lancashire actor who had been recommended as managing director by Granville Barker. 'Not the poet?' queried Iden Payne. 'Yes,' replied Yeats, with not a hint of a smile, 'I am William Butler Yeats. I suppose you might call me a poet.'[2] After the performance, over a whiskey, Yeats invited Iden Payne to come to Dublin to meet his fellow directors, and on Saturday 26 January the young Englishman turned up to tea and buttered toast in Lady Gregory's sitting room at the Nassau Hotel. His first impression of her was of a dowager lady who went well with the heavily upholstered furniture in the tapestry-curtained room. Synge was tense at this first meeting, preoccupied with what lay ahead that night. His *Playboy of the Western World* was having its first performance at the Abbey with Willie Fay playing the lead as Christy Mahon.

Ben Iden Payne was in the audience for the first night and witnessed an amazing theatrical experience that sent shock waves across the whole of the United Kingdom. Before they even entered the theatre, the Dublin theatregoers were suspicious of the new play because its author was Synge and when, in Act 3, Fay spoke the lines, 'It's Pegeen I'm seeking only and what'd I care if you brought me a drift of Mayo girls standing in their shifts itself, maybe,' the theatre erupted.

> The stage became spectators
> And the audience the players
> Whether the play was good or bad
> It really didn't matter
> Whether in comic vein or sad
> Beside the awful clatter
> We couldn't hear a single word
> From rise to fall of curtain.[3]

Substituting 'Mayo girls' for the 'chosen girls' of Synge's script added insult to injury but the real damage was done by the seemingly innocent word 'shifts'. Anger centred on this one word, which was plucked from the play and paraded as an example of the coarseness and depravity in Synge's work. It inspired cartoons, jokes and songs, which were published in a booklet entitled 'The Abbey Row NOT Edited by W. B. Yeats'. On the cover was a lampoon of the device to be found on the Abbey programmes; Mrs Grundy replaced Queen Maeve, carrying an umbrella instead of a quiverful of arrows, and restraining a wolf-hound body with Synge's head. One verse of 'Oh No! We Never Mention it', sung to the air of 'Early Victorian', ran:

Oh no we never mention it, its name is never heard –
Now Ireland sets its face against the one familiar word.
They take me to the Gaelic League where men wear kilts, and
   yet

The simple word of childhood's days I'm bidden to forget!
They tell me no one says it now, but yet to give me ease –
If I must speak they bid me use a word that rhymes with
    'sneeze'.[4]

Annie was not at the Abbey to see Synge's play but she very
soon knew all about it from the headlines and articles in local and
national newspapers in the following days, weeks and months. The
directors were unanimous in agreement that the play must go on
and fulfil the arranged programme for the next week. They would
not give in to the bullying tactics that strove to close the theatre by
fair means or foul. On Monday night the actors went through their
parts, though not a word was heard because of the uproar. The
next night, police lined the walls and rioters were hauled out and
arrested, to appear in court next day. And so it went on through
the week, with rival factions hurling abuse at each other across the
stalls heedless of the play. Finally, on Monday 4 February Yeats
called an open public debate on 'The Freedom of the Theatre',
which gave as much entertainment as the play. One young man
forced his way on to the stage and argued with 'Dossy' Wright,
one of the actors, until a whiskey bottle fell from his pocket and
shattered, when he was thrown down the steps by Dossy to much
cheering and laughing. Yeats senior made a good speech and was
well received until there were cries of 'Kill your father' and 'Get
the loy'.

Annie was both delighted and infuriated by the Irish behaviour.
She recognised that Synge had written a great play and urgently
demanded another from him as soon as possible. She called herself
a worm for not having come over to support him and blamed the
directors for ignoring her offer 'to come and join the fray'. On the
other hand she was not pleased with the behaviour on or off the
stage in the theatre. She sent Yeats a disapproving telegram,
knowing that its contents would very quickly pass round Dublin,
and followed it up with a letter. 'I am informed,' she wrote, 'that
low behaviour (I mean hissing) took place from the stage, and that
the hissing was political. It must be absolutely understood that I
will not allow my theatre to be used for any political purpose
whatever, and the players must be informed that the drunken
vulgarity of the stalls is just as bad as the patriotic vulgarity of the
pit.'[5]

It was just as well that she had not been there in person. She would have seen free fights among the orchestra, Trinity College students singing 'God Save the King', the call boy who was also the general dogsbody, armed with an axe, swearing by all the holy saints to chop off the heads of the first to come over the footlights, the players behind the scenes running around in all directions, while Synge himself sat pale and motionless. The press had a field day, with headlines such as 'A Queer Hero', 'A Dramatic Freak', 'Kill the Author', 'The Language of the Gutter', 'An Insult to the Women of Mayo', 'Police-Protected Drama'. One of the longest was in the Irish *Freeman's Journal* of 30 January: 'Support Abbey Theatre Against Organised Opposition. He Who Strikes at Freedom of Judgement Strikes at the Soul of the Nation.'[6]

Annie collected nearly one hundred and fifty pages of press cuttings relating to the uproar and pandemonium over Synge's play. When tempers had cooled and the atmosphere was calmer, she wrote a letter that was carried by seventeen papers on 12 and 13 February, in which she thanked 'the Press of all shades and opinions for the great amount of space given to the affairs of the Abbey Theatre'.[7] She told them that a great art centre could be made in Dublin which would be the envy of other cities and the opportunity lay in the hands of the general public. But it was not the general public who made their way to the Abbey in Marlborough Street, off the track of the successful commerical theatres, but the nationalists and patriots who wanted to use the theatre to make Ireland great. Annie, knowing this, feared that the general public would never come to her theatre now; they would always associate it with political trouble-makers and nationalist agitators.

Ben Iden Payne had not been put off by the disturbances of opening night on 26 January and was eager to take on the challenge at the Abbey. It was made very clear to him that he would have no hand in the productions of the Irish peasant plays, which were Willie Fay's responsibility. He was to get £5 a week and at once he was resented by Henderson, a business manager, who got thirty shillings a week. Fay knew that the players had to widen their technique and their talents to encompass more than the peasant plays, but he wanted to move slowly. As he saw it, 'it would be time enough to be thinking about getting our light on a candlestick when it was burning steadily enough not to be blown out by the blasts of prejudice and ill-will under which it was even now flickering.'[8] He was not against bringing in Ben Iden Payne but he thought that it was bad timing. But of course the time would never be right, for there would always be prejudice and ill-will while an English woman had any influence or control. Annie sensed trouble ahead and knew that she would be the scapegoat. She tried to forestall it by a letter on 28 January to the directors: 'It must be clearly understood by all concerned that I have had nothing to do with the choice of Mr Payne except that I asked Mr Vedrenne (manager of London's Royal Court) to advise Mr Yeats.'

For the time being tempers remained even, as everyone enjoyed the free publicity brought their way by the *Playboy* rumpus. Yeats was particuarly anxious to take advantage of this and Annie agreed to finance another English tour. There was even talk of an American tour. This possibility could have been the reason for Charles Frohman's arrival at the Abbey one evening. He was a well-known American manager and producer, and had already indicated an interest in the National Theatre Society and their plays. Officially he was in Dublin with J. M. Barrie to see Barrie's new play at one of the other theatres, and the two of them took the opportunity to slip into seats at the Abbey one evening without the actors being aware of their presence. Rumours were soon circulating in the Irish press that Charles Frohman would be taking on the management of the Abbey. Miss Horniman was quick to deny this, assuring everyone that she was pledged privately and publicly to carry on until Christmas 1910.

On 10 April 1907 Yeats joined Lady Gregory, with son Robert as chaperon, on an Italian holiday. It was ironic that he was able to go only because of Annie's generosity that had led to the engagement of first a business manager and now Payne as managing director. While he was taking in the sights of Venice, Siena and Florence, Annie wrote frequently and affectionately to her dear Demon. She was rather wistful that he could never again see Venice for the first time and was glad that his experienced guide had shown it to him in the only way that it could really be appreciated – coming by sea to the steps that lead to the Grand Piazza and to the Duomo of St Mark. Clearly, Annie would have liked to have been her Demon's guide, but she could afford to be magnanimous because she believed that the Abbey was set to move in the

professional direction that she wanted. She gave the directors a
formal warning that if Payne left she would be free 'to refuse any
further aid to the scheme beyond the free use of the theatre, the
subsidy and the payment of half the cost of such things as are used
by my tenants.'[9]

Before the Italian holiday ended, the Irish players went on tour
of Glasgow, Birmingham, Cambridge, Oxford and London, organised by Annie. *The Playboy of the Western World* was in their
repertoire, billed everywhere as the play that caused a riot, and it
brought in the crowds so that takings more than covered expenses.
They decided not to play it at Birmingham because the city had an
Irish element that might have caused a disturbance and the
company wanted to be sure of reaching London. As it was, the
Censor ordered Miss Horniman to consult with the Home Office
and the Lord Chamberlain before the London opening. After the
performances Synge was hailed as a genius but opinions were
unsure on his play. William Archer, the London critic, gave his
verdict: 'If it is a joke, its meaning is not obvious; if it is to be
taken seriously it is surely a libel on the Irish peasant character.
But as a rare piece of writing – in imagination, in colour, in felicity
of phrase – it is a delight from beginning to end.'[10]

When the company reached Oxford Annie finally met up with
her new managing director. Ben Iden Payne saw a slender, self-
assured woman of average height, in 'vaguely medieval' dress. She
appeared to him as a prophetess with the pontifical air she gave
even to the most commonplace remark, breaking the spell by
ending her utterances with a self-mocking twist. He knew of her
English reputation as a good business woman and her Irish
reputation as an impossible woman. This was the public face of
Miss Horniman, and he did not know the shy private side of Annie
and the sense of inadequacy before creative, artistic people that
made her seem pompous and dictatorial. She immediately liked her
new man and was already impressed by his ability. She hoped that
he would be the means of rescuing Yeats' plays which she believed
were in a different class from those of Lady Gregory and William
Boyle which were so popular with Dublin audiences.

Payne was already feeling uncomfortable in his position with the
Irish players, whose casual ways he found very difficult. His first
production, Maeterlinck's *Interior*, had worked well but his next,

Fand, a poetic play by Wilfred Scawen Blunt, was described by
Synge as 'deplorable, it came out as a bastard literary pantomime
put on with many of the worst tricks of the English stage'.[11] Synge
felt inclined to walk out of the theatre and never return,, although
he did concede that Payne was obviously trying his best and might
in time understand their Irish methods. The tour of the English
theatres with English audiences and English appreciation made
Payne realise that he could never achieve the results he wanted in
Dublin, and he left the company after the London run. In his
resignation letter he explained that, though his personal relations
with the company had been entirely friendly, it was useless to hide
the fact that officially they were antagonistic towards an English
managing director.

As soon as Annie heard of his resignation she sent him a note
inviting him to call on her at Montagu Mansions. Over China tea
and toasted teacakes she discovered that she had met an ally. He
was as dispirited as she was over the lack of professionalism at the
Abbey. He could not see what hope there was for players who
stopped in mid-sentence at the cry 'Tea's ready' and disappeared
for tea and cakes and endless talk. Annie shared with him her
feelings of hurt and outrage over her treatment by the company. 'I
want to teach those impossible people in Dublin that I have other
fish to fry,' she declared.[12] Payne removed a cat from his comfortable armchair and told her of his ambitions. He had read Ibsen and
Shaw and was eager to experience the New Drama. As he talked
his eagerness spilled over and Annie knew that she had found the
man who would build with her a new kind of repertory theatre.
Before he left she proposed that he should take charge of her next
theatrical venture, backed by her father's bequest of £25,000. They
discussed the sort of plays they would promote, the kind of theatre
they would run and where it might be situated.

Annie was fairly sure that Yeats would give them his poetic
plays. She had discussed with him many times the need to find a
wider audience. As part of this search for a larger public, she had
already in March guaranteed £1,500 for publication of a limited
edition of his collected plays. With A. H. Bullen of the Shakespeare
Head Press at Stratford, she had agreed terms for publishing a set
of eight volumes; Bullen would take two thirds of the profits, she
would take one third and the author would have reasonable

royalties on the sales. She insisted on new portraits of her playwright – 'whether they are done by an Italian or an Indian or an
Irishman' was immaterial – and in fairness informed Mr Bullen
that Lady Gregory had given some help with the peasant dialogue
in some of the plays. Yeats had pointed this out to her as a reason
why Lady Gregory had 'a certain claim' on the disposal of his
work.[13]

Annie had obviously discussed with Yeats how she might use his
plays when her years of subsidy ran out for the Abbey in 1910, and
Yeats had equally obviously discussed with Lady Gregory what
they could do when the patent ran out. He wanted to please both
ladies, to give them both what they so ardently desired. Lady
Gregory believed that he had been cornered into giving Miss
Horniman a promise against his will and she would never agree to
his taking his plays away from the Abbey. The twelfth in a family
of sixteen children, she had learned from an early age to fight for
what she wanted and to hold on tightly to what she had. She was
more than a match for Annie as Yeats listened to her pleading:

> The more I think of that 'promise' the more urgent does
> the need seem that you should free yourself from it. I
> know you never made it consciously, you may in a hasty
> argument have said something that Miss Horniman took
> hold of and is trying to keep you to. But we have often
> talked of what would happen at the end of the patent,
> and said that she should have a very strong hand,
> theatre renewal of patent, and money, but that we on
> the other side had the plays and the players. You so
> often talked of independence . . . But if that 'promise'
> holds we go into a fight, either at the end of the patent
> term or sooner, with our right hand tied. You will have
> given Miss Horniman one of our strongest possessions
> or weapons. She can take your plays from Ireland
> altogether or force you to put them into some movement
> opposed to your views. You will have betrayed those
> who have been working for you. You will yourself be in
> a humiliating position, seeing your friends and
> comrades dictated to and not being able to take their
> side . . . Those plays were our own children, I was so

proud of them, and loved them, and now I cannot think
of them without the greatest pain.[14]

Against such feminine wiles Annie had little chance. Now that
Payne had resigned from the Abbey she did not want to wait for
the patent to run out before she had Yeats' work. She wanted to
take both playwright and plays with her. But it was not to be. His
reply, undated and unsigned, was simple and true.

> My dear Miss Horniman:
>
> I have thought carefully over your proposal of yesterday
> and have decided that it is impossible so far as I am
> concerned. I am not young enough to change my
> nationality – it would really amount to that. Though I
> wish for a universal audience, in play-writing there is
> always an immediate audience also. If I am to try and
> find the immediate audience in England I would fail
> through lack of understanding on my part, perhaps
> through lack of sympathy. I understand my own race
> and in all my work, lyric or dramatic, I have thought of
> it. If the theatre fails I may or may not write plays – but
> I shall write for my own people – whether in love or
> hate of them matters little – probably I shall not know
> which it is. Nor can I make any permanent allocation of
> my plays while the Irish theatre may at any moment
> need my help. At any moment I may have to ask friends
> for funds with the whole mass of plays for a bait.[15]

With or without Yeats, Annie and her new man were all set for
their next venture. They both knew that London was out of the
question, for the Vedrenne-Barker partnership had already carved
out a niche at the Royal Court Theatre for productions of new and
uncommercial plays and was just ending a very successful three-
year run. In June 1907, at a dinner celebrating his success,
Granville Barker said that what was needed was 'a repertory
theatre, but the difficulty of establishing one in London would be
very great . . . As a good Socialist I am glad to be able to sum up
the chief of these difficulties in the one word rent.'[16] He went on to
suggest that Manchester or Birmingham might be the site of the
first repertory theatre in order to avoid these high costs.

Manchester was the city that came up in conversation in Annie's apartment in that same month of June. Ben Iden Payne favoured Manchester: it was a large city surrounded by towns that could provide plenty of supporters and it was recognised as a cultural and artistic centre, already having a symphony orchestra and a fine quality newspaper with professional theatre critics. He could have added that his father was a Unitarian minister in the city, but Annie was already more than keen. She sent him off to Manchester to scout around for a theatre and to sniff the air for possible support for what would be a wholly new and different kind of theatre.

Although Yeats had rejected her offer, she was still writing in her usual style to him. After her customary 'Dear Demon' in a July letter, she immediately launched into a long tirade against the unclean and unhealthy state in which she had found his London flat. 'There are some moths in your curtains and the books on the top shelves are absolutely filthy. I went upstairs to wash after finding these as my fingers were black. The mattresses are uncovered, the eider-down covers the blankets and that will be *filthy* very soon. The floors are littered with bits of papers, they have not been washed since you left . . .' No wonder Annie had joked to J. B. Yeats that she should marry his son and make him a comfortable home. Her letter continued:

> I hope that now we have got rid of these worrying
> affairs that kept causing disagreeables between us, that
> there will be some peace and quiet. You will find it a
> rest not to be obliged to write me accounts of the
> theatrical doings nor to make vain efforts on my behalf.
> It was a useless task, to try to make the theatre we
> planned at the beginning. But we were right to try our
> best. Let me know if there is anything you want me to
> do for you in London, you know how gladly I will run
> errands!
>
> Yours, Annie.[17]

She had no reason to be angry with her Demon and she had always believed that she was fighting the Irish for his sake.

In August she wrote to him from France, where he had sought

her help on a horoscope reading that he had made for himself. He was obviously in a quandary over what he should do about the constant problems at the Abbey and how he could sort out family and business worries so that he could get back to his own work. Annie, as ever, was there to comfort and support.

> You must be very determined not to take any fresh
> serious course of action under those aspects. I cannot
> help being anxious about you, you ought to be doing
> your greatest work now . . . You are not valued enough
> by your own people, either your relations or your fellow
> country-men. I shall be so glad when you return to
> London in the early Autumn; I want to see you again,
> yourself and myself, not two people worried to death
> about difficulties neither can remove even with the best
> will in the World.'[18]

She was still buying him presents – this time a goatskin water-bag from Tunis – but uppermost in her mind was the fear that he would make some new move when the stars were not favourable and before he had talked it over with her. She once told Synge with her usual twist of humour, 'The study of astrology gives me a beautifully non-libellous means of abusing people.'[19] Yet friends continued to seek her advice on their horoscopes, and the forecast she made for Synge was typical in its accuracy and honesty. She had warned him that strange, unexpected events would turn up in his love affairs to spoil them and that he was unlikely to marry, at the same time comforting him that he was unlikely to become insane despite his attraction to gloomy ideas and his disturbing imagination.

Annie did not need to consult her own horoscope to discover what the future held for her at the Abbey. She knew that there was no hope of reconciliation; feelings were too intense on both sides. Lady Gregory described her as 'like a shilling in a tub of electrified water' – anyone who tried to touch the shilling received a nasty shock. Annie listed their vices to the Reverend Hannay's sympathetic ear: love of power, maniacal vanity, sloth, a queer superstition on all art matters, an absolute absence of a sense of proportion or of duty and, worst of all, using and abusing Mr Yeats, 'wearing out the best years of his working life with their petty quarrels and jealousies'. The Reverend had advised her when she had made such a fuss about political elements in the *Playboy* riots: 'You must either modify the hammer or magnify the nuts . . . I believe you are on the threshold of a school of Drama that might make its mark on Europe . . . Go on, and come more to Dublin.'[20] He was not the only Irishman to encourage and praise. Sir Horace Plunkett, owner of Dublin's *Daily Express* and Unionist MP, had admired her courage and appreciated the good she was doing for his 'unhappy country'. But it was too late. Annie had had enough of the Irish temperament. She would never return to Dublin. She would go to Manchester and if Yeats would not go with her, then he must stay behind. Life was too short to spend in recriminations. It was September 1907 and Annie would be forty-eight in a month's time. She had work to do and no time to lose.

10

The Choice of Manchester

When Annie had visited Manchester with the Irish players and their home-grown plays in 1906, she had dressed as befitted the benefactress of the Abbey Theatre and patroness of Ireland's National Theatre Society. James Agate, Manchester theatre critic, found it hard to decide at the time which had impressed him more – Miss Horniman or the Irish drama. She had worn a gown of rich green brocade with her enormous dragon pendant – over five inches from scaly cheek to coiling tail – flashing across her bosom. This mystical dragon was made of oxidised silver and studded with over three hundred opals which Annie had assiduously collected on holidays abroad. Huge, hypnotic ruby eyes dominated its face, which seemed like an oriental version of the grinning Cheshire cat. It hung by chains of twisted silver links from an opal-studded, shield-shaped brooch which was supported at each side by a stronger linked chain that hung around her neck. It was a mischievously defiant ornament that always caused comment.

The smartly dressed wives of the city's solidly wealthy merchants, who no doubt considered themselves knowledgeable on the latest fashions, must have stared in disbelief at Miss Horniman's stunning appearance. They certainly remembered who she was when they read in their newspapers just over a year later that she was making Manchester the venue for her next theatrical experiment. Her manager, Mr Ben Iden Payne, was already known to them, for he was a local man. His father had been minister at Strangeways Unitarian Chapel and he was an old boy of Manchester Grammar School.

The social centre of the city was the Midland Hotel, an enormous, ornate building that reflected the citizens' wealth and confidence. Within its sturdy shiny-brown brick walls was a ballroom with a stage at one end and a row of pretty boxes down both sides. A direct way led to this hall from the back of the hotel,

which looked towards Central Station. It was a good situation,
Annie thought, in which to test the reaction of the Manchester
people to the new kind of drama that she and Ben Iden Payne
wanted to produce. It also happened to be right in the centre of the
city's thriving theatreland, joining the two main thoroughfares of
Oxford Road and Peter Street. Annie decided to lease the Midland
Theatre for a few experimental weeks.

There were already eight other commercial theatres in the city
centre competing with each other for the people's patronage. They
seemed to offer everything that could possibly be wanted in the
form of entertainment – music halls, variety, spectacle, Shakespeare, serious drama, ballet, opera, circus – and there was a
circuit of suburban theatres. It would have been understandable if
Annie had decided that here was too much competition. Wisely,
she looked beyond the immediate pleasures on offer and contem-
plated the intellectual vigour and business acumen, the artistic
appreciation and political shrewdness that had made Manchester
one of the world's leading cities. The list of its achievements
seemed endless – the Literary and Philosophic Society, the Portico
Library and Club, the Athenaeum, the *Manchester Guardian* and
the *Manchester Courier*, the Royal Manchester Institution, the Art
Treasures Exhibition, the Halle Orchestra and the Royal Manchester College of Music, Manchester University, the Women's
Social and Political Union. The facts of Manchester's thrusting
commercial success had been turned to successful popular fiction:
Mrs Gaskell had written about it in *North and South* and Mrs
Linnaeus Banks in *The Manchester Man*.

The Manchester Ship Canal had brought the world into the heart
of the city and carried her trade back to the four corners of the
world. When one of Annie's actors told her that he could not
possibly stay for long in such a place – 'Why, I've just come from
Venice,' he grandly told her – she answered smoothly, 'We have
canals here too, you know.'[1] Sir Charles Hallé had brought the
music of Berlioz, Brahms, Dvorak, Grieg and Wagner to the city
long before other provincials had the opportunity to hear them and
after Hallé's death Hans Richter had come from the Vienna Opera
and the Vienna Philharmonic to be resident conductor of the Hallé
orchestra. Annie mischievously said that her choice had hinged on
which city had bought the most copies of the Irish plays when they

had toured, and maybe there was more than a hint of truth in this. Manchester had been the first city to open a public library for everyone to use. As for the people, there was an educated, cultured German-Jewish element among the earnest, hard-working and increasingly refined middle classes and a large working class that was thirsty for knowledge as well as entertainment. Annie's ancestors had come from Germany to settle in Devon and her two grandfathers, one English and one Scottish, had made their money in trade. She would feel very much at home in Manchester.

Her first job was to let the people know what she planned to do for them. She had learnt the value of publicity and the usefulness of the press for free advertisement. Over the summer months of 1907 she and Payne fed the papers with news and titbits, so that long before opening night there was a buzz of comment and discussion. He set the ball rolling with his letter of 11 July which several newspapers printed:

> Sir, I am writing to inform you of a scheme which, it is possible, may form the nucleus of a city theatre, the idea of which, I am informed, has been mooted recently in Manchester. Miss A. E. F. Horniman, with myself as her general manager, hopes to form a repertory theatre in Manchester and we shall commence our work in the coming autumn with a series of productions, probably at the Midland Hotel Theatre. This, however, will only be a beginning and we hope in time to have our own theatre.
>
> We have, tentatively, given the name of the Manchester Playgoers' Theatre to our work, and we intend to produce no plays which are not sincere works of art. We shall seek to produce good new plays, to revive old masterpieces and to present translations of the best works of foreign authors. We have chosen Manchester because we feel that of all towns it is the one most ready for such an undertaking, and that there, if anywhere, there will be the support necessary for the success of our scheme. I hope very shortly to give much fuller particulars.
>
> Yours etc., B. Iden Payne[2]

Their intentions were warmly welcomed. An enthusiastic Play-goers' Theatre Club had already been formed in February, while nearby Stockport had a thriving Garrick Society where the members studied plays and gave public performances. Manchester had been the only provincial city to form a branch of the Independent Theatre Society in 1893, two years after London. Their first performance had been George Moore's *The Strike at Arlingford*, three days after London's first performance. The Society had run for five years at the Gentleman's Concert Hall and introduced five Ibsen plays and Shaw's *Candida* to Manchester audiences. Annie was picking up where they had left off and in almost the very same spot, for the Gentleman's Concert Hall had been demolished to make way for the Midland Hotel.

She knew exactly how she would run her company, and she was determined that this time she would be in control. Her actors would have secure contracts but they would be open to dismissal for what she regarded as good reasons. 'If two men come to blows just before the curtain rises, they will get the sack. If the leading man refuses to rehearse with the leading lady – he will be fired.'[3] There would be discipline from the manager down to the callboy. In fact, she had no need to interfere because she had absolute trust in her manager. Payne had been warned by Yeats to make sure that his contract was clear and concise with no room for Miss Horniman to assert her authority. 'She is,' Yeats explained, 'a vulgarian.' He made this remark at a time when she was bending over backwards to be fair and supportive to him and his Irish colleagues. He was obviously smarting from barbs of jealousy that pricked him every time he thought of his benefactress starting a new adventure without him. Perhaps he had hoped his refusal to go with her would deter her. Now he found comfort in ridiculing what she was doing and the plays she had chosen for her first experimental season, as did his fellow directors. 'She claims to have lots of plays,' he wrote to Florence Farr; 'they must be pretty bad if she has.'[4] And Synge wrote to Lady Gregory, 'I am astonished at Payne's repertoire. I fear we must be very ignorant about the classics of the Anglican Drama.'[5] While revealing this meannness of spirit, they were still benefiting from Annie's generosity. Even now she was extending the Abbey's facilities by converting a stable which she had recently acquired into extra dressing-rooms.

Meanwhile, Payne had followed up his letter to the papers with
another, telling the people that their repertory theatre would offer
the best plays of all ages with special emphasis on new and original
drama, performed by a stock company of first-rate actors. The
seats would be at popular prices and he promised efficient productions. Annie had given him a budget within which he went
shopping for capable, dedicated actors whom he knew from
personal experience would work selflessly for the sake of the team.
They were drawn mainly from Granville Barker's company, Frank
Benson's company and William Poel's Elizabethan Stage Society,
all of which Annie admired and respected.

As opening night approached, Payne gave a lecture at the
Midland Theatre to the Playgoers' Theatre Club on the advantages
of a repertory theatre. The rules of the all-male club were altered
to allow female members, specially for Annie's benefit. She sat
centre-stage, dressed in the style that Manchester theatregoers
would recognise – in a rich brocade gown adorned by her famous
dragon – surrounded by her company of actors. Her manager
explained what they meant by repertory, pointing out that the
dictionary meaning of the word was 'storehouse' and this was just
what the company aimed to be. As a library had books on its
shelves waiting to be taken down and used, so would they have
plays that had already been produced and justified themselves
ready to be used again. By changing the play two or three times a
week, the actors would not grow stale and their supporters would
be able to come to the theatre more than once a week. In this way
a community spirit would grown between them and their audience.
The repertory movement was to be a democratic art, reaching the
widest possible public.

Annie engaged a business manager and appointed as acting
manager Edwin Heys, who had been secretary of the Stockport
Garrick Dramatic Society since it was founded. This left Payne
free to concentrate on artistic direction. He and Annie agreed
together on the programme. She read every play that was sent to
her, which, over the years, became an onerous task, and she
became a familiar sight to Mancunians, hopping on and off
tramcars and buses with a bundle of scripts tucked under her arm.

She gave her new company a symbol which was printed on all
their programmes and posters. It was a six-pointed star, the symbol

of glory, fame and success, within which was the sign of Venus, the planet that governs the arts and the house of Libra, which was Annie's birth sign. On one side of Venus was the sign of Mercury, the planet that governs eloquence, speech and writing, and the sign that blessed her personal yellow writing paper. On the other side was the crescent Moon that represents the people, change and growth. Annie wanted her work to be carried out under all the most beneficial astrological currents. In this way she believed that her new venture could only grow from strength to strength. She had done with the ritualistic and transcendental side of her life but she remained true to her belief in this life being only one stage in the evolution of the soul. She knew of other time-scales and could unlock their secrets. Friends would tell her their dreams and Annie would explain their meaning, sometimes referring to events that had yet to happen, but she had no need for such mystic messages for herself. She knew exactly what she wanted to do in Manchester and with the help and support of the people she would achieve it.

On 23 September 1907 the Playgoers' Theatre Company opened their short season of plays at the Midland Theatre. In the first week they introduced Mancunians to Charles McEvoy, an Englishman of Irish extraction whose play *David Ballard* had impressed Annie and Ben Iden Payne on its first showing by the Stage Society in London earlier in the year. It was a realistic drama about lower middle-class life. Payne took the leading part while his wife, the actress Mona Limerick, starred in McEvoy's one-act play *The Helpmate*, which was their curtain raiser. 'Brilliant', was the word that sprang to everyone's lips to describe the opening night – 'brilliant opening', 'brilliant comedy' – but brilliance with a difference, as one critic noted, with 'a refreshing freedom from dramatic conventionalities'.[6]

The four-week programme had been chosen to give Mancunians a taste of what to expect. On offer were realism from Charles McEvoy and from Miss A. L. Williams' new play *The Street*, one light-hearted French farce, one play for a star actress who would be sure to fill the seats, one experimental mood play – Maeterlinck's *The Interior*, which worked wonderfully under Payne's direction – and one play by Bernard Shaw. Annie had hoped for a newer, more popular play from Shaw but he was keeping his material exclusively for Granville Barker at the Royal Court in London. She

felt that he might have repaid the debt that he was publicly
acknowledging he owed to her from the days of the Avenue Theatre
by giving her a new play, but she took *Widowers' Houses* and her
company turned it into a great success. The applause and laughter
rang out in the little Midland Theatre, a remarkable change from
the response to its first performance by the Independent Theatre
Society in London in 1892 when, as St John Ervine recalled, 'the
Socialists in the pit and gallery lustily cheered while the Conserva-
tives in the stalls and dress circle lustily booed.'[7]

C. E. Montague of the *Manchester Guardian* wrote that it was the
best performance that he could recall of any Shaw play. 'The acting
was like Shaw's writing, which has no stupidities and no beauties.
There was no virtuosoish working of any of the actors' special gift,
but every intention of the play was understood and carried out.'
He gave high praise to Mona Limerick's 'dragonsome Blanche' and
thought Shaw would redraft his description of his character Cokane
as played by Charles Bibby.[8] This actor became one of the kingpins
of Miss Horniman's Company. Payne described him as the finest
character actor he had ever known, 'unique in his capacity for
grasping a character in a flash and without effort and apparently
with instinct free from thought, creating *instantaneously* a finished
picture of what he had to represent'.[9]

While the season was in progress, Annie began the work of
spreading the gospel of repertory, work which she carried out with
enthusiasm and dedication for the next twelve years. Her first press
interview was to the *Manchester Courier*, which carried her views
on municipal theatres which, she declared, every German town of
any worth already had. 'When the people want them they will get
them, and not before. We shall have to elect on to the town
councils, or to Parliament, those who are in sympathy with such
an idea and who will push it forward. It must be remembered also,
that when we get a municipal theatre, we shall simply have to pay
for it out of the rates, as we do for our gas and electricity.'[10] A
theatre of art and culture was one of life's essentials to Annie.
Could it be that she was moving into the political arena in order to
achieve her ends?

Her first talk was to the Life Study Association, in a private
room at the Midland Hotel, when she took as her title 'A New
Theatre for Manchester'. She was not the only speaker who was

going up and down the country spreading the news of repertory. Beerbohm Tree had talked to the Liverpool Stage Club in September and Granville Barker had been speaking to the Stockport Garrick Society in October. Ben Iden Payne went up and down the Lancashire towns speaking of their aims for a repertory theatre, and nearer Manchester, Edwin Heys talked to clubs and societies, for even the new business manager was expected to promote their new kind of theatre. People were now receptive to the new ideas that were being worked out on stage and were willing to argue and discuss them – which had not been so at the time of Annie's first theatrical venture more than ten years before. Ibsen and Shaw had gone a long way in changing attitudes and there was a new climate in which Annie's dreams and ideas could grow.

One question being asked by Mancunians was whether Miss Horniman's pocket was deep enough. Expenses at the Theatre Royal in Peter Street were reckoned to be about £300 a week, covering rent, rates, wages, printing, advertising, etc. The Midland Theatre was about half this amount, but here the seats were about half the price – reserved were 5s and 2s 6d, and unreserved 2s and 1s, and of course they were far fewer. The answer really lay in other questions. Was Miss Horniman a wealthy lady who was indulging a whim? Should she be taken seriously? Did she have a sound business head? All these issues were raised in the local papers and discussed through the readers' columns. Annie soon gave them her answer. Although there had been quite a lot of empty seats during the Midland Theatre run, she had found that there was plenty of enthusiasm from the press and a lively interest from the city. With this in mind she went out and bought the Gaiety Theatre in Peter Street, almost opposite the prestigious Theatre Royal where Sir Henry Irving and Ellen Terry had built their reputations over many years. The Tivoli, home of some of music hall's best loved names, was lower down the street.

The Gaiety was old-fashioned and run-down but Annie could afford to remedy these deficiencies. She would not get possession until March 1908 but this did not worry her for she already had plans for her company to tour. First stop was Scarborough and, after that, places large and small from Whitby to Edinburgh. Everywhere they were a success. In Glasgow they followed after the Irish players from the Abbey Theatre and the name of Miss

Horniman provided a connecting link between the two companies which assured people that they would be entertained. 'Our true intent is all for your delight' was the line that the Playgoers' Theatre Company carried in their programme. As the months of the tour went by, the actors got the measure of each other, and of Miss Horniman. There was a mutual liking and trust. Everyone relaxed, worked hard and enjoyed the camaraderie. Their company style of acting was created and loyalties were forged so that before they returned to Manchester and their new permanent home, the Gaiety tradition had been established.

Annie announced through the press that she had bought the Gaiety Theatre and that after a thorough spring-cleaning the theatre would open on Easter Saturday for a six-week season. Over the summer the theatre would be closed for refurbishment. She thought that this was the best way to keep the audience they had already built up at the Midland Theatre. She announced that her aim was to build a theatre that would hold eight hundred people, comfortably seated with a clear view of the stage, with good acoustics and no obstructions such as pillars or ladies' hats. Every seat would be numbered and bookable. She hoped to put on plays by Shaw, Hauptmann and Sudermann. Unfortunately Granville Barker's *Waste* had been banned by the Censor but Edward Garnett's *The Feud* would be staged and Shaw's *Mrs Warren's Profession* 'when the Censor relented or gave up office'. Annie appealed to new and local playwrights to send in their scripts and she undertook to read every new play that was sent to her. Already there was talk of a local school of drama. Alan Monkhouse, Manchester critic and aspiring playwright, wrote that 'We must not imitate the Celtic temper nor Mr Shaw's paradoxes but tragedy and comedy may be found in Lancashire life as well as in the west of Ireland or London.'[11]

From the Midland Hotel where she was staying until she could find lodgings in her adopted city, Annie wrote to her cousins, 'I hope that you will come to Manchester after we have opened at the Gaiety . . . I know that it will be uphill work for a long time, but nothing easy is really worth doing.'[12] She was aiming for an artistic and a business success. Was it possible to have both? Manchester admired her courage and waited to see what she would do.

A New Theatre: The Gaiety, 1908

On Easter Saturday, 11 April 1908, Annie's supporters trooped along to the Gaiety Theatre. They were a motley crowd – 'intellectuals from the University, vegetarians, nature-lovers, weekend hikers in the Derbyshire hills and general marchers in the advance guard of public opinion' was how Basil Dean described them. He was one of the new faces that they had come to see, along with the old favourites among Miss Horniman's players, in Shakespeare's *Measure for Measure*. The worn furniture and faded furnishings, which had been vigorously cleaned, did not matter to them; a spanking new theatre would soon be in existence.

Annie stepped on stage and greeted her audience, 'Here we are again', she promised an interesting and entertaining evening. The first surprise was the bare, Elizabethan-style stage on two levels set within the proscenium arch. The Elizabethan airs played by the orchestra added to the atmosphere. It was a far cry from the Shakespeare plays put on by Mr Flanagan at the Queen's Theatre in Bridge Street, where no expense was spared, and where he would stand on the stage like a master of ceremonies as the curtain rose, bowler hat in his hand, revealing fantastic scenery and superb stage effects. Mr Flanagan went for effect and did not mind sacrificing a large slice of the immortal bard's lines, believing that value for money meant a feast for the eyes, and almost continuous playing from the orchestra (of which he was very proud) even when the actors were declaiming their lines.

The splendid costumes had been brought with him by Mr William Poel, who had come from the Elizabethan Stage Society in order to produce Shakespeare's controversial play with its unpleasant plot and unconvincingly happy ending. He had arranged for an experienced tailor and dressmaker to make the

clothes from the detailed descriptions and pictures which he had
provided. Not for him the usual theatrical costumiers, he liked
everything to be correct 'down to the last gaiter button'. The
absence of scenery went unnoticed in the exhilarating pace of the
production. At the end of the final scene, the whole cast knelt on
stage and repeated the King's Prayer from *Ralph Roister Doister*.

The applause was deafening. Annie took a bow and promised six
weeks of good drama before the workmen moved in to pull apart
the old building and construct a brand new theatre with comfortable seats for all and a fine unrestricted view of the stage. Then
Ben Iden Payne said a few words before everyone disappeared into
the night, well satisfied – even the critics. And Mancunians were
filled with pride when they learnt that Miss Horniman's Company
were planning to take their production to the Shakespeare Festival
at Stratford later in the month.

As artistic director, Ben Iden Payne had chosen the play, which he
wanted William Poel to produce. Poel had founded the Elizabethan
Stage Society in 1894 and had made a name for himself staging
Shakespeare's plays as Elizabethan contemporaries would have
seen them. Poel was not interested in commercial or worldly
success but in scholarly interpretation, and he wanted to educate
his audiences so that they could enjoy and understand. Annie had
not been sure that Manchester was ready for the 'Poel treatment'
but she had entered into an agreement with her new manager that
he had full responsibility over productions and she would honour
her word. Payne went to see William Poel at his Chelsea flat to
persuade him to take on the production for Miss Horniman. When
Payne ran through the names of the actors, Poel commented that
thank goodness they were not established actors, but the last and
least of the names impressed him. The actor had played the Duke
in his production of *The Merchant of Venice*. 'That makes a
difference,' said Poel. 'He can take the tones.'[1] He was referring to
his method of speaking Shakespeare's lines, the unaccented words
spoken very rapidly and staccato-like while the stressed words were
drawn out in an unnatural, rhythmical way. The basic idea was to
make clear Shakespeare's meaning, although the effect was sometimes very comic.

Rehearsals began while the company were on tour in Dublin

because their theatre was not ready to receive them. Basil Dean, who was to play Claudio, remembered one of his lessons with William Poel while Yeats and Synge watched from the side-lines. 'I can see him now with the long ascetic face and flowing hair and spidery fingers enclosed in black woollen mittens. Those fingers drummed ceaselessly upon his knees as he made me repeat the rhythms after him over and over again: a five-finger exercise in words.'[2] The actors found it either excruciatingly funny or exceedingly difficult to speak in the 'Poel' style but, knowing that argument was useless, they complied or ignored, letting off steam in the dressing-room afterwards by mercilessly sending up Poel's strange speech and manner.

Charles Bibby, already a great favourite with the Manchester audiences, was a law unto himself. He was playing the part of Pompey, and happily Poel did not feel the need for 'tones' in comedy parts. Payne was given the part of Lucio and made him into 'a roistering, swashbuckling free-liver, with a cock of the hat and a swirl of the moustache'. He was glad to be back in an acting role. The chance to combine acting with producing had been a strong enticement when Annie had first offered him the job of manager. Poel had cast the parts, rehearsed the actors in his own particular style of acting, taken on the part of Angelo and cut the text to suit his Victorian sense of propriety – Lucio must say 'He will shortly be a father' instead of 'He hath got his friend with child'.[3]

The 'anonymous' Angelo was how the Gaiety audiences referred to Poel's star part because his name was not listed in the programme, which only gave the names of some of the actors. Apparently a compromise had been reached between listing just the characters, which Poel wanted, and printing the names of the whole cast alongside the parts they were playing, which Payne wanted. He knew that their supporters would want to see which of their old favourites from the Midland Theatre season would be appearing and who were the new people who had just joined the company for the opening of the Gaiety. Basil Dean, playing Claudio, had been engaged for thirty-five shillings a week, a low wage, but he was hoping for more as soon as the company became permanent. The heroine Isabella was being played by Sara Allgood, known to Mancunians for her performances with the National

Theatre Society from Dublin. She had been loaned by the Abbey directors because they felt that her experience under William Poel would add to their prestige. She had tried to join the company earlier but was turned down because Annie did not want to poach any players from the National Theatre Society in Dublin 'as long as it holds together'. Miss Allgood had, however, been chosen specially by William Poel, and her beauty and passion made her Isabella a great success with the audiences and the critics.

Annie had been lucky to find talented musicians already installed in the Palm Court Orchestra at the Midland Hotel. They had entertained the audience between acts at the Midland Theatre and Herr Dreschner was only too willing to oblige Miss Horniman with a small orchestra for her Gaiety Theatre. Annie was intent on a more professional atmosphere at the Gaiety than had been achieved at the Abbey, where a solitary violinist played plaintive airs for the patriots, and she wanted music to create the right mood for her programme of plays. Her little orchestra had rehearsed Arnold Dolmetsch's arrangements of Elizabethan songs with great interest and enthusiasm. Dolmetsch, an expert on early music and early instruments, many of which he made, had worked on the music for all the Elizabethan Stage Society's productions and Annie was proud to be able to use his talents in her theatre.

Her decision to open her theatre for a few weeks in its unready state, rather than wait until the renovations had been done and risk losing the loyalty of her newly found supporters, was justified by the first production alone. It had kept up the momentum which had been set going by the season at the Midland Theatre and sustained by the successful tour. The company were already identified with new ideas and a new style of acting, and their opening production was a new approach to Shakespeare that formed a talking point, with comparisons of the merits of a bare stage at the Gaiety with the overflowing extravaganzas at the Queen's.

Shakespeare was followed by Shaw, who had at last been prevailed upon to give Annie his *Candida* on condition that he cast the roles and rehearse the actors. Sybil Thorndike, a newcomer to the company, auditioned for the title-role and Shaw was highly amused by her passion and youthful energy. When she had finished, he cried, 'Splendid, my dear young lady. You go home and learn housekeeping and have four children or six if you'd rather, and then come back and show me Candida.'[4] She did, however, get the understudy role, and the play went on tour before coming back to the Gaiety.

The season ended with St John Hankin's *The Return of the Prodigal*, with the part of Henry, the Prodigal's elder brother, played by Lewis Casson who had joined the company during their tour. Sybil Thorndike wrote of her future husband that he played the part of 'a very prim precise sort of Conservative prig' and that she had 'an awful feeling that he did it so well because he is like that'. She was very happy to be at the Gaiety, and wrote to her brother Russell: 'I have told you nothing yet of Miss Horniman because I only met her a few days ago, and I like her awfully on first acquaintance. She looks as if she'd stepped out of a mid-Victorian picture – tall and dignified and I think just a beautiful face, and she wears the most wonderful clothes all made in the same mid-Victorian style of the loveliest materials.' The compliments did not end there. She went on to praise Annie's enterprise and dedication to the theatre, adding, 'I often wonder whether the people in this City appreciate what she's doing – one wonders if pioneer work is ever appreciated. The Company are certainly all very appreciative and after all that's the main thing.'[5] The actors showed their appreciation by inviting Miss Horniman to join them after the last performance for a farewell supper on stage. They were about to leave for the Shakespeare festival with their production of *Measure for Measure*.

At Stratford Miss Horniman's company were a huge success, despite opposition from a group of local church-goers led by their vicar, who objected to the play's theme of a young man getting a young woman pregnant – even if the langauge had been cut and altered. The actors received high praise for courage and excellence, and the production was voted 'one of the theatrical sensations of my life' by the *Daily Telegraph* critic. In the audience was the young Barry Jackson and his friend, poet and playwright John Drinkwater. Both were bowled over by the directness, simplicity and verve. Jackson said later that he always knew there was something wrong with productions that needed long intervals to set up elaborate scenes that would only last a few minutes. The experience helped to stiffen his resolve to establish the Birmingham Repertory Theatre, which opened in February 1913.

After Stratford Miss Horniman's company went on a summer tour that took them from Llandudno to Brighton, Leeds to Exeter, and Glasgow to Birmingham. Back in Manchester Annie got on with the business of rebuilding and refurbishing her theatre ready for the next – and crucial – opening night. She had received many good wishes from authors and playwrights, and praise from the press for the productions which had already been staged, but she knew that success ultimately depended on whether Mancunians would give her their support. They must come to her theatre week in and week out, and they must like what they saw.

She would start by giving them the cleanest, most modern theatre in the country. She engaged Frank Matcham, the foremost theatrical architect of the day, with offices in London, to redesign the building. He had already been responsible for three Manchester theatres and his beautiful buildings and exquisite interiors could be seen up and down the country. It was estimated that the work would take about three months; the whole of the inside would be torn down and thick iron pillars removed. There would be a complete transformation.

Annie already had her dramatic licence, with Charles Hughes and Charles Rowley as her sureties. They were eminent Manchester men, well-known in theatrical circles, who had been on the committee of the Manchester Independent Theatre Society when it had been formed in 1893. Her application for a drinks licence, however, had been turned down by the Watch Committee. Annie needed the revenue that a drinks licence would bring and, sure that she had been refused because she was a woman, announced that she would reapply every year until the decision was reversed – or until she died, and she intended outliving her grandmother who had lived to be a hundred.

Needing to find less expensive accommodation than the Midland Hotel for her Manchester base, Annie took furnished rooms in Ackers Street, one of the many sooty, house-lined streets in Chorlton but with a reputation for theatrical lodgings. Ben Iden Payne and his wife Mona Limerick lodged there, as did Basil Dean, at Number 32. He recalled that Ackers Street landladies thought the Horniman players an odd lot, 'atheists and I don't know what else, living on nuts and things. It was even rumoured that we indulged in "free love" whereas in point of fact we were just a group of rather high-brow over-earnest young actors and actresses living on humble salaries.' It was a simple tram-ride from Ackers Street up Oxford Road to the Gaiety Theatre, even if the walk home at night through fog and rain past the late-night shops selling tripe and onions and fried fish seemed long, but once home they could talk about the evening performances over steaming mugs of cocoa. Not all of the players had the luck to find rooms in Ackers Street. Esmé Percy, whom Basil Dean described as 'an exotic flower in Miss Horniman's prim herbaceous border', had digs opposite a large cemetery in South Manchester and when he protested about the traffic from the hearses, his landlady retorted, 'Well, we all have to go that way sooner or later.'[6]

Annie's decisions on furnishing and decor for her new theatre were based partly on practicalities and partly on principles. She believed that the theatregoer should not be distracted by obtrusive colour schemes from concentrating fully on the events on stage, so she did away with all the conventional gilt embellishments. It was also cheaper to use white paint everywhere. Annie chose to relieve the white walls with white plaster filigree work and she framed the stage in veined marble. James Agate described the effect scathingly as more like a schoolroom than a theatre. But there were red upholstered tip-up seats and cushioned benches in the Gallery which gave warmth and comfort.

Above the frame of the stage Annie placed a replica of an ancient ship, its square sails billowing as it rode the crest of the waves. This sailing ship was Annie's symbol on all her programmes and it soon became known as the Gaiety ship. It was a symbol of the belief that she had explored in the Golden Dawn years and with her Demon in the Order of Celtic mysteries that the soul is on a voyage of self-enlightenment towards perfection. Yeats' play *The Shadowy Waters* had grown out of these experiences and he had said that the ancient galleon carried 'the great poets and dreamers of the past. It was built long ago, nobody remembers when. From its masthead flies the motto Semper Eadem (always the same way).' Now Annie was taking her ship on a new voyage with herself as pilot and captain, and the symbol she had chosen marked her determination to continue in the best traditions from ancient

Greece to modern Europe, traditions which she and Yeats had tried
to maintain at the Abbey.

Her feet, however, were as always firmly on the ground. She was
as proud of her vacuum-cleaning machinery as she was of her
decorative safety curtain. Her new comfortable tip-up seats, each
one with a good view of the stage, were at popular prices, from five
shillings to sixpence, with boxes from two guineas to twelve
shillings and sixpence, all bookable so that there would be no long
queues blocking the pavements. A few days before opening night,
when the press were shown around, they approved very much of
this measure. 'There will be no crushing and squeezing and
pushing,' the *Manchester Programme* announced, 'and attendants
shouting to angry people to "close up", "sit closer" and so on, an
irritating process that is pursued in all our theatres in regard to the
pit and gallery, and there will be no "early doors" on busy nights.'[7]

The gala reopening night at the newly decorated Gaiety Theatre
took place on Monday 7 September 1908. Manchester's rich and
fashionable filled the stalls and dress circle, while the intellectuals
headed for the pit and gallery. Jew greeted Gentile, Church of
England acknowledged Nonconformist, German accent blended
with Lancashire, in a harmonious mingling of the city's cultures.
The Lord Mayor and Lady Mayoress, proudly displaying their
chains of office, were there, and also the Mayoress of Salford. The
women's elegant dresses and sparkling jewels looked well against
the white walls. Miss Horniman herself was wearing a stunning
geranium-pink silk gown, girdled with jet, and of course her
massive opal-studded dragon. She carried a bouquet of flowers.

Ladies were requested to remove their hats in the auditorium,
and smoking was strictly forbidden. Annie, who was becoming
notorious in Manchester circles for smoking her favourite Turkish
cigarettes through a long holder, felt that if she could manage
without a cigarette during the performance so could everyone else.
She had recently been turned out of the smart Octagon Room of
the Midland Hotel for smoking in public, an incident she related
with glee to the actors on returning to the theatre. They were in
the middle of rehearsing *Marriages are Made in Heaven*, a one-act
play by Basil Dean and the curtain-raiser on opening night. It was
followed by a play by Charles McEvoy, *When the Devil Was Ill*,
with an intervening interval where tea and biscuits, ice-cream,

chocolates and coffee were served. Few jibbed at the absence of alchohol, though the sharp-tongued critic James Agate took pleasure in mocking the 'intellectuals consuming cocoa'. When the final curtain fell, there was enthusiastic applause, and Annie appeared on stage to thank everyone for making the first night of her Gaiety theatre an overwhelming success. Whether the Gaiety succeeded or failed, she told them, would depend on their continuing support in the weeks and months ahead.

The press proclaimed Annie's first Gaiety season an experiment of the highest interest and importance. Of twelve productions in those weeks, three were of new plays having their first staging, three had been produced first by the company on tour, one was the first production in English of a Sudermann play, two were company revivals, one was a bold gamble – Gilbert Murray's translation of Euripedes *Hippolytus*, directed by Lewis Casson and only given at matinees – one was written by a member of the company and the twelfth was their first-night production of McEvoy's play *When the Devil Was Ill*, which had an earwig in the cast and was played, so the programme wittily credited, by Forficula Auricularia. Such a programme would have satisfied the most demanding of London audiences, and Mancunians could derive great satisfaction from the knowledge that they were leading the way in the provinces with the first permanent repertory theatre.

On 4 October 1908 Manchester Playgoers' Club elected Miss Horniman as an honorary member and gave a six-course dinner at the Albion Hotel in her honour, with the dessert entitled 'Bombe Horniman'. A toast was proposed by Charles Hughes, who praised her international vision, her encouragement of new talent in acting and writing, and her sound business head. Annie responded by saying that she had chosen Manchester for her dramatic experiment because she knew it to be a city of sensible people (laughter), and she was determined to make a great theatre (cheers). Charles Rowley proposed a toast 'To The Drama'.

Annie wrote to cousin Bella on 28 December, 'There is such a crowd at the Booking Office, it never stopped from ten to six today. This is most gratifying to me personally, as to give these particular plays at Xmas was a fancy out of my own head.'[8] She was referring to their Christmas programme, which featured Beaumont and Fletcher's long-forgotten Elizabethan comedy, *The*

Knight of the Burning Pestle, which had been dug out and the cobwebs blown away in a rollicking production that was fun for both actors and audience. It was advertised as 'A Pantomine of Three Hundred Years Ago' and it certainly intrigued the people. It was also a clever way to compete with the traditional pantomimes that were on offer in the city. Once inside the Gaiety, the theatregoer was transported back in time. Actresses, dressed as Elizabethan serving girls, sold chocolate-filled oranges, while actors in Elizabethan dress moved freely between the stage and the stalls with long clay pipes which they proceeded to fill with tobacco. There were folk dancers and Elizabethan airs. It was a holidyay for everyone, with no serious message or educational intent. Annie's legal advisers could be forgiven for not knowing who Beaumont and Fletcher were and demanding from Ben Iden Payne their present address so that they could receive due payment of royalties! Along with this play, Annie gave the children their own special matinee delight: *Alice In Wonderland* performed by Ben Greet's company.

Annie was having a wonderful time. She knew exactly what was going on at her theatre from box-office receipts to the state of the lavatories. High standards of hygiene were as important to her as high standards of acting. 'I see after it myself,' she wrote to cousin Bella, 'but when part of the public bring in fleas and another part write indignant letters to the Business Manager we can only apply Keating [powder to kill vermin] to every hole and corner.'[9] One way of keeping pests under control was to have a cat on the premises and one item on her expense account was for 'mouser's milk'. Alas, Trixie the Gaiety cat was killed by the safety curtain.

Basil Dean might have renamed his opening night curtain-raiser *Marriages are Made in Miss Horniman's Company*, for by the end of the year the romance between Lewis Casson and Sybil Thorndike, together on stage for the first time, resulted in marriage. For the wedding on 22 December the bridegroom wore his *David Ballard* suit, changing into his second act *Widowers' Houses* suit to go away in. Annie's gift to the happy couple was a month's leave of absence from the company. She may have been known as Lady Bountiful to some people in Manchester who thought that she had a bottomless purse into which she dipped to fund her theatrical enterprise. She may have been called Hornibags by a few others, perhaps men dismayed to see a woman achieving what men could only talk about. But her actors and actresses were happy to belong to her innovative and acclaimed company, and they all looked forward to the next year.

12

Ties That Bind

Across the Irish Sea the mood was very different. The squabbles among the players that had begun before Annie joined them, and had continued while she was there, had not stopped since she had left them. Her tarot cards had warned her that Willie Fay and Yeats would not work easily together. Lady Gregory had been aware of the friction between them and by Christmas 1907 she and Yeats decided that Fay must go. When Iden Payne left, Fay had tried to take control as manager and producer because he felt that he was the one best qualified to make all decisions and he needed to have authority over the actors and actresses. Annie had complained loudly after the Scottish tour of 1906 about inefficiencies, lowering standards and slovenly behaviour, and now Fay was making the same criticisms about the company. The directors retaliated with the same about Fay. Synge was critical of Willie Fay, who was critical of Mollie Allgood. Yeats talked of 'a disciplinary committee'. Lady Gregory complained, 'We all have artistic temperaments if we chose to flaunt them.'[1] Annie's prophetic words that 'disappointment in friendship crowns all' were proving uncomfortably true.

Fay would have to go but Yeats was 'anxious not to seem to push him out. I want the pushing to come from the company.' He confided in Lady Gregory, who hoped Fay would make some move that would make it impossible for him to stay and thus leave them with nothing to reproach themselves with. Looking back over the years since the founding of the Irish Literary Society which became the Irish National Theatre Society, the path was strewn with victims of Yeats' inability to work amicably alongside others and to face the fact that he was quite incapable of running every department single-handed while at the same time writing the masterpieces that were required of him. He was like a cuckoo in the nest. He managed to get rid of all those who stunted his personal growth, beginning with Edward Martyn and George Moore, then George Russell (A.E.), and finally Annie.

She had become a convenient scapegoat, the focus of all the abuse that might have been, and should have been, hurled from one to another in the Society. Yeats was to be pitied, the others thought, because he was dominated by Miss Horniman. Against his better judgement, she had forced him to bring in an English manager, and presumably the English actresses Florence Farr and Miss Darragh, and later Mrs Patrick Campbell for his *Deirdre*. In fact, Yeats had written to Lady Gregory that if the choice lay between filling the country's stomach or enlarging its brains by importing precise knowledge, then he was for ignoring its stomach, and Lady Gregory had agreed that the expedient path was the wise one for them to take. One of the very few in the Abbey camp to give Annie any credit was Joseph Holloway, who wrote to her at the time of her Easter opening of the Gaiety in 1908, wishing her well in Manchester. He believed that she had been right in her criticisms of Willie Fay who, Holloway felt, gave her 'dog's abuse and deserved to be kicked for his pains'.

The departure of Willie Fay left Yeats master of all that he surveyed at the Abbey, with his faithful and formidable ally, Lady Gregory, by his side. According to Padraic Colum, 'It was she who estimated the forces, who countered the dissident elements, who precipitated the situations.'[2] Together they would rewrite history. Officially it was stated that there had been a difference of opinion on theatre policy and that the parting had been amicable, but rumours were rife in Dublin as Willie Fay sailed away to England taking with him his wife Brigit O'Dempsey and his brother Frank. Within a week or two of his arrival in London he received a letter from James Barrie inviting him to his home at Lancaster Gate. Fay told his side of the story and learned that the famous playwright had seen every one of his performances with the Irish players. A week later Fay was invited by Charles Frohman to produce and play an Irish one-act play, as a curtain-raiser for Barrie's *The Admirable Crichton* at the Duke of York's.

Willie Fay was bowled over by his good luck in landing a West End engagement so quickly. In fact it did not come to fruition but the alternative was just as exciting. By early February the three Irish refugees were sailing to America to put on, under Frohman's management, some Irish plays including two of Lady Gregory's comedies. They had no written contract but the word of Charles Frohman was good enough for Willie Fay. He explained: 'Perhaps travelling the road makes me sceptical about the all-compelling power of documents; perhaps also, it helps one to know an honest man.' They played in New York and Chicago, and gave Americans their first taste of modern theatre, with an Irish flavour. The Americans loved it even if they did not understand. One critic did not know whether Mr Fay's acting was 'pure genius or pure ignorance'.[3]

There were no hard feelings between Annie and Willie Fay and he looked back in gratitude for all that she had done for the Abbey. He maintained that she was 'the real sage-femme of the Abbey' and although there had been harsh words between them inside the company, Annie defended him to outsiders, declaring that he was a gentleman. It was J. M. Barrie's invitation that had set the ball rolling and he kept a kindly eye on developments, sending a letter of good wishes to Fay on the day of sailing. Maybe Annie put in a good word for the Fays. She certainly corresponded with Barrie early in 1908 because on 1 April he sent her his best wishes for success with her repertory theatre, regretting that she could not have any of his plays for her new company as they were tied up to another management. She could be relied on to give a sound, honest judgement and she had more first-hand knowledge of working with the Fays than any other English manager. A hint from Miss Horniman in the right direction would go a long way – in 1913 Beerbohm Tree asked her opinion of Basil Dean's ability as a producer, adding as a postscript, 'Pray send your message enigmatically if necessary but I will be most scrupulous in discretion.'[4]

Remarkably, Annie was still on good terms with Yeats, who had seen her company's performance of *Measure for Measure* at Stratford and had been impressed by the high standard of acting. It seems he had got over his pique at her independent move to Manchester and accepted that she was not coming back to the Abbey. He was probably relieved, but worried about the theatre's economic future. Annie's funding had given the company an artistic freedom which they would not be able to enjoy any longer. She had enabled him to make such statements as 'It is not the business of a poet to make himself understood, but it is the business of the people to understand him.'[5] The business of paying the bills was Annie's and had to be balanced against what she saw as her responsibility to art. She tried to make the new manager at the Abbey, Norreys Connell, understand that she could manage to go on with her subsidies '*if I thought it right* but I don't'.

She underlined this point in a letter of 27 February 1908 to her Demon. Annie's involvement with the Abbey has been personalised, trivialised and romanticised, and how distorted has been the view of her is obvious in this letter. She wanted him to appreciate what she thought he had known all the time – that she had not just been in the business of promoting his own personal ideas, they were part of a much wider scheme. She wrote, 'Why, the same sum of money as the subsidy spent each year on a week of matinees of your good work at a good London theatre done *decently* would do more for your reputation and as there would be some receipts, the expense would be less.' She added, 'Don't bother about answering this letter, it is only to impress on you that I never imagined for a moment that you were practically exploiting me . . . You are a great deal too stupid.'[6]

These were strong home truths and Annie lashed out with more. In May she wrote from London: 'Most polite Demon! Greetings! Is it influenza or Conscience that has made you so civil? . . . One dozen astrological forms & three penny stamps enclosed – the latter to replace some I took from your rooms to-day.' She went on in her usual bantering tone: 'The Sargent picture is excellent, it makes you look very young but with more vigour than you had in your youth. Many thanks for sending it.' (This was the portrait chosen for the collected edition of Yeats' works published in the autumn.) Then she had to include one of her customary scoldings: 'Why on earth are bits of mostly fur kept carefully in your drawers, I opened them in search of the keys. Your undergarments will get moth-eaten & then I'll have to annoy Mrs Old again with naptha-line. I suppose that they have tumbled off your fur rug.' She ended with a little pat on the head, 'You have grown much tidier now-a-days.'[7]

Perhaps Yeats enjoyed being privately brought to heel by Annie. She certainly enjoyed handing out the discipline. At any rate, their friendship continued. In January 1909 he stayed in Manchester and slept on the floor of her rooms in Ackers Street. She was busy organising the next production at the Gaiety, John Galsworthy's *The Silver Box*, which Mancunians would see for the first time on 1 February. The author came along to rehearsals and was most impressed with the extras in his trial scene. Edwin Heys had rounded up a dozen unemployed from Manchester streets and they gave just the right touch of realism. Before he left, Galsworthy was moved to give Iden Payne £10 to add to their fee, making the point that nothing was to be said about it to anyone. His play was a great theatrical experience and at the same time a box-office success, a rare combination. Manchester's Lord Mayor was in the minority when he refused to go to it on the grounds that he could see such happenings in the local police court every day.

Annie continued her resolve of giving the people new plays about real life. In April there was the first performance of Edward Garnett's *The Feud* and in May John Masefield's first Manchester performance of *Nan*. All her playwrights were very conscious of the debt they owed to her and wrote appreciatively of her courage and pioneering spirit. Edward Garnett told her that she was having 'a more potent and far-reaching influence on the English Drama' than perhaps she realised.[8] John Masefield wrote that she gave them three things: 'the very rare and very precious gift of encouragement, and the useful gift of the possibility of experiment, and the priceless gift of understanding.' Annie, her head not turned by all these compliments, would only say, 'We are beginning only, everything must grow and go on growing.'[9]

She had learnt from her years at the Abbey that a London season set the seal on any success and her next target was a visit to the Coronet Theatre at Notting Hill in June – not exactly the West End but easily accessible and not too expensive. For three weeks from 7 to 26 June her actors played their repertoire of plays and London audiences and critics were astounded by the high standards of this provincial company. On the opening night Shaw was there to see how they performed his *Widowers' Houses* and in the box opposite his was the legendary Ellen Terry, who paid Miss Horniman the compliment of two return visits. Critical opinions on the plays varied but all were agreed on the brilliant ensemble performances. E. A. Baughan of the *Daily News* urged his readers, 'Go to the Coronet and see the company turn itself inside out from night to night so that you don't know which side they shine most', and William Archer, perhaps the most influential London critic, wrote in *The Nation*; 'I wish to express my deliberate opinion that this Manchester Movement is the most important fact in our theatrical history since the opening of the Vedrenne-Barker campaign at the Court Theatre . . . The flexibility, the adaptability of the company was altogether admirable and the sense of living artistic endeavour gave excellence a new charm.'[10]

Annie became an overnight celebrity, for it was Miss Horniman's company that was being talked about. The glory belonged to Iden Payne and Annie acknowledged this but, naturally, she enjoyed the recognition of her achievements. She gave interviews, accepted invitations to speak, to chair meetings, to be guest of honour at dinners, always using her access to the public to further the cause of repertory. William Archer paid homage to the woman who was using her money 'to remedy the starvation and malnutrition of dramatic art' and he wondered in what way Manchester proposed to show its gratitude to her, suggesting that 'the best way would certainly be to vote her a subsidy'.[11]

Did he really expect hard-headed businessmen to behave so philanthropically? Annie had her own ideas about the reasons for the undernourished state of the English theatre. She saw the problems as different in London from the provinces. In London there were long dinner hours, so that people only had the time and inclination for short and flimsy plays. In the provinces musical comedies and lurid melodramas or touring plays with worn-out stars were the usual fare. In Manchester she was still fighting to get a drinks licence for her theatre and having a lot of trouble with the local clergy about it. Dean Welldon was trying to suggest that the Gaiety was failing as a business because Miss Horniman needed a drinks licence to boost her profits. Annie, furious, wrote to him that if he made similar public statements about a grocer he would find the outcome unpleasant and advised him to contact her accountant, Mr Oswald, who would provide the facts, adding that she would continue with her application even if the profits reached the four thousand pounds mark. She had become a well-known personality in her own right and would stand no patronising from the likes of Dean Welldon.

She was also at this time taken up by the suffragette movement.

She had already been on the platform of the Free Trade Hall in Manchester at a meeting of the less militant suffragists. In March 1908 she had allowed her Gaiety Theatre to give a matinee in aid of a new Women's Union building for Manchester University, the aim being to provide facilities for use by both sexes. In June she had spoken on suffrage at the Queen's Hall in London, the first of many such speeches. She told one of her relations, 'My speaking is *very light* – really of the after-dinner species. Yet it takes very well after the audience has got over the shock of no notes and no neatly typed manuscript.'[12] She developed a style that was all her own, always opening with the neatly turned phrase 'Gentlemen and Ladies'. Here was a business woman owning a theatre, managing her own theatrical company, employing men and women, yet she had no say in what kind of Member of Parliament could make decisions that would alter her life or what kind of government should rule over her. At one meeting in Manchester when she was challenged by a bald-headed heckler to say what he could do that she could not, she retorted 'Go around with a bald head'. Her reputation for wit and her outspokenness grew. 'We can forgive a woman for wanting the vote, but not for convincing us that she has a sense of humour,' the *Daily Sketch* observed acutely. [13]

Annie was not interested in the militant activities of the suffragettes. She thought that the best way to prove equality of the sexes was for women to show by their own achievements that they could do as well and better than men. But she did feel that she had a duty to her fellow sisters to speak out against injustice now that she was in a position to do so. She also realised that speaking anywhere on anything brought publicity for the Gaiety and was a way of drawing attention to the need for repertory theatres in circles where theatres were not normally discussed. So out she went to literary and dramatic societies, to working men's clubs, to Methodist and Unitarian chapels, to the Co-op Debating Society, to Bolton, Marple, Sheffield, Bury, Barrow, Halifax, Worcester, Bristol, to name just a few of the towns that listened to her. Wherever her company performed, she would speak. 'Speech with her' wrote one newspaper, was 'a liberal education after the moth-eaten conventions that permeate the patter of the ordinary managers.'[14]

But politics were still taboo and no actor under contract to her, whether in Dublin or Manchester, was allowed to get involved. The Abbey players were in London in June 1909 for a season that overlapped with the Gaiety. One of their plays was Yeats' *Deirdre* with Mrs Patrick Campbell, who asked Sarah Allgood, now back with the Irish players, to take her place in reading a short story at a concert organised by Lady Alfred Lyttelton. Lord Alfred Lyttelton was Commander-in-Chief of the British Army in Ireland and Miss Horniman, interpreting Miss Allgood's action as political, demanded apologies from one and all, even from Norreys Connell the new director at the Abbey. He wrote to Yeats saying that he had received an 'incomprehensible' letter from Miss Horniman commanding an apology. 'I cannot imagine', he went on, 'what politics Sally has in common with Mrs Lyttelton but I am quite certain that this is the last straw upon the camel's back and that I have finally done with the Abbey Theatre. Please delete my name from the list of directors and believe that I shall always be proud to have been associated with you in this work.'[15]

Annie had indeed become quite paranoid about the Irish, believing that politics lurked behind their every action and that every action was an intended insult against herself. She maintained that Yeats should have prevented Sarah Allgood from speaking and when she discovered that Miss Allgood had acted on her own initiative, she still held the Abbey directors responsible. She did get letters of apology from Yeats, Lady Gregory, Lady Lyttelton and Mrs Campbell, none of which is traceable, but Annie's response to Mrs Campbell's apology – that it did her as little credit as any letter she ever wrote – leaves room to imagine how perfunctory were the other letters. It seems likely that Yeats had words with Sarah Allgood, for she promised that while she was under contract she would in future seek permission before appearing on stage. This issue of consultation was what had sparked Annie's unreasonable behaviour. If she had been asked for permission, she would surely have granted it, for reading a story on stage could hardly be considered political if Annie's own speaking on the suffragist platform was not.

Connell's stay at the Abbey had been brief. He had come in when Synge was very ill and stayed on after Synge's death in March 1909. Annie was greatly saddened by the news of his death. She may not have always liked Synge as a person but she never doubted his genius and did all that she could to promote his work. She sent her own wreath from London with the message, 'To our leader and our friend – goodbye'. Synge had led them along exciting new dramatic paths that had brought recognition and prestige to their company although he had been too realistic and uncompromising for the ordinary Dubliner. Annie knew that the fights over *The Playboy of the Western World* had helped to put the Irish players on the theatrical map and she was delighted to see the fight now being taken up on behalf of Bernard Shaw's play, *The Shewing Up of Blanco Posnet.*

Annie had tried to obtain a licence for this Shaw play to be performed at the Gaiety but the Censor refused unless there were alterations to the script. So Annie took another of Shaw's plays, *Press Cuttings* which had at first been banned because some of the characters could be identified with politicians of the day. She was always ready to have a go at the Censor, or 'any man in a position to bully me' she told Shaw. The Reader of Plays in the Lord Chamberlain's Office was G. A. Redford, described by St John Ervine as a respectable solicitor, 'better placed as Clerk to a Diocesan Board than as a judge of literature or morals'.[16] Shaw liked to think that Mr Redford had 'a fixed delusion that I am a dangerous and disreputable person, a blasphemer and a blackguard'.[17]

In Dublin Yeats and Lady Gregory were crossing swords with the Castle officials over Shaw's play. The Lord Lieutenant was away when Lady Gregory called at the Castle but the Under-Secretary, while at great pains to assure her that Lord Aberdeen was a supporter of the drama – 'he was one of Sir Henry Irving's pall-bearers' – nevertheless pointed out that it would place him in an invidious position if he were expected to overrule the Censor in London. Yeats wrote a long letter to Annie with all the comings and goings to Dublin Castle to meet now the Under-Secretary now the Lord Lieutenant and yet again his Under-Secretary. Nothing was gained except 'much admirable folk lore' for Lady Gregory. Yeats was determined to fight the censorship and knew that their patent was at risk. He wrote, 'I told him that I was entirely confident of your support to the utmost, that you were so opposed to the English Censorship that I knew you would be prepared to sacrifice the patent in its defence.' If they lost it, they would appeal for money from Ireland and England to take over the theatre, buy out Annie and compensate her for the loss of lets. If they did not succeed, they would come to 'a glorious end' and Annie would be no worse off than if they had ended 'ingloriously from mere lack of money'. 'Whatever happens we shall have done something by having resisted first of all Cardinal Logue over the *Countess Cathleen*, then the mob over *The Playboy* and now the Castle over *Posnet*. We shall leave behind us a tradition of an Irish theatre which will produce its effect though maybe not at once.' For the first time Annie's intention of not going on with the Abbey Theatre once her patent ran out at the end of 1910 was given as an accepted fact between them. This was to be kept very secret because, as Yeats pointed out, 'if we are to make anything out of being martyrs we must insist on the reality of the firewood and the matches'.[18]

The Shewing Up of Blanco Posnet was performed at the Abbey on 25 August 1909. It was the week of the Dublin Horse Show and every seat at the theatre was sold out because of all the publicity over the censor row. Guineas were being offered for standing room in the wings. At curtain fall there was a great outburst of cheering that carried out into the street so that a passerby asked what was going on. Back came the answer, 'They are defying the Lord Lieutenant.' Once again the press had a field day. It was not the merits of the play that were discussed but the question of censorship. 'Censored Play in Dublin', 'Warning from the Viceroy to be Ignored' ran the headlines. Annie collected over a hundred pages of press cuttings in her scrapbooks.

Over in Manchester Annie was rehearsing *Press Cuttings*. Shaw was delighted to have Miss Horniman in his corner against the Censor. 'I think I shall get our horoscopes cast; for our stars certainly are in the same constellation.' Annie was flattered by his approval but her choice of his play was a business matter. She liked to ask herself about a play, 'Would it suit my eighteen-penny public?', and she had wisely decided that *Press Cuttings* would give them plenty to laugh about. It opened at the Gaiety to a packed house on 27 September 1909, the publicity over the initial banning of the play helping to draw in the crowds, who hugely enjoyed Shaw's satirical romp. The names of two of the characters had been changed to suit the Censor: Prime Minister Balsquith (Asquith) became Johnson and the War Minister Mitchener (Kitchener)

Bones but everyone knew who were the real politicians. The audience dissolved into laughter at the scene in which Prime Minister Johnson, disguised as a militant suffragette as the only way he could get out of Downing Street, was dragged into the War Office. Once inside, he stripped off his feminine attire and revealed his true identity to the astonished War Minister, who exclaimed 'Good Heavens! Johnson!' It was a case of mistaken identity twice over.

As the year drew to a close, the Gaiety went from success to success. Galsworthy's *Strife* ran for three weeks, followed by Ben Jonson's *Every Man in his Humour*, and for Christmas another Shakespeare, this time *Much Ado About Nothing*. Miss Horniman promised: 'If Manchester will support me, Manchester shall have the finest theatre in the empire.' Her satisfaction with events in Manchester only served to throw into stark contrast her dissatisfaction with events in Dublin. There it was muddle and trouble. With Norreys Connell gone, Yeats and Lady Gregory were trying to do all the jobs of management and production and find time to write. Not surprisingly the accounts were not up to date. After a London meeting with Annie in December, Yeats wrote to Lady Gregory that Miss Horniman had been very cross because they had not submitted their second statement and added, 'I thought her unusually mad'.

While Annie had hoped to become her Demon's saviour she had suffered the slings and arrows of his careless, thoughtless and sometimes downright cruel behaviour towards her. She had allowed herself to be soothed by his soft words and Irish charm but compliments and pleasing phrases no longer had the power to placate her. She ran a business organisation at her Gaiety Theatre that worked efficiently and harmoniously, and at last she was able to see all too clearly how she had been manipulated and abused by the Abbey directors. Yet she was unwilling to sever all links with her old Demon friend. In the days between Christmas 1909 and the New Year she wrote at least four times to him, going over and over the way in which she saw that their relationship had changed. On 23 December she wrote, 'I have a duty towards you, my old friend, and I shall do my best to prevent you from injuring yourself by hurting me in public.' She went on to speak of his superiority and her role as his slave. 'Long ago I warned you that Supermen cannot prevent a revolt of slaves and the time has not yet come that the supermen are completely paramount, or that revolt is impossible.'[19] Her years of subservience to Yeats' literary genius were over, as were his years of playing the courtier to her wealth.

She would continue to pay the subsidy to the Abbey Theatre until her agreement ran out at the end of 1910. She was already considering the future. On Christmas Day she wrote, 'How glad I shall be when I am free of the Abbey and you will no longer be urged by Dublin atmosphere to exhibit Dublin ways in regard to me.' Her fourth letter, written on New Year's Eve, said only, 'My dear Demon, Just a few lines to wish you a most prosperous and happy year in 1910. May all the old worries take flight. Yours Annie.'[20] She was looking forward to a new relationship once she had shaken off her Abbey responsibilities. How wrong she was. The last and public battle was yet to be fought and when it was over, both sides claimed the victory and neither had won. All that remained was hurt and bitterness.

13

1910

In 1910 Annie was in her fiftieth year. As the months unfolded she found her share of pain and disappointment centred, as always, on Dublin. Its Irishness she had once called 'a mere geographical detail' and the extent of her mistake continued to haunt her. In May the death of King Edward VII triggered off a sequence of events that finally and irrevocably severed her links with the Abbey and sounded the knell of her friendship with her Demon. It was a messy, drawn-out public affair. The news of the king's death was carried in the Saturday morning papers of 7 May, and at once eighty London theatres and concert halls and over four hundred provincial places of entertainment decided to cancel their performances that day as a mark of respect. The Abbey Theatre did not follow suit.

The new manager, Lennox Robinson, was young and inexperienced. When Yeats and Lady Gregory had engaged him on a salary of £150 a year he had admitted that he knew nothing about stage management. He had thought them crazy to appoint him, but that did not stop him from accepting their offer on the spot. He was sent to learn his craft for a few weeks in London, watching Shaw, Boucicault and Granville Barker at work. Back in Dublin he was soon left in sole control while Lady Gregory went home to Coole Park in County Galway and Yeats went to visit Maud Gonne MacBride in France. When Robinson read of the king's death he felt that whatever decision he made on opening or closing the theatre would be taken as a political act. In a difficult position, he decided that to close would be seen as bowing to the wishes of the Castle. He sought confirmation by telegram from Lady Gregory, but, for reasons that have never been satisfactorily explained, the telegraph boy took three hours to make the return journey of four miles between Gort Post Office and Coole Park. By the time that Lady Gregory's advice to close as a mark of courtesy reached him, the matinee was already under way. It was too late to put notices in Dublin's evening papers cancelling the evening performances and, with the thought that if there were any crime in opening it had already been committed, he chose to carry on.

On 9 May Annie received the returns from the Abbey, which included what she described as 'circumstantial evidence' about the theatre's opening. She took it as a deliberate personal insult and an openly defiant political act. She was incensed and sent telegrams to Lady Gregory, to Henderson the business secretary and to Lennox Robinson: 'Opening last Saturday was disgraceful. Performance on day of funeral would stop subsidy automatically.' She was not appeased by answering letters that reached her on 11 May. She sent further wires to Henderson and Lady Gregory: 'Subsidy ceases now unless directors and Robinson express regret in Dublin press that decent example was not followed.'[1]

Her next act was to write to the Dublin papers and to the magazines *Stage* and *Era* demanding a public apology from the directors and from Robinson. If it were not forthcoming, she threatened to withdraw her subsidy immediately. She sent Lady Gregory a telegram with the same message. She believed that acting so swiftly made sound business sense, for Robinson's action had put at risk the patent which would be up for renewal in a few months. If Dublin Castle officials thought that there were political agitators working behind the scenes in the Abbey Theatre, they would be unlikely to view their petition to renew the patent with any favour. The new young manager had to be sacrificed to make their position secure.

On 11 May Miss Horniman's letter appeared in the Dublin press, as did Lady Gregory's apology. (Yeats was still not back from France.) Annie was seeking an abject admission of guilt and expression of sorrow, but what she got was a proud statement of regret that included an announcement that the next play at the Abbey would be *Harvest*, a new work by S. L. Robinson. It was publicity for the very culprit of the deed! Furthermore, Lady Gregory artfully worded the apology so that it read that the theatre had remained open 'owing to accident'. Annie took the apology as intentionally ambiguous and therefore unacceptable to her. James Flannery in his book on her and the Abbey has written of her 'blind hatred of patriotism', 'her vitriolic fluids', and accused her of using the opening on 7 May 1910 as a means of saving £400 of subsidy money. William Murphy in his book on J. B. Yeats has written that Miss Horniman 'allowed herself to be outraged'. However unfairly she has been so condemned, what is beyond question is that there followed a battle to the death, for nationalists predictably took the apology as bowing the knee and dared Yeats to do the same, which of course he refused to do on his return from France.

Annie's fury was personal as much as it was political. To try to untangle the two means going back fifteen years to the time when her mother had died and her father had taken up a political life. Politics were all part of the male world that she despised. Her father had used his wealth and position to dazzle a young woman into bed and a speedy marriage, and Annie had never forgiven him. Her only brother, who had at one time shared her artistic dreams, had also ended up as a Member of Parliament and she had found herself being patronised by her sister-in-law. As she saw it, 'the lords of creation' wasted a great deal of valuable time in useless talk and politicians were a prime example of the species. In her opinion, deeds were far better than words and her experiences in Dublin had only confirmed her prejudices. She saw their politics as 'the curse' of the country, teaching them 'to hate each other so intensely'.

It rankled too that she had never been officially informed that Lennox Robinson had been appointed manager at the Abbey and she did not know that he was in charge alone at the time of the King's death. She felt sure that the theatre would close and that any directive from her would be taken as interference. She was hurt and angered that Robinson had not thought to seek her advice as well as Lady Gregory's on the matter of closure. Yeats was equally furious with her for what he regarded as her high-handed attitude and unbending response. Annie's fury was fuelled by the knowledge that Yeats had put his own pleasures first, carelessly abandoning his responsibilities at the Abbey to a young and inexperienced man. The rift between them was too deep to heal. The dreams that she and her Demon had shared of building an intellectual and artistic theatre that would reach across international boundaries to the European stage had crumbled into dust. The evidence that they would fail had been there for some time but they had refused to acknowledge it. Yeats had written in October 1908, 'All the praise we have had from the most intellectual critics cannot bring the Irish educated classes, and all the abuse we have had from the least intellectual cannot keep the less educated classes away.'[2]

When Yeats returned from France he declared that Miss Horniman had been appeased sufficiently by the apology. Robinson would not be sacked. In June, while the Irish players were in London for a season of plays, the news broke that Miss Horniman was withdrawing her support from the Abbey Theatre. Annie believed that the National Theatre Society had forfeited their right to any further instalments of her subsidy by this last outrage, which she insisted on interpreting as a political act. She withheld her June payment to them. Yeats and Lady Gregory scurried frantically around London canvassing financial support to replace her backing. Lady Gregory called on all her aristocratic contacts and held drawing-room meetings for the rich and famous at her nephew's home in Cheyne Walk, Chelsea. An Abbey Theatre Endowment Fund was set up and a committee formed.

Annie was only too willing for other people of substance to take over her burden. She would not back down on her decision not to pay the June subsidy and neither would she pay the December instalment. Yeats and Lady Gregory retaliated by refusing to pay the £1,000 that they had agreed for the transference of the Abbey Theatre into their ownership. It was a particularly sad state of affairs given the generosity of Annie's original offer. Annie wrote to Joseph Holloway, one of her few remaining friends in Dublin, telling him exactly how much she had lost over the Abbey venture. She estimated that she had spent £10,350, not including the losses of English tours (any profits were always handed to the directors). The shop and house in Abbey Street and the stable behind the theatre had cost £1,428, and she was giving all the contents of the buildings. She told him that it had taken her a long time to realise that Dublin had no use for a middle-class educated woman with a great love of the arts. On 1 November Dublin's *Evening Telegraph* noted that it was the day that the Abbey Theatre patent expired and added, 'Our Drama loses the best friend it ever had in parting with Miss Horniman today.'[3]

In Manchester there was plenty to concentrate Annie's mind.

She now had comfortable rooms in High Street in Rusholme, where she lived with her cats and her books, the play manuscripts which arrived at the rate of forty a week piled up on chairs and floor to await her attention. She read them all, giving short shrift to the obviously hopeless, and during 1910 chose twelve new plays for first performances at the Gaiety Theatre. Payne, still her artistic director, wondered how many potentially good plays were being rejected by Miss Horniman. He was not sure of her ability to judge, describing her as 'the only person I have ever met who could see a play only from the visual point of view'.[4] Annie's artistic training certainly directed her attention to the visual details on stage – she remembered one London production for the realistic detail of water dripping from the pots as they were raised from a well and dismissed another for using a green grass mat in a scene set in Italy in the autumn. She disconcerted one of her Gaiety actresses by complimenting her choice of a small hat in one scene and saying nothing of her superbly tragic performance. But many times she spoke out against expensive scenery that distracted from the acting and stage effects that took preference over plots. She believed that when audience attention was held by good acting, the props were superfluous.

One of the Gaiety's greatest successes in 1910 was their April production of Sheridan's *The Critic*. It was one of Annie's favourite plays and she believed that the Puffs and the Sneers and the Dangles could be enjoyed as much by twentieth-century audiences as by those of the eighteenth. The Manchester *Courier* declared that in Payne's Mr Puff, 'No actor has a finer sense of burlesque nor tears a passion to tatters more flamboyantly or with better grace.'

Meanwhile Annie was busy enlarging her business enterprise. She now had a full-time stage manager and permanent scenic designer. Scenery, stage props and costumes were made on the Gaiety premises. By 1910 the staff on her payroll, from carpenters and electricians to call-boys and programme sellers, amounted to eighty. There were enough actors to divide into two companies, which allowed for half to rehearse or to tour while the other half played at home. According to Whitford Kane, one of her actors, it was an ideal arrangement because it combined the creative with the interpretative and gave actors a chance to experience both and to try out a great variety of roles from leading parts to walk-ons. Of course there were jealousies but they were healthy and stimulating and soon dissolved in the happy atmosphere. Her actors had the security of a forty-week contract which expired each year but was immediately taken up again for a further year. She would not tie them down for longer periods because she believed that it was in everyone's interest that they should stay because they wanted to, not because they were legally bound to her. During the 'off' season there was the chance of a London showing or the fun of a summer tour, and salaries covered rehearsal time. They would have been hard put to find a fairer or more generous employer. Wages ranged between three and twelve pounds, which was the average rate even in London except for the stars. There was no star system at the Gaiety but Annie kept her talented players because of the good working conditions that she created for them and because of the artistic and dramatic opportunities that she offered. Rehearsals started at 10.30 a.m. and went on until 4 p.m., with a coffee break mid-morning at Miss Horniman's expense.

Next door to the theatre was a small public house, the Swan, which made a convivial meeting place for actors, journalists and aspiring playwrights. They called themselves the Swan club and over a glass of ale spent happy hours arguing extravagantly over politics and personalities. It all added to the feeling of comradeship at the Gaiety. The more active members of the company formed a sports club for hockey in the winter and cricket in the summer, and their families would turn up on Sunday afternoons to give support in matches against local rival teams. By having a permanent home at the Gaiety the actors could settle down to a normal life outside the theatre and many put down roots in and around Manchester.

Henry Austin, probably Annie's oldest actor at fifty-eight, decided to edit a Gaiety Theatre Christmas Annual and collected contributions from as many of the company as he could persuade. He was a charming Mancunian, an actor with no acting technique but who sometimes managed a brilliant performance. Iden Payne said that when rightly cast he was perfect, but he had the exasperating habit of 'creative' acting – bringing in new dialogue quite spontaneously or quoting from an entirely different play. Sporting a rimless monocle, he played all his parts in the same suit of clothes and got away with it, so Basil Dean thought. His Christmas Annual carried photographs of the actors, articles, reviews, poems, short stories, and advertisements to pay for it all. Annie was asked to contribute to the first edition, which appeared at Christmas 1909, and she sent in a few lines on the ideals of conduct. They were not her own words but a quote from a first-century Roman emperor. One dictum was 'That which is not good for the beehive is not good for the bee.' She could feel very happy about the community spirit in the Gaiety beehive.

Those who left during these years of growth went on with her blessing to spread the gospel of repertory elsewhere. Not only did she not place obstacles in their way, she actively encouraged them. Lewis Casson and Sybil Thorndike left after the first London season to try their luck on the London stage. Basil Dean and Miss Darragh left in the summer of 1910 to start their own repertory system at Liverpool, at first with a short experimental season. Along with Granville Barker, Annie spoke at a meeting at Liverpool University Club one hot June afternoon when, having resisted an invitation to establish a theatre for them, she gave a rallying call to the city's 'merchant princes' to help endow a theatre, one with comfortable seats and a modern box-office system. Perhaps she had made her seats too comfortable, she humorously suggested, because the rich and fashionable chose to occupy the pit stalls instead of the more expensive circle. They seemed to think that she was enormously wealthy and was not interested in making a profit at the Gaiety. How wrong they were. She wanted her repertory theatre to be an artistic and a financial success. She believed it could be done, unlike James Agate, who said that a repertory theatre existed for the production of plays that could not get a staging in the commercial theatre. Comments like this made her shrug off the label 'repertory' because she felt that it was used disparagingly.

Annie's ambition was to see a civilised theatre in every big town in the land. Glasgow was the first to follow her example in April 1909, under the founding hand of Alfred Waering who had worked with her on the Scottish tour of 1906. The big difference at the Royalty Theatre was that the company was financed by a group of Glasgow businessmen who gave £1,000 to secure a lease on the theatre, which was used at other times by touring companies.

Throughout 1910 the movement for a repertory theatre was growing in Liverpool but enough people had to be found to guarantee the money to cover the expenses for the first season. It was said that Glasgow's expenses were £400 a week and their receipts only around £300. Annie admitted that she had yet to make a profit. Lord Derby headed the list of guarantors at Liverpool and opening night came eventually on 20 February 1911. Lord Derby sat in one of the boxes, John Masefield in another with Miss Horniman by his side in her finest brocade gown decorated with her opal dragon. John Galsworthy and William Archer were in the stalls. Annie lent them Whitford Kane to play the strike leader Roberts in Galsworthy's *Strife* and he was billed as appearing by courtesy of Miss Horniman. She helped them as much as she could by lending them scenery and costumes, releasing actors to appear in their plays, persuading authors to give their new work, all the time knowing that her theatre would be the worse financially because it would lose some of its audience that had regularly made the journey from Liverpool. Their trial season was a great success and ended with a profit of £1,600.

Next on Annie's list for its own theatre was Sheffield. She hectored and cajoled the worthy citizens:

> When you go to a theatre and see a play, good, bad or
> indifferent, tell your friends about it. Have strong
> opinions, quarrel about it if you like. But be honest.
> For the most perfect curse that weighs upon theatres,
> music and art of all kinds in England is this; that a few
> people go and see the thing for themselves, and the
> other wretched people talk about it without having
> been. As a manager of a theatre I say it is not
> commercially honest.

She was severe with them: 'You have allowed yourselves to be treated like children, and given the cast-off things not good enough for London. You have swallowed what even London would not swallow,' adding a touch of humour to soften the rebuke, 'and goodness knows London will swallow a great deal.'[5]

The high spot of the year for Annie came in July, three months before her fiftieth birthday. The University of Manchester recognised her contribution to her adopted city and to the cause of

drama by conferring on her an honorary MA degree. Professor
Conway, who introduced her at the ceremony, expressed 'the
gratitude of a community which cannot have too many protectors
from its own Philistine instincts.'[6] Another woman was honoured
at the same time, Mary Dendy, for her work for the handicapped,
proving the professor's point that distinctions were in no way
limited by sex. Annie was immensely proud of her degree and wore
her cap and gown whenever she could. She gave photographs of
herself in her academic robes to friends, and there is even one of
her in cap and gown and opal dragon.

October was the month in which the Gaiety Theatre mounted
two of its finest productions. On the 3rd the first performance in
English of Verhaeren's *The Cloister* was given, with William Poel
persuaded back to Manchester to play the main part of Balthazar,
a monk who murders his father and allows another to be punished
for the crime. Unable to live with his conscience, he confesses
publicly in the monastery chapel, which leads his angry brothers to
throw him out physically into the outside world. Iden Payne
remembered that Poel gave 'a penetrating and poignant delineation
of a difficult character'.[7] He also remembered the actor's vainly
eccentric behaviour over a wig. As a Dominican brother, Poel's
head with its bald patch was just right in its natural state but Poel
wanted a wig with long unkempt hair. He managed to persuade
Iden Payne that the wig would be suitable, the condition being that
it would be dressed, but the actor carefully carried the wig home
with him each night in a little black bag so that the producer would
not lay his hands on it.

The play had only one set – an impressive monastery interior –
and an all-male cast. The result, in Rex Pogson's eyes, was 'a
balanced beauty and harmony rarely achieved by the Gaiety
company'. But it did not appeal to Manchester theatregoers and
Annie had an artistic success but a financial flop on her hands.
Galsworthy's *Justice*, opening on 24 October for three weeks,
helped to balance the books. His powerful play had been seen by
London audiences in February as the opening to Granville Barker's
repertory season at the Duke of York's Theatre, backed by Charles
Frohman. It dealt with the harsh treatment of convicted criminals
and led to Winston Churchill, then Home Secretary, ordering a
review of the penal system that brought reform to the system of

solitary confinement. The first night audience at the Gaiety were stunned by the performance but they got their breath back in time to cheer and applaud the actors, who took one curtain call after another until at last the exhilarated but exhausted cast came on stage in their dressing-gowns. Only then were they allowed to go. It pleased the critics as much as the audiences and was a sell out. It also pleased the author, who wrote, 'Dear Miss Horniman, . . . I am delighted that Manchester is taking its dose with such an apparently willing mouth . . . We ought all of us to be most grateful to you for your pluck and obstinacy . . . for who will hold the flag aloft if you cease to?'[8]

As Annie turned fifty her star was still climbing ever higher. Her actors were popular at home and successful in London. She was in great demand as a celebrity speaker; giving as her only qualification that she was a member of the audience and as such was indispensable to playwrights and performers, she spoke on all manner of subjects. Photographs, portraits and even cartoons of her appeared. Her secret of success was that she was a woman unafraid to speak in a man's world, where she was considered eccentric of behaviour and illogical of thought. Lewis Casson said that when he laid a proposition before her she would discuss it briefly, then abruptly change the subject entirely, and then after an interval of vague talk jump back to the proposition with her decision. Eden Phillpotts, one of her playwrights, described her mind as like a fly's, darting up and down, which was exactly how Virginia Woolf described the mind: 'the most capricious of insects – flittering, fluttering.' At the age of fifty, Annie had the confidence to be herself, to talk as she thought. Her fame spread overseas, invitations poured in from Paris to Philadelphia. She talked of an open-air theatre along the lines of Oberammergau. What did it matter if the English climate were unpredictable? She had sat in the pouring rain in Germany. She talked of a chain of theatres taking in America. Nothing seemed impossible.

Yet there remained like a thorn in her flesh the problem of the final resolution of the Abbey Theatre affairs. Years later she could be philosophical about her Irish experiences. 'When one is going through a bad time it is well to remember that if one can have the pluck one can learn a great deal,' she wrote.[9] Now she dug in her heels and would not compromise, and Yeats and Lady Gregory did the same. The year ahead would decide the issue once and for all.

14

Legal Battles and Atlantic Crossings

From Manchester on 11 January 1911 Annie wrote a cold formal letter to her old Demon:

> Dear Sir,
>
> As the Directors have now possession of the Abbey I must protest against bills being sent to me like the enclosed. Unless the £1,000 due to me be paid before Jan 23rd, when I shall return here from London, I must consult my lawyers as to taking proceedings against the Directors. They have possession of my property & have not paid for it. Any quibble as to my not paying the subsidy would injure them in the public eye. They accepted my condition as to no politics at the Abbey & broke this condition on May 7th. They made no application for the subsidy, they made no public protest against my letter to the press, they did not protest at the remarks reported at the application for the renewal of the Patent & that £400 was not in the Accountant's statement in December as a debt. This would I believe be called 'consent' by the law & at any rate unless I am paid there will be a scandal of the directors' own making which will damage the future of the Abbey,
>
> Yours truly A. E. F. HORNIMAN[1]

She poured out her grievances to her old friend Helen Rand who, in February, wrote to Yeats on Annie's behalf, maintaining that, in her opinion, Annie had made clear to him from the start that she would have no politics in her theatre. Helen Rand had been present at one of their detailed discussions and she reminded Yeats that Annie's view had been perfectly plain to everyone. Yeats of course wanted to have it both ways – he wanted the freedom of the artist, unshackled by political considerations, and he wanted to be his country's spokesman and work for the glory of Ireland. The difficulty was about when national feelings became political.

Although in a letter to Bernard Shaw Annie had written that she did not want to damage Yeats, she maintained her aggressive stance. She would give no favours that might be interpreted as womanly weakness. She was behaving just as she had done in her final year in the Order of the Golden Dawn. She seemed to lose all sense of proportion whenever her 'self-respect' was threatened.

In March both sides consulted their lawyers. Annie would not pay her last two subsidy payments amounting to £400. Lady Gregory and Yeats took legal action to recover the money. C. P. Scott, editor of the *Manchester Guardian*, known to both sides and respected by all, was asked to arbitrate. The public scrapping ended on 29 April. He gave his judgement that 'Miss Horniman was and is not justified in refusing to pay the two instalments of subsidy' because of events before 20 February 1910 and particularly over the opening of the theatre on 7 May 1910.' By 'events' was meant the various activities that Annie had condemned as political which she believed had broken the contract that she had first made with the Irish National Theatre Company. C. P. Scott went on to say that 'In making this award I wish to state my opinion that Miss Horniman has throughout the transaction submitted to me acted with generosity and perfect good faith. I assess the costs of the Award at £5 15s 6d.'[2]

On hearing the verdict, Lady Gregory and Yeats wrote to Annie that, because of her past generosity, they did not intend to press the legal point. They had acted according to their principles, and, if she could not accept this, they could not accept her money. Annie replied that she did not accept the integrity of their actions. Her final word to Yeats, no longer 'her dear Demon', was a telegram on 5 May 1911: 'You have shewn me that I do not matter in your eyes. The money is paid. Supermen cannot associate with slaves. May time reawaken your sense of honour then you may find your friend again but repentance must come first. Horniman'[3]

Annie maintained that Yeats' attitude towards her had deteriorated from the time he had first crossed the Atlantic for America. This was way back in 1903 when she had been working on costumes for *The King's Threshold* and before she had decided to give so much of her time and money to Irish affairs. She had brought it to his attention many times in the hope that he would try to be more considerate towards her and more appreciative of her position at the Abbey Theatre. It had been like water off a duck's back. Whenever she thought about these years, as she once wrote to her cousin Marjorie, 'I always considered that Mr Yeats came under a Nietsche influence which crippled his genius.'[4]

The man who had been responsible for introducing Yeats to Nietzchean philosophy was John Quinn, a successful Irish-American lawyer who had come over to Europe in 1902, met the Yeats' family and all the Irish artists, intellectuals and nationalists, and appointed himself as their godfather. He organised the American tour which took Yeats from east coast to west and back again, lecturing to immense and enthusiastic crowds all the way. As William Murphy explains in his book on J. B. Yeats: 'Quinn, a brilliant, self-made man, would of course regard with favour Nietzche's doctrine of the natural superiority of a few men over all others, and it was not difficult to convince WBY that he was a member of the tribe too.'[5] Annie was not alone in noticing Yeats' increasingly arrogant posturing. George Moore remarked that he was 'lately returned from the States with a paunch, a huge stride, and an immense fur overcoat'.[6]

The relationship between herself and Lady Gregory was quite a different matter. They could never have been friends but they could have been allies. They both wanted the same kind of theatre and Annie admired her plays. She wrote to Yeats in November 1906 that she was proud of Lady Gregory 'because she makes the people laugh in a witty way'. But there were jealousies and suspicions harboured by both women that spread malignantly. Many years later, when Lennox Robinson was writing the history of the Abbey Theatre he sent Lady Gregory his notes for her comments. She used them to light a fire and wrote in her diary, 'Quite untrue about the founding of the theatre, Miss Horniman made the *building* not the theatre.'[7] Yeats senior told his daughter Lily of his feelings on the matter: 'On the whole I am very glad that Lady Gregory "got" Willie . . . though it is not easy personally to like her' (a sentiment that was probably echoed by many of the Irish).[8] Bernard Shaw's wife described her as 'Loving-cold. Womanly-cold. Enthusiastic-cold. Faithful-cold. Poetic-cold. Very calculating, dutiful, courageous, purposeful."⁹ She could have added that she reserved all her warmth for men. Lady Gregory did not like her own sex and saw no reason to try to do so. When she took on the management of W. B. Yeats she had already made a play for father and brother Jack and lost. They had an independence of spirit that would bow to no woman while W. B. lapped up the little luxuries and special privileges at Coole Park. A little loss of manhood was a small price to pay for the finest bedroom, the best vintage wine, trays of tempting snacks, from beef tea to eggs and bacon, and thick rugs laid either side of his door to muffle any loud noises that might disturb his muse.

There was no animosity between Annie and the Abbey actors and she welcomed them to use her Gaiety Theatre when her company were playing away, as happened from time to time. Twelve of them signed a testimonial in appreciation of all her endeavours. Henderson and Holloway added their names and gave Annie a silver chalice. She was deeply touched and hung the testimonial on her office wall at the Gaiety. How much of her side of the story Annie ever told is unknown but she had the support and sympathy of some of her Manchester team. Edwin Heys, her business manager, was one to be counted on her side. He gave a talk to the Leeds Playgoers' Society about this time, taking as his subject 'The Irish National Society', and he told them that the Abbey on which Miss Horniman had spent about £11,000 had never been intended as merely the local theatre that it had become. This was roughly the figure that Annie had given in a letter to Joseph Holloway the previous year.

Annie and Yeats had shared too many experiences to remain locked in enmity. As she told Bernard Shaw, there had been many exchanges of friendship between them in the past. Even last year they had been able to meet and push aside the disagreeable business of the Abbey. They had been together in April at the Stage Society's Annual Dinner at the Criterion in London, both speaking on their theatrical experiences. They had been guests of Birmingham Dramatic and Literary Club for the Shakespeare Commemorative Banquet. In September, when Uncle George Pollexfen had died, Yeats had sat down to write to her on his return from the funeral, remembering how deeply the three of them had worked on magical matters over the years. Now there was a frozen waste between them and although reconciliation would follow, it would not be for many years and then without the old intimacy. In 1934 he would send her a copy of his *Collected Plays*, a gesture that moved Annie. She found his alterations to the original playscripts most interesting and she wrote to thank her 'Dear Old Friend', ending her letter, 'In a few years' time no one will believe the tales of the odd happenings near to the Liffey.'

She filled only one more scrapbook with cuttings of events relating to the Abbey Theatre and the Irish players. Perhaps this was because Yeats too untangled himself from the theatre after two or three more years and its management was continued by Lennox Robinson. The latter's memories of Miss Horniman were not unkind and he felt that, as 'a sturdy Englishwoman', she had been justified in dismissing him. Annie kept just one small cutting from the *Freeman's Journal* of 25 October 1917 that reported the marriage of W. B. Yeats to Miss Hyde-Lees at a London register office. There were no details and no comments added. As the years passed, the cuttings dwindled away. 'If ever a real history of the Irish affair be written', Annie told the librarian of John Rylands Library when she gave him her scrapbooks of Irish press cuttings in 1918, 'I'll be glad to give information. But the points which are the most interesting are just those which could not be published.'[10]

She could have taken up an offer for a book to be published on her theatrical experiences from Sidgwick & Jackson who felt that she must have a store of anecdotes and opinions. If she had given her story at least the record would have been set straight. As it is, the new Abbey Theatre built in 1966 to replace the old theatre that was burnt down in 1951 carries a plaque on the exterior to commemmorate its founders – the names of Yeats, Lady Gregory, Synge and the Fays but not of Miss Annie Horniman. Inside on the foyer walls the largest and most prominent portrait is of W. B. Yeats. Lady Gregory hangs there along with others who have served the Abbey Theatre but not Miss Horniman. She has to take her turn along with some fifty other paintings that hang on the walls of the first-floor lounge, the Green Room and the rehearsal areas.

When Joseph Holloway remembered her sixty-sixth birthday, Annie wrote to say how 'delightfully kind' of him, adding 'so the Abbey still lives – will it ever lead to a *real* theatre: I mean with properly paid good actors and dramatists from all the world?'[11] She hoped so, for this is what she had wanted and was achieving in 1911 for her Gaiety Theatre. She was still working hard to get a drinks licence and was still being obstructed by certain members of the Temperance Society, supported by the city's churches and chapels. Dean Welldon, in a fine piece of tortuous thinking, said that Miss Horniman's experiment of running a theatre without a bar had failed, and he knew that it had because she was so anxious to get one. The local press called her 'A New Portia' as she went to plead her case to the Town Hall. She was turned down by the Watch Committee by one vote, but her eloquence obviously swayed the City Council. She called no witnesses, but relied, like Shakespeare's heroine, on her own arguments. The local papers reported the town hall proceedings:

> She had good reason to believe that the absence of the licence had roused a certain prejudice against the Gaiety. There were those who thought that it was a place of instruction, an innovation, a place where they would have a tract given them (laughter) and perhaps hear a harmonium playing the tune the old cow died of (more laughter) or go to sleep – or be bored. That was not fair to her. She did not want to be put under the slur of superiority. It was a superiority she could do very well without.[12]

Annie's persuasion finally won the day – by one vote. Fifty-nine councillors voted for her, fifty-eight against. That night her theatre was playing *What the Public Wants* by Arnold Bennett and when one of the characters spoke the lines, 'Haven't I put your place in order? Didn't I get you a licence?', the audience exploded into laughter. When the curtain went down and Miss Horniman appeared on stage, they clapped and shouted their approval of her performance earlier that day at the town hall. The decision to give the Gaiety an excise licence was of course attacked by Dean Welldon in his Lenten address at St Ann's Church in the city centre. The matter was well aired by the local press, who decided that it was a good moment to investigate the religious past of the Gaiety players: Miss Horniman had been brought up a Dissenter in a London Suburb, Ben Iden Payne's father had been a Unitarian minister, Edwin Heys had been organist at a Stockport church, Hilda Davies was a member of Moss Side Unitarian Church. The gossip was as good for sales as the drinks licence.

Mrs Pankhurst took the time to write with her congratulations, 'for you have had a long struggle to obtain fair treatment. I hope now that not only will your theatre continue to have the artistic success which under your enlightened management has always attended it but that financial success will be yours also. You have done so much for dramatic art in this country that you have won our gratitude. It is an added pleasure to me that you are a woman.'[13] Annie returned the compliment by speaking with her usual dash of wit on the Conciliation Bill that would give the vote to women householders. She raised a laugh when she told her audience, 'They could be sure that when women got the vote they would go to the poll sober.'[14]

In May Annie accepted an invitation from a Montreal business-man for her company to visit Canada. Jack Hoare of His Majesty's Theatre wanted to show what could be done with moderate capital, a good company and much enthusiasm. He guaranteed a backing of £2,000 and offered to pay first-class travelling expenses for all the company. Annie accepted without hesitation and with delight. Here was a chance to prove that she was no mere amateur philanthropist but a business woman to be taken seriously. It was agreed that the season would begin on 12 February 1912. She was aready getting publicity across the Atlantic from Lewis Casson, who was in America under contract to Charles Frohman and was following the Horniman tradition of lecturing on the repertory movement whenever he had the opportunity. In February he talked to the Boston Dramatic Society about Miss Horniman's success in Dublin and Manchester.

More publicity came from the Abbey Theatre players, who made their first trip to America five months ahead of her. They toured Boston, Washington, New York, Philadelphia, Chicago and towns in between, and every time they performed *The Playboy of the Western World* there was public opposition that frequently erupted into rioting. In Washington they were denounced from the altar by Catholic priests. In New York they were showered with vegetables and nauseating capsules that burst on impact. In Philadelphia the entire cast was arrested under a law forbidding immoral and indecent plays. In Chicago Lady Gregory was sent an abusive threatening letter that if the play went on she would 'never see the hills of Connemara again'. Their notoriety brought in the crowds but the reviews were mixed. *The New York Times* wrote of 'a lack of method which has been unduly regarded as a sign of greatness', while the *New York Tribune* said, 'Americans must understand the romance of the Irish players.' 'There is nothing so sensitive as a sensitive Irishman' reported the city's *Evening News*. Newspaper reporters fell over themselves for interviews and articles, and, not surprisingly, stories of Miss Horniman spilled out. A San Francisco headline ran, 'Miss Horniman of England Spends Dividends Supporting Theater. American Rail Shares Assist Dramatic Art.'[15] His Majesty's Theatre in Montreal, where her actors were due to open in February, began their advance publicity with a programme article on her as early as October.

Before the Atlantic crossing there were big changes at the Gaiety. Annie sadly said goodbye to Ben Iden Payne with whom she had worked so happily for four years. It had been an ideal partnership, based on mutual respect and trust. At first Annie was often at her theatre in the daytime attending to practical details, and she would sit in rehearsals. When Payne found that her presence distracted the actors he asked her not to attend and she accepted his decision without question. She was proud of her artistic director, she had confidence in him and in her actors, and they returned the compliment. Milton Rosmer, who joined the Gaiety in the summer of 1910 from Glasgow Repertory Theatre, called her 'an actor's best friend'.

Maybe she was to many of them, but Mona Limerick did not get on with Miss Horniman. Payne's wife and one of the company's star players, Miss Limerick was a beautiful and tempestuous actress whose grand manner fitted with difficulty into the company's style of group acting. She was acclaimed by the critics, although their praises were usually barbed. They made the same point that Miss Limerick had an exciting talent but that it needed discipline and restraint. Max Beerbohm was the exception; he went overboard for her 'mystical flamboyance' which he claimed fitted her only for great parts. His cartoonist's eye pictured her as a twentieth-century 'Delilah or a Madonnah or a Cassandra'. No doubt so much singling out for excessive attention was disliked by Annie, who perceived that it made the actress even more unrestrained. In any case the two women had little in common, and it showed. Iden Payne told of an occasion when he and his wife were sitting next to Miss Horniman at a public dinner. Conversation turned to Wagner's *Parsifal* which, Annie told everyone within earshot, she had seen many times at the Bayreuth Festival. '"Really," said Mona in her always penetrating tones. "You must be able to whistle it all the way through!" Miss Horniman was not amused.'[16] A more ruthless employer might have made a sharp remark but Annie showed her annoyance only by her flushed cheeks, and an awkward silence followed.

Mona Limerick was ambitious for herself and her husband and she encouraged him to form their own acting company, which toured for two summers before Payne finally resigned from the Gaiety. He and Annie parted on good terms. She had been her usual generous self by putting before him a chance to make his name in America. She had been approached by a group of Chicago businessmen to bring her company to their Fine Arts Theatre and, already committed to her Canadian tour, she had recommended her artistic director. Payne's first American trip was brief and not a success. He felt that American audiences were not yet ready for his kind of theatre and he came back to the Gaiety with his company for a summer season while Miss Horniman's company was touring. America beckoned again and he returned this time to Philadelphia.

He went on to spend five years on Broadway in the Charles Frohman Company, an appointment which he took with 'a bitter sense of shame', driven by financial pressure from his wife, who had remained in England with their two daughters. It was an unhappy and frustrating time for him, working in a star system which he condemned as 'a soul-destructive shackling of the art of the theatre'. In the war-torn year of 1917, when Annie was holding on to her theatre by her fingernails, she asked him if he would return to the Gaiety to work again as her partner. He was very tempted. 'I *do* like working with you better than any possible committee or organisation and I know of no individual with whom I can be in such harmony', he wrote, but he doubted that it was the right time for carrying out her ideas.[17] The times were certainly out of joint. His letter went down on the mail ship, *Laconia*, which was torpedoed in the Atlantic, but it was strangely saved, water-marked throughout but with the date clearly visible: 24 February 1917. (Payne's luck turned and his talent was recognised. He turned to academic work in Pittsburg which gave him the opportunity for Shakespeare productions that led him back to England to work at the Shakespeare Memorial Theatre, Stratford. Shakespeare had been his first love and through his academic work he was able to share this love with the next and future generations.)

Lewis Casson was in Salt Lake City, also under contract to Charles Frohman, when the call came that he was needed at the Gaiety to fill the post of artistic director, with acting parts for his wife, Sybil Thorndike. His first big production and a great success was *Twelfth Night* for the Christmas season of 1911, after which all eyes turned westward for the company's first crossing of the Atlantic. Annie went ahead to organise and to promote interest. After the last curtain call of *Twelfth Night*, she excitedly said goodbye to her enthusiastic supporters. She promised to tell the people of Canada about her theatre, that it was not very big and not always as crowded as she would like but she was very proud of it and of everyone involved with it. She received their good wishes and God speed, and everyone joined hands to sing 'Auld Lang Syne'.

In a letter to her cousins, Annie wrote quite simply, 'I am going to Canada in January for several months to see after my show in Montreal.'[18] She told the *Daily News*, 'I am going to make money – and Fame and to show that an Englishwoman has the courage to do what New York millionaires tried to hire men to do.' On 19 January 1912 she sailed on the *Grampian*, looking forward to a long rest and hoping that the captain would allow her to smoke in her berth. Her group of eighteen actors and her business manager Edwin Heys, armed with eleven plays for which over fifty tons of scenery and props had already been sent in advance, set sail from Liverpool on the s.s. *Corsican* on 2 February. By this time Annie had made the Corona Hotel in Montreal her publicity headquarters and was having great fun as a personality and a novelty to the Canadians, who loved her style. She gave talks on her work in Manchester, her idea of a civilised theatre and the state of the drama. She never used notes and no one seemed to mind if she wandered from her chosen topic. Her one lecture in Boston was billed as 'The Plays and Players of the Gaiety Theatre, Manchester England' but, as one reporter noted, 'She gave her views on almost everything but that'.[19] As ever she was generous to her colleagues and paid tribute to Ben Iden Payne's work.

The repertory idea of a changing programme and the group responsibility of acting whereby an actor played a minor character in one play and a star part in another was new to Montreal audiences and they responded with great enthusiasm and approval. *Candida, Man and Superman, The Silver Box, Nan* and *She Stoops to Conquer* were some of the plays in the repertoire. They clamoured for a return visit but Annie would make no promises as she sailed for home with her actors.

When she landed at Liverpool she had a fund of good stories for the awaiting press, like the performance where she noticed an elderly lady asleep in the stalls. 'I thought it better not to rouse her,' she laughed, 'lest I might discover she was a hostile critic.' And she had plenty to say on Canadian audiences:

> Well, there is plenty of culture among them, and they
> are appreciative, but we missed that solid background of
> applause which comes from the pit and gallery in an
> English theatre. As time went on the audiences
> improved. At first we had only the fashionable people
> and university students, but later we began to get the
> general class of people, and these are always the best
> because they are so much more alive – they have not
> had so long and heavy a meal; they are more active and
> will applaud. People seemed to have been labouring
> under the delusion that the plays were too recondite and
> deep for the average intelligence, but this fallacy we
> soon dispelled.

To the question of a return visit, she quipped, 'I will not be hustled into an agreement – like a mere man. Montreal now knows what management by a woman means . . . Selling amusement is a matter of business the same as selling coal or any other commodity.' She said that she had very much missed her morning and evening papers 'written in English or some language I could understand. French or German I would have managed but not American' – a comment which would not have endeared her to her newly won Canadian fans.[20]

While the company had been abroad, the theatre had been taken over by Miss Darragh, who had brought her company for a repertory season. She and Basil Dean now had a new home at the newly decorated and newly named Playhouse in Liverpool. Annie had been there for their opening night the previous October and was very much in favour of the two theatres running exchange seasons. Now, on 6 April 1912, there was a triumphant welcome home at the Gaiety. As every actor appeared on the stage, there were shouts, cheers and clapping. The orchestra played 'Home Sweet Home' and American tunes, and at the curtain call Miss Horniman was showered with flowers. She would never be more dearly loved by the Manchester audiences than at this moment. She had made the city internationally famous and she had brought her actors home to their just deserts. That night the play was immaterial, for no one cared to be critical.

The Gaiety ship was riding the crest of the wave. Ahead of them lay a six-week season at the Coronet Theatre in London. Next year there would be three months in Canada and America, and nine weeks at the Royal Court Theatre in London. How Miss Horniman and her actors would handle their fame and unqualified success, and how Mancunians would react to being left for so long remained to be seen.

15

A Star in its Zenith, 1912

On 6 May 1912 Annie was back in London with her actors for a seven-week season at the Coronet Theatre, and they were a wild success. There was nothing but superlatives on all the critics' lips – 'excellent company Miss Horniman has pioneered', 'all round efficiency', 'excellent repertory company', the notices ran. Annie was seized upon eagerly by the suffragists in town. She spoke at the Actresses Franchise League's 'At Home' in the Grand Hall of the Criterion Restaurant, at the Women's Social and Political Union in the London Pavilion and at the Annual Ladies' Dinner of the Savage Club. The *Daily Herald* of 22 May gave her a headline 'Famous Theatrical Manageress Gives Her Views', which were that 'Of course the vote will come. It must. All the talk of the anti-suffragists can never stop it.' The *Weekly Guardian* on 15 June fairly described her as 'no militant suffragist but playing the iconoclast in a much more sensible fashion, wisely directing her energies to the breaking down of conventions and uninformed prejudices regarding the drama.'[1]

If Annie's greatest moment of triumph in Manchester had been her welcome home from the Canadian tour the previous year, her highest point of glory and acclaim in London came now in the last week of the Coronet season. She had been asked by the Stage Society to provide a new play, preferably dealing with local issues, for its thirteenth season. The idea of a playwright drawing on his own environment for inspiration had begun with the Irish movement and was now being taken up enthusiastically by the English. One of Annie's young Manchester playwrights, Stanley Houghton, had written a play on Lancashire life which he described as 'rather serious and of more ambitious quality than some of my recent efforts, called *Hindle Wakes*. It is about Lancashire people and is practically in dialect, though not barbaric. It will be of no use for London . . . It is of no use to anybody but the Gaiety here.'[2]

Annie thought differently. She paid him £100 for the sole rights to the play and offered it to the Stage Society, who gave it the very first performance on Sunday evening, 14 June, at the Aldwych Theatre, followed by a matinee on Monday afternoon. The event was billed as a visit by Miss Horniman's company from the Manchester Repertory Theatre. The actors had rehearsed in moments snatched after and between performances at the Coronet, and Lewis Casson had found time from his work there to direct them. He was no stranger to the Stage Society for he had played two small parts in their production of Yeats' *Where There is Nothing* in June 1904 at the Royal Court Theatre.

When *Hindle Wakes* was given its licence, the Examiner noted that the subject of the play was painfully realistic. Fanny Hawthorne, mill-girl, has already had her weekend in Llandudno with Alan Jeffcote, the millowner's son, before the play opens. The action centres on the parents' reactions when they learn about it and Fanny's spirited refusal to marry Alan just because parents and convention demand. Alan is prepared to sacrifice himself and his fiancée, the beautiful, genteel and pure Beatrice, in order to marry Fanny and obey society's rules. But Fanny will not have him; he was good enough for a weekend but not for marriage.

The play was an immediate success and Annie included it in Wednesday's programme at the Coronet and again on Friday. Edyth Goodall, a Manchester actress, played Fanny and Herbert Lomas, a Lancashire actor, took on the part of Jeffcote senior. Sybil Thorndike was the matchless Beatrice. The whole cast fitted their parts perfectly and could not have been bettered by any London company. 'To see every member of the cast of a long play acting his or her part with absolute sincerity and seemingly without a thought of the audience on the other side of the footlights is a rare joy in a London theatre these days' wrote the critic of the *Pall Mall Gazette*. 'Being Miss Horniman's company, the interpretation is as nearly perfect as we can hope for' reported the *Evening Standard*. The *Daily Telegraph* admitted, 'We know nothing of the work of Mr Stanley Houghton, the author.'[3] This was about to be remedied.

Annie arranged for Cyril Maude to put on *Hindle Wakes* at the Playhouse, opening on 16 July with the original cast. It became the most discussed play in London. 'Should Fanny marry Alan?' was the question that everyone was asking. Stanley Houghton was challenging a code of conduct that had been exclusively male, just as Ibsen had challenged it in *A Doll's House*. The inevitable uproar boosted the play's publicity, until everyone had heard of Stanley Houghton. The press had a field day and considerations of drama were left far behind as morality overtook art. Headlines in the *Sketch* ran 'The Girl Who Wouldn't Be Righted' and in the *Graphic* 'The Play With The Strongest Grip in London'. Annie and her playwright were delighted.

On 13 August Stanley Houghton wrote from the Marine Hotel, Criccieth:

> Dear Miss Horniman,
>
> . . . Charles Hawtrey believes so much in the play that he sent a friend (the actor Reginald Owen) up here to see me about it. He wants to take up your company in it if by any chance Maude (at Playhouse) loses heart and wants to stop . . . he personally believes there is a fortune (and if for him – for you and me) in it for London. He will find a theatre and put it on as soon as Maude tires. I have told Mr Casson all this and he has written Hawtrey agreeing, I believe. At the same time it should be kept absolutely secret between the three of us, I think . . . I can never thank you enough for the chance you have given me of getting a footing and the encouragement and experience your production of my plays have given me.[4]

All Stanley Houghton's plays had been written for the Gaiety from the time when Annie had chosen his one-act play *The Dear Departed* out of her weekly pile of manuscripts and used it as a curtain-raiser to Shaw's *Widowers' Houses* back in November 1908. At that time he was a bashful twenty-seven-year-old, earning his living by selling textiles, but his ability to observe local character acutely and to write about it with honesty and humour made him an instant success with the Gaiety audiences. Annie had invited him and his mother to share her box on the opening night of his first play and she almost had to push him on to the stage for his curtain call, so shy was he of the people's applause. His next play for her had been full-length, *Independent Means*, which was put on in August 1909, and he followed it the next year with *The Younger Generation*. He was very sensitive of the debt that he owed her: 'I started to write expressly and absolutely for you. Had the Gaiety not been there, I wouldn't have written a line. I can assure you that I shall never forget it, and if ever I can do you and the Gaiety a good turn you have only to command me.'[5]

Stanley Houghton was just one of Annie's protégés. She was like a mother hen spreading her wings and gathering in many young hopeful and talented artists. In Dublin her brood had been Irish. In Manchester she was doing all she could to encourage anyone who had any talent for writing plays. Experienced authors like John Todhunter and Arthur Symons sent her their new work, hoping that their manuscripts might appeal, as well as quite unknown and most unlikely people. Marie Stopes, proving herself as persevering in this as in her championing of birth control and women's suffrage, wrote in 1915: 'My dear Miss Horniman, . . . Years ago you told me that I could not write plays and you were right, I could not – then. I was too young. Now I can . . . (enclosed play).'[6] Annie had to be very firm in declining her. She was polite and patient and if she could not use the material she was sometimes able to recommend the author to another theatre manager, as she did with some of Harold Brighouse's plays. Just occasionally she found the need to let off steam, and once her cousin Marjorie felt the blast – 'I need hardly say that Victoria Cross play was more "impossible" than even her unspeakable novels. She is such a stupid woman to talk to.'[7]

There was a group of local young playwrights who came to all the Gaiety Theatre productions, caught up by the excitement, the buzz of ideas, the new approach that gave every player an equal share of responsibility. They were fired with enthusiasm to write their own masterpieces and they knew that Miss Horniman had promised to read all the plays that were sent to her. Alan Monkhouse was theatre critic on the *Manchester Guardian* when his one-act play *Reaping the Whirlwind* was put on during the Gaiety's first season. He went on to write two more curtain-raisers and a full-length play for Annie, as well as writing plays for other theatres. Harold Brighouse was a cotton salesman when, in 1909, his one-act play *The Doorway* was chosen from three that he had

offered to the Gaiety and his full-length play *Dealing in Futures* was
a great success at the opening of the 1910 season. It also provided
a marvellous introduction for Manchester audiences to two young
actors, Irene Rooke and Milton Rosmer. The *Manchester Guardian*
wrote of their performances: 'one sat back in one's seat with that
feeling of calm and even pleasure which comes of seeing a thing
supremely done.'[8] Stanley Houghton had been at the first night
and afterwards wrote to congratulate the author, first apologising
for his boorish behaviour at their meeting. 'It is my cursed self-
consciousness again. I am so afraid of being suspected of covering
up insincerity by an affectation of warmth.' He went on to praise
'the constant atmosphere of drama. You were excited about what
was going to happen next, about what people were going to say
about the reply that would be made to a certain question – that
surely is very high testimony to the force and grip of your
dialogue.'[9]

The Gaiety playwrights were pleased to be identified at this time
as the Manchester School of Dramatists and to be recognised as
part of Miss Horniman's fame. They were big fish in a little pond.
Besides Ben Iden Payne himself, Stanley Houghton, Harold Brighouse, Gilbert Cannan, Jack Kahane and James Agate were old
boys of Manchester Grammar School. They were members of the
Swan Club, all proud to be Mancunians. Harold Brighouse
described his fellow playwrights as men of their time who had been
influenced by Shaw's and Ibsen's social plays. Annie urged them
to write about real life and this they did with humour and warmth.
Ernest Marriott, librarian of the Portico Library and a talented
artist, made caricatures of his fellow-members of the Swan Club,
depicting Stanley Houghton eavesdropping over the chimney pots
and writing down the conversation that drifts upwards with the
swirling smoke.

In 1912 Harold Brighouse had still to write his masterpiece,
Hobson's Choice which would prove to be one of the most popular
successes of all time. It was written after he had joined the Air
Force in 1914, although he had had the title earlier. According to
Ben Iden Payne's story, he had been chatting with Houghton and
Brighouse in the Midland Hotel's American Bar and remarked that
a particular actor had been the only one available for a certain part
– a case of Hobson's choice – which, he added, would make a good

title for a play. As each young man fancied the title for himself, Payne suggested that they should toss for it, and Brighouse won. When the play was written he was unable to find anyone in wartime London interested in it so he sent a copy to Payne in New York who persuaded an American impresario to put it on. The play ran for months at the Comedy Theatre in New York with Iden Payne directing and Whitford Kane playing Will Mossop (two of Annie's old team). When the play came to London in 1916 one of Miss Horniman's actresses played Maggie and, according to Brighouse, she was the best Maggie ever.

It has been said that *Hobson's Choice* has been played every week somewhere in the world. It has certainly created its own stories of fame and legend and has helped to strengthen Miss Horniman's reputation, even though it was independent of her. It was in the opening repertoire of the National Theatre, London; it was taken to Russia by Sir Laurence Olivier; Charles Laughton played Will Mossop in the film version; Wilfred Pickles played the same part for fifteen weeks in a Blackpool season; there has been a musical version on Broadway and, in 1989, a ballet version. Its creation surely owes something to Annie's choice of Manchester for her Gaiety theatre. Stanley Houghton believed that he and Brighouse were the only two Manchester men whose plays were likely to be worth anything. They both wrote one classic, and Houghton's, closely entwined with Miss Horniman's reputation, came first.

Miss Horniman's company played *Hindle Wakes* at the Playhouse for a month before moving to the Royal Court. Soon public argument over the play's morality closed around the subject of women's independence. Day after day letters appeared in the papers praising or denouncing Fanny Hawthorn and it was only a matter of time before mud was being slung not just at the character but at the actress who dared to play the part and she was called upon to defend herself. As one actress pointed out, did one have to be a queen to play a queen or have incestuous desires to play Phedre? And how did Sarah Bernhardt cope when she played Joan of Arc in a matinee and the Lady of the Camellias in the evening? By the end of the year the questions were being aired up and down the country and as far away as Chicago when *Hindle Wakes* opened there. The Vice-Chancellor of Oxford University tried to ban the play from Oxford theatres but he had to make do with placing the play out of bounds to his students. Annie declared that he was wasting his time on a passing tradition 'that lords of creation are to be allowed a lower morality than the unenfranchised helots'.[10] She wondered why he should wish to blinker the younger generation when the Prince of Wales and Prince Albert had been to see the play in London.

In July Annie's business manager Edwin Heys had married and she made him a wedding present of the touring rights of *Hindle Wakes*. In this way she lost control of the provincial productions outside the Gaiety and the excellent services of her business manager, who left to take charge of the tours which he organised. She had already lost some of her best actors and actresses to the London production of *Hindle Wakes*. She did not have the American rights of the play but she gave Stanley Houghton all the help that she could as he arranged for his play to cross the Atlantic. On 31 August 1912 he wrote:

> Dear Miss Horniman,
>
> . . . I shall soon be in the throes of engaging a company here to go to America. Brady should open on Dec 1st at the 48th Street Theatre. Whom do you recommend to produce it? I suppose you wouldn't let Mr Casson – not even if we sent the company to rehearse in Manchester? Who else? Can you suggest any actors?
>
> Yours very sincerely,
> Stanley Houghton[11]

His play was going well in London. He mentioned that £800 was made last week.

Annie's generosity was remarkably selfless and might even be seen as irresponsibility or folly on a superficial business level, but in the long run it all added to her reputation. In March 1913, when her company was in America during a ten-week tour, the *Chicago Journal* could write of her company as 'the most widely known repertoire company in the English speaking world'. She sent seventeen of her players under Milton Rosmer with a selection of plays – some Galsworthy and Shaw, a little of their new drama, some old English comedies and a Shakespeare play. They toured from Montreal to Chicago to Ottawa to Boston. They did not of course please everyone but theatregoers were keenly interested in their new style, none of the 'high-salaried but superficial players' of the 'average stock company production'.

Hindle Wakes was playing in Chicago while they were there and it did not pass without notice that Miss Horniman was the link between them. The city had recently seen the Irish players and the worthy citizens were reminded that she was 'the real fairy god-mother in their early days'. The city's *Evening Post* of 15 March believed that 'Miss A. E. F. Horniman the founder of the Horniman Company even more than Lady Gregory is responsible for the present Celtic and Anglo-Saxon revival of interest in the repertory theatre'.[12] These comparisons continued throughout the tour and even in Boston, that most Irish of American cities, Miss Horniman's players scored more points than the Irish players for a wider repertoire. There was no doubting their success as theatrical entrepreneurs fought to sign them up for future tours. Their invitations showed how little they understood Annie's temperament or her ambitions. One theatre manager in Montreal wanted her to sign a contract that would include her established actors for a twenty-week season for the next five years. This went right against Annie's policy of leaving her actors free each year to choose whether to stay with her or to move on. A Chicago millionaire, clearly unaware of quite what he was asking, was reported as wanting to invite Miss Horniman and Lady Gregory to join forces for a season of plays.

Annie was not on the tour to receive these invitations in person and to give her inimitable witty replies. She had intended going with her actors but, in December, she was knocked down by a London taxi and taken back to her flat suffering from concussion that kept her in bed for three weeks. She was very annoyed to miss all the fun but, as she recovered and her sense of humour reasserted itself, she sent a message to Manchester that she wished her teetotal friends to be informed that the accident had occurred before lunch and that she had nothing but tea for breakfast.

At the time of the accident, she had been showing her newest protégée, a young music student, the way to the nearest post office from her flat in Portman Square. Miss Rainier was newly arrived from South Africa in order to study music. Annie had met her at Southampton and, as arranged between them, had worn a black hat and a bunch of violets so that she would be recognised. There were three Rainier sisters and Annie was a kind friend to each of them over many years. She had first heard about the eldest sister Nella from Winifred Pullen-Burry, known to Annie from the Golden Dawn days. Winifred had gone out to South Africa to teach and had made friends with Nella, whom she described in a letter to Annie as 'the most sought after mistress and the worst paid' in the school, for she did not have the necessary English qualifications. Annie offered to pay for her ticket to England and for expenses while she studied at the Royal Academy of Music. Once qualified, Nella returned to a good job in Capetown and, in her turn, helped her two sisters to become educated. One of the sisters was Priaulx Rainier, who became first a music teacher and then a composer of such talent that Yehudi Menuhin commissioned her to write a violin concerto that was performed at the Proms in September 1978. He said that it was his wife's idea that he should commission a violin concerto from Miss Rainier; 'the result is a fascinating work, beautifully suited to the violin sound.' Priaulx Rainier lived to be eighty-three and in March 1987 there was a recital in celebration of her life and work at the Wigmore Hall that included a range of her compositions over a span of fifty years – pieces for cello and piano, clarinet and piano, a string quartet, and an elegy for the unaccompanied voice which she wrote for Peter Pears in 1953. She did not start composing until her late thirties, which was too late for Annie to share in her successes.

It would have been Nella Rainier who was with Annie when she was knocked down and who quickly found digs close by so that she could visit her every day until she was well again. Annie was at least a generation older than the Rainier sisters and she took pleasure in behaving towards them like a fond aunt. She took them on holidays abroad, bought them presents, allowed them to call her Tabbie. According to a story about one of these holidays, on the train journey to Munich the customs inspector asked to see inside Annie's small travelling case that she carried on her lap. She demurred with good humour but he persisted and Annie was forced to open her case and reveal a spare set of false teeth without which she never travelled. The customs officer exited, covered in confusion, much to the merriment of Annie and friend. Annie was generous and warm-hearted, modest and egalitarian towards the young sisters, as to other young protégées and when she died she left each of them a gift of two thousand pounds.

This was the private and intimate side of Annie's life that few discovered and certainly not those who shared in her Manchester circle that revolved around the theatre. Sybil Thorndike felt that there was always a certain reserve, a 'keep off the grass' attitude that prevented her from getting close to Miss Horniman, whom she could like and respect but could not love as she could Miss Baylis of the Old Vic. She thought that Miss Horniman was the oddest person that she had ever worked for until she met Miss Baylis. Perhaps Annie deliberately created for herself a certain mystique and cultivated her little eccentric ways as a means of maintaining her self-confidence and authority among actors and people of the theatre who worked in their own world of fantasy. Basil Dean thought that she was eccentric to the point of silliness but he detected a determination 'beneath all the flim-flam'. Lewis Casson sensed her longing to make an impression in the world of art without the ability of the creative artist, but Eden Phillpotts, whose plays were performed at the Gaiety, disagreed. He wrote to Annie in November 1912: 'Your influence on the art of the theatre and the instinct that has borne fruit in better plays and better acting belongs to creation. You are emphatically a great artist and the weird power to make your fellow artists greater than they would have been had they not known you, is creative.'[13] How Annie must have purred at this.

As 1912 ended and Annie looked ahead into her fifty-third year, she made two New Year wishes: that she should have a vote and that London should have a civilised theatre under her control. She did not intend to abandon Manchester. Indeed she was planning to spend more money on alterations and decoration of the Gaiety. She would remove the boxes which, she declared, were 'places to put your enemies'. She also intended to go on with her repertory crusade. But she had become a well-known name in London and she wanted to use this to her and to the city's advantage. She had already let it be known that she was seeking a rich capitalist who would provide the money for a London theatre and leave her to run the business. She told the *Pall Mall* reporter:

> I would like someone to buy me the Coronet, rearrange
> it as my experience shows would be profitable and

convenient, and supply the necessary capital for running
it for three years. He should have the honour and glory,
his statue in the vestibule, his coat of arms over the
proscenium, and the knighthood which is the probable
reward that awaits the founder of the first repertory
theatre that can be made to succeed in London. In
addition to these lighter laurels, at the end of two or
three years he would have a magnificent property,
because I would undertake to improve the character and
status of whatever theatre was supplied to me, in the
same way that I have increased the financial position of
the Gaiety Theatre, Manchester, which, when I bought
it, had an unspeakable past.[14]

Whether she was casting her net widely over all wealthy businessmen with artistic interests and a weakness for aristocratic
trimmings or whether she was hoping to ensnare one particular
individual is speculation but Bernard Shaw did not think her idea
was a good one and told her so. 'It would certainly be very jolly if
you got the Coronet, but I am not sure that your present plan of
using it just when you want it has not its advantages.'[15] He did not
go into details but his advice was sound. Annie's successful and
much talked of forays into the London scene had the advantages of
novelty and limited supply. With a permanent London base she
would lose these advantages. She wanted to repeat her Manchester
experiment in London – no star system and no high salaries, good
plays and no freakish productions, herself in full control – but she
did not have the wealth to do this alone.

As the new year opened, reactions to Miss Horniman's proposals
came from all quarters. All things being equal, her ideas could
have been floated, but events beyond her control cut the ground
from beneath her feet and Annie had to fight to hold on to what
she already had. She was always a fighter.

16

Decline

The reputation of Miss Horniman's company had peaked. By 1913 Annie's six-pointed star, symbol of 'glory, fame and success' on all the Gaiety posters and programmes, was losing a little of its lustre. Within her star was the crescent moon, full of promise and potential and by its very nature open to change and growth. For five years her company had adjusted to change as actors came, stayed for a while and moved on but it had always continued to grow in size and reputation. The biggest change had taken place when Ben Iden Payne handed over to Lewis Casson, and the emphasis in direction at the Gaiety had shifted from imaginative to realistic. Into the gap left by Payne had come many talented actors who had built up a standard of sustained excellence. Good new plays had given them the material upon which they worked their talents. But most of the actors who had created the Gaiety successes over the past six years had left, and the last exodus had been the cast of *Hindle Wakes* for the London run. Annie had lost about a dozen of her best people.

While she lay concussed at her London flat early in 1913 Milton Rosmer took half of her actors to the States and Canada on a twelve-week tour. From 11 February to 5 May much of the Gaiety's best talent was away from home. Lewis Casson was in charge at the Gaiety and even his home team went off to Cambridge for two weeks, leaving outsiders at the theatre. It was not surprising if the atmosphere in the theatre had become sluggish and uninspiring. The Horniman company was spreading itself too thinly for any cream to form. Manchester audiences began to grumble that they were being offered second best, that Miss Horniman was neglecting her loyal supporters. The grumblings grew louder when the touring company returned from abroad and within a week went off to the Royal Court Theatre in London for a three-week season, leaving the Gaiety closed.

Ironically, Annie's difficulties became entrenched by the success of one of her own playwrights. She had given Stanley Houghton his big chance with a London production of *Hindle Wakes* and it had changed many fortunes. It made the names of those actors who took on the leading roles – Herbert Lomas pointed to this play as the one that gave him the big break – and it brought fame and financial success to the author, who moved first to London and then to Paris. But the play was not seen by Manchester audiences until four months after the London opening, and this rankled with them. When it arrived at the Gaiety it was such a popular success that it brought to the theatre people who had never been there before and who had no sense of the old loyalties.

Annie said that her crescent moon represented the people, or rather that section of the people who mattered in the theatre – the audience. Public loyalty is a fickle affair and the very people who had applauded now began to criticise and attack. The most outraged and articulate was the editor of the *Manchester Playgoer*, who spoke of failure at the Gaiety. He granted that it was a financial success, but that was not what the Gaiety should aim to be, that could be left to the commercial theatres. He lashed out against recent tawdry productions, against an air of smugness and complacency, against pleasure in the mediocre and artistic impotence. Some of these arrows hit their mark, for there had been some poor plays and weak performances at the Gaiety as well as mediocre entertainments brought in to fill the theatre when the residents were away. Shining performances from Sybil Thorndike in two vastly different new plays, *The Whispering Well*, a Lancashire fairy story, and St John Ervine's powerfully realistic *Jane Clegg*, were not sufficient to dispel the dullness.

The *Courier* on 16 May reported with sarcasm: 'Miss Horniman's American Company passed by yesterday. This particular model is a very locomotory one. From fascinating America it moved straight on to capture London. While spreading clouds of glory abroad the earth, it passed none of its lustre on Manchester.'[1] A second London season for eight weeks at the Royal Court in the autumn left Mancunians wondering where Miss Horniman's loyalties and ambitions lay. This was the theatre that had been the home of Granville Barker's repertory experiments in 1904 and they wondered if Miss Horniman was planning to take up the mantle which he had worn so successfully for a brief while. After all, her two best Manchester playwrights, Houghton and Brighouse, were now entertaining London audiences.

Annie had met with similar jealousies years ago when the Abbey players were acclaimed by the London critics and then returned to hostilities in Dublin. She had been used to criticisms and complaints from the Irish, it had always been so, but they were quite a new departure in Manchester. She wanted a London theatre but her first loyalty was to Manchester and she turned to repairing the Gaiety bridges that were in danger of collapse through neglect.

She and Lewis Casson knew that they had to come up with some good new drama that would sell seats for the autumn of 1913 but they were trying to work with another Royal Court eight-week season at the same time. *Hindle Wakes*, a sure winner to fill the theatre, opened the season at the Gaiety and then went on to open the London season, where it ran for four weeks. For the Gaiety alone Annie had a little jewel, a one-act play by Alan Monkhouse. *Nothing Like Leather* was a biting romp laughing against the very company that was performing it. It was a hilarious success and became the talk of the town, not least because Miss Horniman played the character of herself. She did not have to speak on stage, only assume her role of elegantly eccentric dame. James Agate was transformed into the character of Topaz. He lent one of his famous larger-than-life overcoats for the part and invited the actor to spend the afternoon with him to catch the flavour and nuance of such phrases as 'My dear chap! You don't suppose I am going to confine my notice to your blooming play?' and 'I can write about masterpieces, I can write about rubbish. I've no middle register.' Lewis Casson was neatly turned into the character of Mr Push the producer who 'reduced the art of the theatre to an imaginative manipulation of this table and that chair'.[2]

John Galsworthy's powerful tragedy *The Silver Box*, a good box-office draw, came after Alan Monkhouse's half-hour of fun. So far so good, and the next play in the repertory was a new offering, *The Shadow*, by Eden Phillpotts, who sent the play to Annie with the message that he had written a big part for a woman this time. Sybil Thorndike's acting was superb and certainly pleased the critics but not the general public, who failed to buy the tickets. While this play went on to London, the Gaiety staged a Shakespearean production. Shakespeare was always popular at the Gaiety and Annie was hoping to recoup some of her losses. *Julius Caesar* opened on 13 October 1913 and ran for a fortnight. Lewis Casson produced it and played Brutus. The critics either loved it or hated it but still the people stayed away. Perhaps they were put off by the reviews that called it an unconventional, freakish, 'Gordon Craigy' production with Brutus striding around in what looked like a dressing-gown and the soldiers' leather armour 'looking like a new line in corsetry'.

Annie had watched some of the rehearsals and had offered no criticisms. Was it the mention of Gordon Craig that sent her blood pressure soaring and herself rushing into the theatre the morning after the first night to have words with Lewis Casson? Her instinctive reaction was that here was a self-indulgent production, experiment for the sake of it and not because the text called for it. She abhorred any artistic inspiration that owed allegiance to Gordon Craig. She placed him in the same black box as George Moore, for both had mocked and ridiculed her at some time and she hated their masculine arrogance and coarseness which cancelled out for her their obvious talent. Three years previously Gordon Craig had cruelly attacked her in his art journal *The Mask* at a time when she was particularly vulnerable because of her painful split with Yeats. Craig had written of her as naturally unpleasant, ungraciously blundering into the Irish theatre,

> one can only beg the insensate lady to get a man . . . a
> strong man . . . behind her as soon as possible. Rosa
> Bonheur was a bad painter, George Elliot and George
> Sand disgraceful writers, and Catherine of Russia a
> disgusting queen. If she wishes to rule let Miss
> Horniman emulate our loved queen, Victoria, that true
> Englishwoman and let her learn that woman is nothing
> but a selfish accident drifting aimlessly or to the bad
> without the guiding influence of a man.[3]

To have a production at her theatre compared in any way to the artistic principles advocated by Craig was more than Annie could bear. 'Freakish' was a word that she would not allow to be applied to work in her theatre. Lewis Casson did not attempt to placate her as Yeats or Iden Payne might have done. He could be just as forthright and unbending as Annie and when their outspokenness had run its course, she had cancelled his next Shakespearian production of *The Tempest* and he had tendered his resignation. A public front of sweet reasonableness was assumed and in December it was announced that *Colombine* and *Jane Clegg* would be Mr Casson's last productions. He would have a well-earned rest before taking up the post of director with the Glasgow Repertory Company.

If Annie ever regretted losing her director, she never said so and she did stay friends with him and more so with Sybil Thorndike. They went with her blessing to continue their excellent work in the theatre. Lewis Casson's ideas of what was needed at this time to whip up the flagging fortunes of the Gaiety and to restore the people's confidence in them were different from Annie's. He wanted to continue the repertory idea of two or three changes of programme in a week and to push ahead with experimental intellectual drama. Annie, with a need to balance the books, knew that experimental drama had to be paid for by good commercial success. She had already dispensed with her orchestra, which was a saving of around £1,000 in a year. She was moving away from the true repertory model to one play a week and was using more frequently the word 'civilised' to describe her theatre.

Through the autumn and winter into the spring of 1914 she had a heavy load of lectures up and down the country. In October she was in Watford, in November Leeds, in December she spoke to the Sesame Club in London, in January she was in Chorlton, February in Hull, Harrogate and Hampshire, and in March she travelled from Liskeard to Stoke-on-Trent. Everywhere she went she spoke on the state of the drama, the importance of the theatre, and she was biting in her criticism of Manchester whose inhabitants were only interested in cotton and money. The *Manchester Guardian* seemed to agree with her when it maintained that 'If we lose our best artists we have only ourselves to blame.' In a letter to the paper, James Agate praised Miss Horniman and her directors for 'the noblest, the best-sustained and most consistent theatrical achievement that this city has ever known' but he went on to argue that a theatre cannot thrive on the intellectual set alone, that it must have the smart set as well.[4] Annie was well aware of this and she was fighting against the idea that intelligent theatre meant highbrow and boring. This was why she objected to the word 'Repertory'. 'It is a new importation into the English Language during the last few years . . . that means something dull, slightly improper, somewhat immature and not worth having.'[5]

In December 1913 Stanley Houghton lay dying at his parents' home in Manchester. He had been convalescing in Venice, his mother staying with him as he recovered from a lung operation. After coming home his condition suddenly deteriorated and on 11 December he died, unaware that he had just notched up another mark of success – an entry in the *Who's Who* issue for 1914 that came out on 10 December. He was only thirty-two. Annie wrote sadly to the local paper in appreciation of her young playwright: 'Now he has gone from us and we can only wonder why it should be so.' He was one of the younger generation whom Annie had trusted to carry on the fight against injustice, against authority, against the complacency of the establishment. 'You younger people must go on growling for the sake of the future generations,' Annie wrote to a young friend when she was seventy-four.[6] In his play *The Perfect Cure* Stanley Houghton put into the mouth of one of his characters, described as a 'jolly, honest lady of middle age', words that might well have been spoken by Miss Horniman: 'There's a struggle between every generation. It's terrible and cruel; but it's bound to come . . . the younger generation is bound to win. That's how the world goes on.' These last two lines were inscribed on a bronze plaque which Annie was asked to unveil in his memory on 10 February 1915 in the presence of the city's dignitaries and the Houghton family.

Five days after Stanley Houghton's funeral it was time to say goodbye to Lewis Casson. He was given a farewell dinner at the Midland Hotel and, responding to speeches of good wishes, he spoke out against the people of Manchester who were failing to support the Gaiety Theatre that had made their town famous throughout the world. 'Manchester hadn't founded it, didn't work for it and didn't pay for it.'[7] These words were a far cry from the sentiments that he had voiced in Boston in 1911 before he experienced the frustrations of being the director of the theatre. Then he had declared, 'if ever Miss Horniman wishes to lay down the work I am convinced the town will carry it on.' There is no doubt that his resignation came at a bad time for Annie. Rex

Pogson believed that 'his departure was the beginning of the end of Miss Horniman's undertaking'. But Annie's moon was already past its zenith. Change at the Gaiety had brought poorer plays, less talented actors and less inspiring productions.

There were two new men in charge at the Gaiety. Annie had promoted W. Roberts-Marshall from bookings manager to replace Edwin Heys as business manager and she now chose Douglas Gordon to be the new artistic director, a sound rather than an exciting appointment. Nevertheless, the new 1914 season got off to a good start in February with three new plays. It was still Annie's top priority to comb through quantities of manuscripts to find good new drama and she chose *Loving as We Do* by Gertrude Robbins as a curtain-raiser to Harold Brighouse's *Garside's Career*, which some said was the best play he had written. The next week saw a new comedy by a local Jewish solicitor. The theme of *Consequences*, by H. F. Rubenstein, was mixed marriage between a Jew and a Gentile with the suffragette movement in the background. When the author had submitted his manuscript his friends had warned him not to expect anything to come of it. Even when Miss Horniman offered him what he described as 'an incredibly generous contract' they pointed out that he was not being given a definite date for production and it probably would never happen. In his wildest dreams he had never imagined a London production and when Annie included it in her repertoire he was quite over-whelmed. 'Frankly events have exceeded even my most sanguine expectations. I sincerely trust you will get some return for it all in *this* world if not in the other,' he gratefully wrote.[8]

Along with the new plays Annie gave Manchester its first staging of Shaw's *Major Barbara*, sandwiched between two plays by John Galsworthy. *Justice* could always be relied on to bring in the crowds and it ran for the first week in March 1914, while *The Mob* was given two weeks' staging. This new play, about the outbreak of the Boer War with Lloyd George thinly disguised as the hero, was enjoyed by the audiences but the critics were not impressed. The *Daily Telegraph* reported that the audience hissed at some of the scenes. 'Would that they had', Annie wrote in her scrapbook beside the press cutting, 'I love a row.'

All these plays were in the repertoire for yet another London season at the Coronet theatre on 20 April 1914. The opening programme ran for two weeks with weekly changes thereafter and two weeks of *Lonesome Like* and *Consequences* to end the nine-week season. During their stay two years before there had been nightly changes of programme. Now they had to work hard for their publicity, which had come easily when they were an exciting new sensation. Opportunities came with Galsworthy's plays. A child actress was needed for a scene in *The Mob* and Westminster magistrates refused a licence for one to perform after 10 p.m. Annie appealed to the Home Secretary but was turned down so the scene had to be cut. *Justice* had been directly responsible for bringing about penal reform when it was first staged, and this seemed a good reason for giving a special matinee for the entire judicial bench of the High Court and all London magistrates, with the Lord Mayor and the Lord Chief Justice as special guests. Annie put in her usual round of lectures and after-dinner speeches, which kept her name before the public.

Back in Manchester the Gaiety audiences were enjoying a week of Stanley Houghton plays put on by their old director Ben Iden Payne. He loved the theatre and was back from America for a second summer season. When it was over he presented Annie's manager with a pair of early Victorian candlesticks as a token of his appreciation of all the help that he had been given by the Gaiety staff.

Once again new acting contracts were taken up and preparations were under way for the next season, but in August England declared war against Germany. The First World War was about to unleash its fury and misery. This was when the 1890s truly ended; optimism was destroyed, experiment was killed. At first Annie determined to ignore the war apart from a few minor changes to her plans. She would put on 'cheery plays', she announced, 'the more sober brethren will go on the shelf – until you start mafficking, then they'll be done to restore youth's sanity.'[9] In December she wrote to her cousin that she was giving talks about her 'chap' to keep people cheerful but, infuriatingly, did not say whether this was one of her new young playwrights or one of the older established ones. All those who said that the war would be over by Christmas were proved tragically wrong. It was four weary years before peace came.

Annie kept going for three years with diminishing resources.

Her German and Jewish supporters, who had made up at least a quarter of her audience soon stopped coming. All the able-bodied actors went off to join the fighting forces and she was left with a surplus of actresses and old men. There was a lack of materials for her scenery shop and props department, and as the war years dragged on she found there were more urgent needs than in her theatre. She sent one of her heavy brocade dresses to France to be used as a vestment for a priest. She wrote to her cousin that 'any old leather (not boots or shoes) bags, boxes, straps, portmanteaux are all wanted. They are being used to make into *stiff* boots for wounded soldiers . . . there must be hundreds of leather hat-boxes in garrets which no one needs now-a-days.'[10]

In these circumstances she managed to run an amazingly varied programme at the Gaiety, from Shakespeare to Pinero to Somerset Maugham, but always comedy. Over the first wartime Christmas *Twelfth Night* was staged and over the second *The Comedy of Errors*, with a translation of Molière's *Les Femmes Savantes* under the title of *The Blue Stockings*. And of course there was always *Hindle Wakes*, revived each year in Manchester and London. In September 1915 Annie took a lease on the Duke of York's theatre for a season of plays, reopening it for the first time since the death of Charles Frohman, who had been one of the hundreds of passengers drowned when the *Lusitania* was torpedoed off the coast of Ireland in May.

London's bombing raids did not deter her and she used to watch from her window. She wrote to cousin Marjorie, 'We had a splendid view on Wednesday and saw two zeps, the bombs falling, the searchlights and the counter-firing. I thought that the bombs were dropping just west of Holborn Viaduct and found it to be so when I went to explore a day or two afterwards.' She was back at the Duke of York's in December and felt lucky to have secured the theatre for she wrote, 'two days ago there was not *one* (theatre) to let in the West End. That shows how we have driven off and forgotten the zeps. If you are writing to anyone abroad please mention that – it is such an answer to the Americans who imagine that we are panic-stricken and in want of food.'[11]

Rumours in the press that she had taken a two-year lease on the Duke of York's annoyed her. She still wanted a new theatre to be built for her in London when the wretched war was over, 'one without those horrid proscenium boxes that give the spectators a stiff neck and prevent a good view of the stage'.[12] Meanwhile, she would make do with renting and in December 1916 she was at the Royal Court for five weeks and then on to Wimbledon and Hammersmith. Her company had built up a reputation for excellent drama and intelligent acting, and Miss Horniman could be relied upon to deliver. Theatre business was undeniably good in London during these war years. *Chu Chin Chow* opened at His Majesty's in August 1916 and ran until 22 July 1921. *A Little Bit of Fluff* opened at the Criterion on 27 October 1915 and ran until late May 1918. People wanted a chance to escape from the horrors of war and musical comedies provided it.

At the Gaiety it was a different story. Annie tried hard to keep the doors open and to give the people what they wanted. There were many new diverting little comedies from local playwrights that entertained but left no lasting impression. Concerts were given to raise funds for tanks and ambulances, and to help the wounded soldiers. There were always free seats at the box-office for soldiers and nurses in uniform. News of her actors and playwrights who were fighting abroad filtered through from time to time. Captain Frank Stayton was serving with the Mediterannean Expeditionary Force when Annie accepted his comedy *The Joan Danvers*. He was recovering from wounds in a Cairo hospital when he learned that his play was so successful in Manchester that the Gaiety had retained it for a second week. Esmé Percy, who had joined her company in its first season, ended the war as a lieutenant and in May 1919 he formed the British Rhine Army Dramatic Company and put on fifty plays in the Deutsches Theater, Cologne. There were many less lucky ones. Charles Bibby was killed in action, as was Harold Chapin and George Calderon. Charles McEvoy, whose play had launched them into the Manchester scene from the Midland Hotel Theatre, was dead and Gilbert Cannan would not recover from mental illness.

Each year, despite all difficulties, Annie renewed her contracts with her actors – until the summer of 1917. In May and June her company was at the Grand Theatre Blackpool, and their last play was a comedy, *Cousin Kate*. On 4 August she wrote to the newspapers, 'Owing to the present state of affairs I have been obliged to suspend my company for the present but I hope and intend to revive it in the future.' The *Manchester Guardian* wrote that Miss Horniman and her Gaiety company had vanished so quietly that they could hardly believe that they had gone. 'Let us hope that she will soon be on the Gaiety stage again making her time-honoured speech, "Here we are again".'[13]

17

The Years After

How much longer would this wretched war go on was the question everyone was asking by Christmas 1917. Annie's answer was, 'When the martial spirit has worn itself out so that peace may rule in the world.'[1] Strongly influenced in her early years by her family's Quaker principles, she believed that now the way forward for individuals and for nations was through friendship and peace. There was little that she could do to influence world events but she did add her signature, A. E. F. Horniman, to a list of many names – Bernard Shaw, Jerome K. Jerome, Rowntree, Israel Zangwill – who sent a Christmas message to the men and women of Germany on that last Christmas Eve of the war.

When peace did come, Annie knew what she would do – '*two new dressing-gowns (one to keep in Manchester), a fresh supply of yellow writing paper, chairs to be recovered and curtains dyed and further efforts to get my claws into London in the West End, in a theatre built for me*'. Then she added in this letter to cousin Marjorie, 'You won't mind turning thirty like we did, soon it will mean becoming a person with a vote.'[2] In June 1918, five months before the end of the war, a Parliamentary Bill removed the privilege of suffrage from adult male householders and £10 lodgers. All men except peers, madmen and a few criminals could now vote. At the same time the right was extended to married women, women householders and women graduates over thirty. At last, in the General Election that followed swiftly on the ending of the war, Annie was able to cast her vote. She, now fifty-eight, had waited nearly fifty years for this moment. 'I do not expect you to believe that but it is true,' she told Marjorie.

After her company of actors disbanded in the summer of 1917, the Gaiety was leased to other companies. Annie kept a close eye on their productions, always reading the plays before they were performed. She was like a strict landlady who cared deeply for the reputation of her lodging house and sized up the tenants before she accepted them. One of the most successful plays in the Gaiety's history was put on by a visiting company. A. A. Milne's comedy *Mr Pin Passes By*, produced by Dion Boucicault, broke all records in box-office takings, all of which were badly needed for there was a new iniquitous entertainment tax. Annie told a *Manchester Guardian* reporter that between May 1919 and May 1920 she paid out £6,735 in entertainment tax, which was nearly twenty per cent of the money paid in by the public for seats. She was still dependent on comedies, for this was what the people still wanted – all kinds of comedies, from fairy stories like *Through The Green Door*, written by her friend and Manchester theatre director Maud Vernon, to Shakespeare's *The Merry Wives of Windsor*. In May 1920 Noel Coward's *I'll Leave It To You* came to the Gaiety with the twenty-year-old author taking a part. He was billed as 'grandson of Dr Coward, late famous organist of Crystal Palace and godson of R. D. Blackmore of *Lorna Doone*.'

But the Gaiety as a lodging house was intended only as a temporary measure. Annie was constantly talking about restarting her Gaiety company and every other month there was a rumour picked up by the local papers that this was about to happen – it was desired so fervently by a dedicated few who wanted to see Manchester regain its position on the theatrical map. In February 1920 the weekly *Manchester Chronicle* reported that it was impossible to fix a date yet. In private letters and public announcements her message was the same – I'll be back. One earnest young man who went to all the Gaiety productions and longed to see Miss Horniman's company back in residence was Tom Bass. He was in love with the world beyond the footlights and hung around the stage door after performances to catch a glimpse of his heroes. He took the liberty of writing a letter of admiration and appreciation to Miss Horniman in August 1919, using Louis Calvert, an ex-Gaiety member, as go-between. 'I will try to deserve the way in which you write about me,' Annie wrote in reply.[3]

There followed a warm but formal friendship between them that lasted for eighteen years. It never reached beyond the polite address of Mr Bass and Miss Horniman. He was not allowed any intimacies and probably never knew of Annie's pet name of Tabbie. She became his mentor, teaching, correcting, encouraging, advising this young student of life who so valued his correspondence with the great Miss Horniman. All manner of subjects were discussed between them – Italian paintings, sculpture, music, reincarnation, Egyptian religion, teeth, fascism, her youth. He asked for a photograph of her and she sent him one of her in cap and gown and dragon brooch. 'A real photograph of Miss Horniman' he wrote in his diary. In 1923 she told him to buy an encyclopaedia and she would pay up to £30. In 1928 he sent her a photograph of himself and she wrote, 'I have only had a glimpse of you once at the Gaiety stage door and yet I remember that you were like that only younger.' She sent him books that she felt he should read and he sent her little birthday presents like a dainty handkerchief.

Tom Bass was only one of many who were waiting for Miss Horniman to resume business at the Gaiety, but Annie had not been idle since the war ended. She had sat on a committee chaired by William Poel that spearheaded a movement to gather parliamentary support for the dramatic arts. A letter was sent to members of Parliament and prospective candidates advising them that the drama had 'no organised existence, and no organic voice and it is obscured by the purely commercial aspect of the theatre'. As always Annie was impatient with those who sat and talked. Even before the war ended she had advocated less talk and more action. In a letter to the *Daily Express* she wrote that 'those who want a National Theatre should help to prepare for one by supporting what is good on the present stage and avoiding what is worthless, however lovely the dresses and the chrous and however enthralling the ragtime music'.[4] She criticised the lack of information from the National Theatre Committee and begged for a report that would reveal what had happened to her tiny subscription to the fund. William Archer was not amused by her scorn of men who sat and talked in what seemed to Annie to be an exercise in self-justification. Yet since the opening of the twentieth century he and Granville Barker had been saying that a National Theatre would surely come.

In 1919 there was a step in the right direction with the founding of the British Drama League, with Barker as chairman of its council. In August the League organised a two-week conference at Stratford as part of the effort to establish a Shakespeare Memorial

Theatre. Annie was one of the speakers and once again she was urging them to stop talking and get on with doing.

On 3 October 1920 Annie had her sixtieth birthday. Did she intend to retire? On 5 November the *Daily Herald* carried this headline, 'Miss Horniman Compelled To Sell Manchester Gaiety. Heavy Blow To Drama.' Soon all the Manchester papers had the story. The facts were simple. Annie had a huge overdraft that had been with her for a long time and would not go away. She called it 'The Old Man of the Sea' but Sinbad was able to release his burden by making the Old Man drunk. Annie's overdraft was a burden that she could not shake off. She said that she had no idea that it had grown so large, and privately told cousin Marjorie that there had been some concealment from her of her business affairs, adding that just lately the theatre had been running most successfully. She appealed to the people of Manchester not to let their theatre die; she would stay on and run the theatre if she could be paid a salary. Letters poured in to the press with expressions of regret but no offers of financial rescue. Bernard Shaw thundered against the wretched city that would not pay off her overdraft. St John Ervine wrote that 'the splendour belongs entirely to Miss Horniman while the failure is entirely Manchester's . . . Manchester through Miss Horniman's exertions was put in a position theatrically which made it almost unique among the cities of the world. But was Manchester grateful? Not a bit of it.'[5] The only practical move was that the Manchester Playgoers' Club set up a committee to drum up funds but although there was plenty of talk, no one came up with the money.

On 30 December 1920 Annie signed the contract that agreed to sell her theatre for £52,500 to Mr Abe Hollander, owner of the Futurist Picture House. He had plans to expand his cinema empire. There was a sudden eleventh hour reprieve when Mr Hollander announced that he was willing to suspend his plans to turn the theatre into a cinema for a week or so to give the people who wanted to preserve the Gaiety for drama a chance to come up with an alternative scheme. He declared that he did not want to take from the people of Manchester anything that they wanted. Miss Horniman announced through the press, 'It is for the young people to make up their minds whether they will remain content with football and such-like games in the daytime and the movies in the evening.'[6] Mr Sam Fitton, a Manchester stockbroker stepped forward to head a board of directors that included Edwin Heys, Annie's former business manager, and Louise Holbrooke, a former Gaiety actress. They tried to sell shilling shares to provide capital to relaunch the Gaiety as a repertory but the scheme foundered.

On 8 April 1921 an advertisement appeared in *The Stage*:

> Gaiety Theatre, Manchester
> Wanted May 9
> First-class company
> Edwin T. Heys
> Mile End, Stockport

The committee had decided to run a last season of plays and, almost to prove the perversity of mankind, there were full houses every night. When she was asked if she intended being present at the final performance, Annie replied spiritedly, 'Of course I shall be there. Every corpse must attend its own funeral.' For the final two weeks there was a Stanley Houghton Festival which, in the circumstances, seemed the right way to end Annie's years in Manchester. She certainly needed her sense of humour to rescue her from despair and bitterness on that last night as she saw the stalls overflowing with the smart rich who had neglected to give her the support that would have kept her theatre alive. After the last performance of *Hindle Wakes* the actress who played Fanny was photographed by the press locking the door of the Gaiety for the last time. Annie stuck the photograph in her scrapbook with the comment, 'This door fastens with a bar inside. There is no key-hole there.'[7]

It was all over. 'You did your best to keep me,' Annie wrote to the *Manchester Guardian*. 'I have always felt that you have acted towards me as a kindly chaperone, and that if I had done anything irregular you would have chided me.' She packed up all her belongings and prepared to leave. She gave her Durer engravings, which used to hang in her room at the theatre, to Manchester Grammar School and her Rossetti painting 'Jolie Coeur' to the City Art Gallery. She pasted her last cutting into her scrapbook; dated 18 July 1921, it was a report of the Gaiety reopening for one night to celebrate Ellen Terry's sixty-five years on the stage. The famous actress was there in person to read extracts from Shakespeare. After this last item Annie wrote:

R.I.P
A. E. F. Horniman,.
1H Montagu Mansions,
London W1
Late – Gaiety Theatre[8]

Then she parcelled up her seventeen scrapbooks and sent them to join the ten Irish scrapbooks which she had already given to the John Rylands Library, Manchester. She presented to the Drama League, which its founder Geoffrey Whitworth described as 'a central aid station for amateur and small professional groups', all her prompt copies of plays produced at the Gaiety Theatre together with a full set of actor's parts. There were 176 plays.

When she was asked her immediate plans she said that she would 'seek some clean cities, sit out of doors under a clear sky in a comfortable climate' – and that is what she did for a large part of the next seventeen years, consistently turning down invitations to speak about the theatre. 'My life has moved away from the theatre and so there would be nothing for me to tell,' she would say.[9] It was not entirely true. She remained a passionate theatregoer for another ten years and in 1932 was writing, 'I can go to theatres and concerts by myself and do so.' On some of these occasions, when her feet were swollen by rheumatism, she would put on slippers which no one noticed beneath her long skirts. She kept in touch with playwrights and authors, writing to praise new productions and to make observant comments. Lewis Casson said that he looked to her for valuable and intelligent criticism. She was no longer interested in giving talks on her theatre; there had once been a purpose in it but now it would be talk for the sake of talk. It was pleasant not to be forgotten but 'perhaps the same things said by fresh voices might be more effectual' she wrote in response to yet another invitation.[10] She made an exception to speak at Ibsen's centenary dinner in 1928. She thought that 'the Norwegian Minister and Mr Grein both seemed pleased when I spoke for seven minutes, just to say what I thought of the great dramatist'.[11]

She turned down an invitation to stand for Parliament as a Liberal candidate in a Manchester constituency. Her excuse was

that she objected to three-cornered fights and that she believed that
the Capital Levy would injure the national credit – 'But rather that
than Protection so I voted here for Labour.' In characteristic
fashion she had used her vote independently. Her grandfather,
father and brother may have been staunchly Liberal but she would
never toe the party line.

Part of her time was spent travelling – in 1921 Morocco and
Spain, 1923 France and Austria, 1924 Florence, Cairo and the
Nile, 1925 Genoa, Amsterdam, Munich and Cologne, 1926 Italy,
1928 Brussels and Carlsbad, 1930 Madeira and Oberammergau,
1931 her beloved Bayreuth. Sometimes she went in search of relief
for the rheumatism that attacked her hands and feet, for 'a cat with
swollen hindpaws is a nuisance to herself and everyone else'.
Sometimes her trips were purely for pleasure and the experience.
In May 1923 she was in Arles to attend a bullfight – 'I want to
watch the *public* and I hope not to be sick.' Her closest friends now
were her oldest, like Helen Rand and the Rainier sisters, and one
of them usually travelled with her. To all of them she was Tabbie
and in one of her letters she confided that she was so used to being
called Tabbie that it was an effort to write Annie but she tried to
sign properly to people who expected it. Her language was full of
'purrs' and 'miaus' and one letter begins, 'If this be a fractious
letter, blame the head and not the poor old Cat who does her best
to purr nicely,' and ends, 'Many purrs from your arthritic Cousin
Tabbie'.[12]

She left Manchester to carry out its post-mortem on why Miss
Horniman and the Gaiety Theatre failed and who should bear the
blame. It has continued down the years – too many gloomy dramas,
too many popular successes, too little artistic experiment, too
intellectual, too few long runs, too many. There have been some
harsh criticisms and Annie has been turned into a caricature that
bears little resemblance to the real person. Jack Kahane, ex-
Manchester Grammar School boy and member of the Swan Club,
who tried to write plays and novels until turning to publishing after
the 1914–18 War, was particularly bitter, judgemental and abusive:
'I despise Miss Horniman, the ugly bedizened spinster in whose
veins ran tea, as it does in most elderly virgins; I despise her for
having begun a fine scheme, set alight a fine blaze of endeavour,

and then wrecked it, doused it for I know not what stupid, spoiled woman's whim.'[13]

C. E. Montague of the *Manchester Guardian* wrote in 1922 more truly and sensitively that:

> the keener flavours of playgoing went when Miss Horniman closed the Gaiety doors. The lively minded audience that she had collected and animated quickly dissolved; the actors who had become really a company, with a real company's permanent power of mutual stimulation became once more atoms – now part of this and now of that fortuitous group of atoms; that sovereign pleasure to be had in the theatre, the first night of a play that is an artistic adventure, when the air in the house as the lights go down for the curtain to rise is all astir with the delights of a shared effort and hazard, making one eager creature of all on both sides of the arch – that is not to be had any more in our city.[14]

His appreciation was part of an article on the Liverpool Playhouse. This theatre had kept going during the war years by forming a Commonwealth that guaranteed the actors a minimum wage and gave the public a diet of light comedy and established successes.

Of the other theatres that Annie had nurtured, Glasgow was the first to lose its repertory theatre. Lewis Casson, who had gone to be their director after his fracas with Annie, had volunteered for the services at the outbreak of war in 1914. The Royalty Theatre proprietors did not renew the lease for the company. Bristol's repertory theatre had only lived a short time. The citizens had been fired with enthusiasm after Miss Horniman's company had brought *Candida* and *Hindle Wakes* to the Theatre Royal in December 1913 and Annie had lectured to them on the need for every civilised city to have their own repertory theatre. One of her players had organised a season of plays there but the experiment folded in May 1915. Sheffield's repertory was run by amateurs. Birmingham still had its repertory theatre in 1920, due to the devotion of Barry Jackson whose family money, like Annie's, came from trade. (His was made by the chain of Maypole Dairies.) Apart from personal wealth, he shared another essential with Annie: he had a talented playwright who provided him with some fine plays. In 1918, when

John Drinkwater's play *Abraham Lincoln* moved from the Birmingham Repertory Theatre to a London production at the Lyric Theatre Hammersmith, it carried Jackson's reputation with it and went on to lay the foundations for success for Nigel Playfair at this theatre. Annie would never have achieved her success at the Abbey Theatre Dublin without W. B. Yeats and Synge, and *Hindle Wakes* could not be separated from the Horniman name in people's memories. In 1924 Barry Jackson had to appeal to his season ticket holders to take shares so that he could realise more money, and Birmingham audiences, unlike Manchester, did not let him down.

Over in Dublin the Abbey Theatre had managed to keep open during the war years by touring in America and Great Britain and by becoming at home a popular theatre relying on its folk drama. It was a pale shadow of the theatre dreamed of by Annie and her poet-playwright and its existence was a triumph for Lady Gregory, who wrote to Yeats about the closure of the Gaiety. 'I hope we won't have to give up the Abbey as Miss Horniman has done. I am glad we have outlasted her, and we have faith.'[15] In June 1924 she and Yeats offered the Abbey Theatre to the Irish nation and it was accepted through the interest and enthusiasm of the then Minister of Finance, who succeeded in persuading the Irish Government to provide an annual subsidy of £850. The Irish National Theatre became the first state-subsidised theatre in the English-speaking world.

The Gaiety had been everything that a municipal theatre ought to be and Manchester should have had the vision to maintain it. Annie had wanted to forge a link with other repertory theatres, foreseeing a chain of theatres across the country exchanging programmes and with a London outlet. Each would have its distinctive character and all would be mutually supportive. It was Manchester's loss that it did not take Miss Horniman seriously and let her go. Londoners had more sense and after the 1914–18 War Miss Lilian Baylis ran the Old Vic with increasing success along the lines first pioneered by Annie.

As early as 1920 John Masefield had recognised that her work had been 'a glorious success, for all over England, in towns and villages, the theatre is springing up with quite new wonderful life'.[16] But it took thirteen years for any national recognition. In May 1933 'a long envelope without a stamp and with OHMS' stamped across it dropped on to Annie's doormat at 1H Montagu Mansions. She thought it was an Income Tax demand, but it was to inform her that she had been made a member of the Order of Companions of Honour, of which there were only fifty, 'and you can look in Whittakers Almanac to see who they are,' she wrote to Tom Bass. With great delight she went to Buckingham Palace to receive her honour from King George V, and described the scene with amusing and eccentric detail to her cousin Marjorie:

> They let me take my umbrella into Buckingham Palace
> and, when I went into the Investiture Room, I handed it
> to a gentleman and behold it was returned to me when I
> left by another door. We assembled in a Picture Gallery
> and I spotted a lovely Vermeer and a late Rembrandt. I
> was lined up with the first batch, three men with many
> medals went in and I saw ribbons put over their heads
> and one of them was knighted as well. I could see the
> King's paws tidying the ribbons – that movement which
> is made by someone who feels weak. A little bronze
> hook had been put on my dress – I was told to go in. I
> walked into a dim light and I bowed, the badge
> appeared on a cushion – George hooked it on, we stared
> hard at each other and shook hands and I passed out. In
> the anteroom my badge (and the hook) were removed, a
> ribbon bar was added, then popped into a neat little box
> and returned to me. Then I was handed a gigantic white
> envelope and the *un*decorated man in yellowish khaki
> who had talked to me most nicely before, came and
> asked about the umbrella. I had wondered what on
> earth he could be, so inconspicuous, not any medals of
> any importance. Like everyone else, he knew my name,
> probably because I was the only C.H. in the Birthday
> List. Next day I found that I had a C.H. companion
> and he was the Rev. Philip Clayton, generally known as
> 'Tubbie' . . . Yours Tabbie[17]

The two young men whom Annie had first helped at the Avenue Theatre in 1894 had received due recognition and honour long ago. In 1923 W. B. Yeats was awarded the Nobel Prize for Literature and Bernard Shaw followed him for the same prize in 1926.

In her last winter Annie fought back from a severe attack of pneumonia that she said *ought* to have killed her and in April 1937 she could write, 'But the cough is nearly gone now, thanks to the sweet company of my two Tabby Cats . . . some human beings have been very kind and patient too.' For the previous five years she had fought against bronchitis and rheumatism. 'I won't become a cripple, mind or body if I can fight against it,' she told cousin Marjorie.[18] Old friends came to visit her: Sybil Casson bringing love from Lewis, Ben Iden Payne and, at last seeking her company again, Yeats. He found her bed-ridden 'but her mind lively and vigorous'. He hoped to see more of her, 'there was so much that we and nobody else could talk about', but he had left it too late.[19] Annie died peacefully in her sleep on 6 August 1937 at Shere in Surrey. 'She was as generous with her time as with her money,' Yeats wrote on hearing of her death, and Bernard Shaw declared that she should be buried in Westminster Abbey. This was not at all what Annie wanted. She had given orders that her body should be cremated in a simple and inexpensive manner. A handful of her oldest and closest friends carried out her wishes and scattered her ashes over the Garden of Remembrance at Woking.

The letters that appeared in the press after her death suggested that Miss Horniman would be remembered more for her distinctive style of dressing than for her pioneer work for British drama. One particular dress, brocaded in peacock tails, must have been seen by half of England. As Annie once told a friend:

> I wore it for years and years and it wouldn't wear out.
> At last I had it altered into an opera cloak, and I wore it
> and wore it. It was still as good as ever but I was getting
> a little tired of it so I had a petticoat made of it. Still it
> endured, and eventually I gave it to a young friend. One
> evening she was at a party of mine and I noticed what a
> smart skirt she was wearing. After a while she came up
> to me and behold! The smart skirt was the last of my
> peacock dress. Or at least the last I ever saw of it, for I
> have no doubt it figured again, since my young friend
> was of the contriving kind, as an opera cloak, then
> perhaps as an opera hood or a theatre bag, and there
> may be to this day fragments of it adorning a patchwork

cushion or hidden away in a piece bag ready to be
produced on occasion.

Her true worth was, however, recognised by the man whose
youthful genius she had herself recognised, and unstintingly
financed, over forty years earlier at the Avenue Theatre. On her
death Bernard Shaw declared that Miss Horniman's work deserved
to live and should live as long as the British Theatre.

In the summer of 1949 there was a Repertory Theatre Festival in
London with repertory companies from Manchester, Glasgow,
Bristol and Nottingham taking part.

In 1958 Manchester celebrated the fiftieth anniversary of the
opening of the Gaiety, recognising at last the contribution Miss
Horniman and her company had made to the city's heritage. Lewis
Casson was there and made a speech in which he compared Miss
Horniman to a small Australian tree that the natives called 'the
good mother because it has to die before its seeds can germinate
and blossom'.

In 1959 the Gaiety Theatre building was demolished to make
way for a multi-storey office block called 'Television House'. The
local press carried a photograph of Dame Sybil Thorndike among
the ruins, with her only comment, 'It's heart-breaking.' A plaque
in the foyer of the new building records the dates of Miss A. E. F.
Horniman and her Gaiety Theatre.

In 1976 the new National Theatre opened on the South Bank,
London. It is a repertory theatre, holding a collection of plays in
store which it alternates in its programme while rehearsing new
ones to add to its repertoire. It produces Shakespeare, the classics,
translations of foreign plays and good modern plays. It encourages
new dramatists. It has a permanent group of players who work
together.

Sources

1 The Avenue Theatre, 1894

1. Letter Horniman to Tom Bass, 6 October 1930; Central Library, Manchester
2. *Sporting & Dramatic News*, April 1894; quoted in Bernard Shaw, *Major Critical Essays*, p.94 (Penguin, London, 1986)
3. Richard Findlater, *Banned. A Review of Theatrical Censorship*, p.74 (MacGibbon & Kee, 1967)
4. Scrapbook N, Horniman Collections, John Rylands University Library of Manchester
5. Michael Holroyd, *Bernard Shaw*, vol.1, p.248 (Chatto & Windus, London, 1988)
6. G. K. Chesterton, *Autobiography*, p.150 (Hutchinson, London, 1936)
7. George Moore, *Ave*, p.34 (Heinemann, London, 1933)
8. Quoted in Simon Wilson, *Beardsley*, plate 17 (Phaidon, Oxford, 1983)
9. W. B. Yeats, *Autobiographies*, p.282 (Papermac, London, 1980)
10. Quoted in St John Ervine, *Bernard Shaw. His Life, Work and Friends*, p.266 (Constable, London, 1956)
11. Letter Shaw to Charrington, 1 March 1895; quoted in Dan H. Laurence, ed., *Collected Letters 1874–1897* (Max Reinhardt, London, 1965)
12. Letter Shaw to Horniman, 14 September 1904; microfilm 5131524, Central Library, Manchester
13. Letter Horniman to Shaw, 22 June 1907; MS 50538, British Library
14. Letter Horniman to Farr, 5 December 1905; quoted in Josephine Johnson, *Florence Farr. Bernard Shaw's New Woman*, p.62 (Colin Smythe, Gerrards Cross, 1975)

2 The Horniman Family

1. Letter Horniman to Garrod, 5 December 1932; Horniman Collections, John Rylands University Library of Manchester

2. Rex Pogson, *Annie Horniman and the Gaiety Theatre Manchester*, p.2 (Rockliff, London, 1952)
3. Letter Horniman to Bass, 6 October 1930; Central Library, Manchester
4. G. K. Chesterton, op.cit., p.15
5. Letter Horniman to Bass, 17 January 1924; Central Library, Manchester
6. Letter Horniman to Pierce, 16 February 1932; Horniman Collections, John Rylands University Library of Manchester
7. Letter Horniman to Garrod, 17 October 1932; Horniman Collections, John Rylands University Library of Manchester

3 Annie's Student Years

1. Chesterton, op.cit. p.143
2. Scrapbook Q, Horniman Collections, John Rylands University Library of Manchester
3. Yeats, op.cit., p.122
4. Ellic Howe, *The Magicians of The Golden Dawn*, p.42 (Aquarian Press, Wellingborough, 1985)
5. Letter Horniman to Bass, 1 April 1934; Central Library, Manchester
6. Helen Pullen-Burry's unpublished reminiscences; Horniman Collections, John Rylands University Library of Manchester
7. Holroyd, op.cit., p.268
8. William Plomer, *Autobiography*, p.42 (Jonathan Cape, London, 1975)
9. Letter Horniman to Garrod, 16 October 1932; Horniman Collections, John Rylands University Library of Manchester
10. *Forest Hill News*, 28 December 1889
11. Yeats, op.cit., p.182
12. Frank Tuohy, *Yeats*, p.49 (Macmillan, London, 1976)
13. Howe, op.cit., p.59
14. Yeats, 'Essay on Magic' in *Essays and Introductions* (Macmillan, London, 1961)
15. Howe, op.cit., p.76
16. Private Collection, by courtesy R. A. Gilbert
17. Howe, op.cit., pp.85, 110
18. Yeats, *Autobiographies*, p.335

4 The Years of Mystery, 1893–1903

1. Flying Roll XVIII; quoted in Francis King, *Astral Magic & Alchemy* (Neville Spearman, London, 1972)

2. Howe, op.cit., pp.118, 132
3. Ibid., pp.132, 136
4. Plomer, op.cit., p.92
5. Letter Emslie to Annie, 5 March 1906; Horniman Collections, John Rylands University Library of Manchester
6. Yeats, 'Essay on Magic' in *Essays*, op.cit., pp.28, 51
7. Ibid., p.29
8. Ibid., p.43
9. Letter Yeats to Gregory, 25 April 1900; in Allan Wade, ed., *The Letters of W. B. Yeats* (Macmillan, New York, 1955)
10. Private Collection, by courtesy R. A. Gilbert
11. Ibid.
12. Letter Yeats to Russell, May 1900; in Wade, op.cit.
13. George Mills Harper, *Yeats's Golden Dawn*, p.53 (Aquarian Press, Wellingborough, 1987)
14. Howe, op.cit., p.174
15. Helen Pullen-Burry's unpublished reminiscences; Horniman Collections, John Rylands University Library of Manchester
16. George Moore, *Vale*, p.548 (Heinemann, London, 1933)
17. Yeats, *Autobiographies*, p.391
18. St John Ervine, op.cit., p.264
19. MS 13568; National Library of Ireland, Dublin
20. Yeats, *Autobiographies*, p.254

5 Dublin, 1903

1. Letter Yeats to Sturge Moore, early 1903; in Ursula Bridge, ed., *W. B. Yeats and T. Sturge Moore. Their Correspondence 1901–1937* (Routledge Kegan Paul, London, 1953)
2. Letter Yeats to Horton, 5 May 1896; in Wade, op.cit.
3. *Saturday Review*, 'In Dublin', 13 May 1899; quoted in Liam Miller, *The Noble Drama of W. B. Yeats*, p.43 (Dolmen Press, Dublin, 1977)
4. Letter J. B. Yeats to Sarah Purser, 24 December 1900; in William Murphy, *Letters From Bedford Park: A Selection from the Correspondence (1890–1901) of John Butler Yeats* (Cuala Press, Dublin, 1972)
5. Ann Saddlemyer, ed., *Theatre Business*, p.14 (Colin Smythe, Gerrards Cross, 1982)
6. W. G. Fay and Catherine Carswell, *The Fays of the Abbey Theatre*, p.126 (Rich & Cowan, London, 1935)
7. Ibid., pp.108, 142
8. Ibid., p.119

9. Ibid., p.140
10. Irish Scrapbook 1, Horniman Collections, John Rylands University Library of Manchester
11. Marie Nic Shiublaigh, *The Splendid Years*, pp.57–8 (James Duffy, Dublin, 1955)
12. Letter Horniman to Yeats, 10 October 1903; MS 13068, National Library of Ireland, Dublin
13. Letter Yeats to Frank Fay, January 1904; in Wade, op.cit.
14. Fay, op.cit., p.151
15. Irish Scrapbook 1, Horniman Collections, John Rylands University Library of Manchester
16. Fay, op.cit., p.159

6 The Abbey Theatre

1. Joseph Holloway, 'Impressions of a Dublin Playgoer', MS, National Library of Ireland; quoted in Miller, op.cit., p.105
2. W. B. Yeats, ed., *Samhaim*, December 1904 (T. Fisher Unwin, London, 1904)
3. Letter Horniman to Rev. Hannay, 17 July 1907; MS 2259, National Library of Ireland, Dublin
4. Letter J. B. Yeats to Lady Gregory, 4 February 1899; in Wade, op.cit.
5. Moore, *Ave*, p.279
6. Letter J. B. Yeats to Lily Yeats, 26 June 1904: in Murphy, op.cit.
7. St John Ervine, op.cit., p.189
8. Scrapbook K, Horniman Collections, John Rylands University Library of Manchester
9. Letter Horniman to Yeats, 22 July 1906; in Richard J. Finneran et al, eds, *Letters to W. B. Yeats*, vol.1 (Macmillan, London, 1977)
10. Letter Yeats to Gregory, 4 August 1904; in Wade, op.cit.
11. Quoted in Lady Gregory, *Our Irish Theatre*, p.42 (Capricorn Books, New York, 1965)
12. Letter Yeats to Gregory, 4 August 1904; in Wade, op.cit.
13. Letter Horniman to Sarah Purser, 21 September 1904; MS 15781, National Library of Ireland, Dublin
14. Silvester Sparrow, 'The Stained Glass of the Future', *Art Workers Quarterly*, 111, 9, January 1904
15. Letter Yeats to Frank Fay, 9 August 1903; in Wade, op.cit.

7 Opening Night and the Tarot Cards

1. Shiublaigh, op.cit., pp.64–5
2. Ibid.

3. Quoted in Miller, op.cit., p.112
4. Quoted in Russell Thorndike, *Sybil Thorndike*, p.71 (Thornton Butterworth, London, 1929)
5. Fay, op.cit., p.105
6. Quoted in Miller op.cit., p.128
7. Quoted in Lennox Robinson, *Ireland's Abbey Theatre. A History 1899–1951*, pp.76–7 (Sidgwick & Jackson, London, 1951)
8. Letter Yeats to Frank Fay, January 1903; in Wade, op.cit.
9. Letter Yeats to Frank Fay, 21 April 1902; in Wade, op.cit.
10. Letter Yeats to Gregory, June 1903; in Wade, op.cit.
11. Letter Yeats to Farr, 7 October 1907; in Wade, op.cit.
12. Tarot readings, MS 18312; National Library of Ireland, Dublin
13. 'Old Memory', in W. B. Yeats, *Collected Poems* (Macmillan, London, 1961)
14. Irish Scrapbook 1, Horniman Collections, John Rylands University Library of Manchester
15. Yeats, *Autobiographies*, p.205
16. Ibid., p.412
17. Helen Pullen-Burry's unpublished reminiscences; Horniman Collections, John Rylands University Library of Manchester

8 From Democracy to Professionalism 1905–7

1. Letter Horniman to Synge, May 1904; quoted in David H. Greene and Edward M. Stephens, *J. M. Synge 1871–1909*, p.163 (University Press, Columbia, 1959)
2. Letter Yeats to Farr, 6 October 1905; in Wade, op.cit.
3. Letter Horniman to Yeats, 26 September 1905; Roberts MS 13272, National Library of Ireland, Dublin
4. Mary Stocks, *My Commonplace Book*, p.105 (Peter Davies, London, 1970)
5. Fay, op.cit., p.181
6. *United Irishman*, 10 March 1906; quoted in Robert Hogan and James Kilroy, *The Abbey Theatre: The Years of Synge 1905–1909*, p.64 (Dolmen Press, Dublin, 1978)
7. Irish Scrapbook 11, Horniman Collection, John Rylands University Library of Manchester
8. Letter Lady Gregory to Yeats, 3 January 1906; in Saddlemyer, op.cit., p.86
9. Letter Lady Gregory to Synge, 10 January 1906; ibid., p.107
10. Letter Lady Gregory to Synge, 27 February 1906; ibid., p.116
11. Letter Horniman to Synge, January 1906; in Hogan and Kilroy, op.cit., p.59

12. Fay, op.cit., p.203
13. Letter Synge to Lady Gregory, 4 July 1906; in Saddlemyer, op.cit., p.131
14. Letter Annie to Emslie, 15 March 1906; Horniman Collections, John Rylands University Library of Manchester
15. Letter Horniman to Yeats, 24 June 1906; in Finneran, op.cit.
16. Letter Horniman to Yeats, 14 August 1906; MS 13068, National Library of Ireland, Dublin
17. Letter Yeats to Farr, 30 September 1906; in Clifford Bax, ed;, *Florence Farr, Bernard Shaw, W. B. Yeats Letters* (Home & Van Thal, London, 1946)
18. Letter Yeats to father, 21 July 1906; in Wade, op.cit.
19. Fay, op.cit., p.208
20. Letters Horniman to Yeats, 14 August, 3 September, 26 October 1906; MSS 10956, 13068, National Library of Ireland, Dublin
21. Letter Horniman to Yeats, 12 December 1906; MS 13068, National Library of Ireland, Dublin
22. Letter Horniman to Yeats, 17 December 1906; in Saddlemyer, op.cit., p.182
23. Letter Horniman to Yeats, 31 December 1906; MS 10952, National Library of Ireland, Dublin

9 The Playboy and the English MD

1. Letter Horniman to Yeats, 28 December 1906; in Saddlemyer, op.cit., p.195
2. Ben Iden Payne, *Life in a Wooden O*, p.65 (Yale, 1977)
3. Irish Scrapbook 111, Horniman Collections, John Rylands University Library of Manchester
4. Ibid.
5. Letter Horniman to Yeats, January 1907; in Joseph Hone, *W. B. Yeats 1865–1939*, p.217 (Macmillan, London, 1965)
6. Irish Scrapbook 111, Horniman Collections, John Rylands University Library of Manchester
7. Ibid.
8. Fay, op.cit., p.223
9. Quoted in Saddlemyer, op.cit., p.214
10. Irish Scrapbook IV, Horniman Collections, John Rylands University Library of Manchester
11. Quoted in Saddlemyer, op.cit., p.220
12. Payne, op.cit., p.78
13. Letter Horniman to Bullen 14 March 1907; MS 30586, National Library of Ireland, Dublin

14. Letter Gregory to Yeats, undated; in Saddlemyer, op.cit., p.202
15. Letter Yeats to Horniman, undated; in Wade, op.cit., pp.500–1
16. Denis Kennedy, *Granville Barker and The Dream of a Theatre*, p.193 (CUP, Cambridge, 1985)
17. Letter Horniman to Yeats, July 1907; in Finneran, op.cit.
18. Letter Horniman to Yeats, August 1907; ibid.
19. Letter Horniman to Synge, 26 May 1904; Trinity College, Dublin
20. Letter Rev. Hannay to Horniman 20 February 1907; microfilm 5131524. Central Library, Manchester

10 The Choice of Manchester

1. Basil Dean, *Seven Ages 1880–1927*, vol.1, pp.56–7 (Hutchinson, London, 1970)
2. *Manchester Guardian*, 11 July 1907
3. Letter Horniman to Rev. Hannay, July 1907; MS 2259, National Library of Ireland, Dublin
4. Letter Yeats to Farr, 7 September 1908; in Bax, op.cit.
5. Letter Synge to Gregory, 21 August 1907; in Saddlemyer, op.cit., p.238
6. Scrapbook A, Horniman Collections, John Rylands University Library of Manchester
7. St John Ervine, op.cit., p.245
8. Quoted in Pogson, op.cit., p.34 (Rockliff, London, 1952)
9. Payne, op.cit., p.89
10. Scrapbook A, Horniman Collections, John Rylands University Library of Manchester
11. Ibid.
12. Letter Horniman to Pierce, 28 January 1908; Horniman Collections, John Rylands University Library of Manchester

11 Annie's New Theatre: The Gaiety, 1908

1. Payne, op.cit., p.86
2. Basil Dean, 'Miss Horniman – A Glorious Amateur'; MS Th792094273, Central Library, Manchester
3. Payne, op.cit., pp.92, 88.
4. Quoted in Diana Devlin, *A Speaking Part. Lewis Casson and the Theatre of His Time*, p.50 (Hodder & Stoughton, London, 1982)
5. Quoted in Russell Thorndike, *Sybil Thorndike*, p.71 (Thornton Butterworth, London 1929)
6. Dean, *Seven Ages*, pp.15–17
7. *Manchester Programme*, 7 September 1908; Central Library, Manchester

8. Letter Horniman to Pierce, 28 December 1908; Horniman Collections, John Rylands University Library of Manchester
9. Ibid.

12 Ties That Bind

1. Quoted in Saddlemyer, op.cit., p.261
2. Padraic Colum, 'Early Days of the Irish Theatre', quoted in E. H. Mikhail, ed., *The Abbey Theatre Interviews & Recollections*, p.67 (Macmillan London, 1988)
3. Fay, op.cit., pp.242–3
4. Letter Tree to Horniman, 30 September 1913; Horniman Collections, John Rylands University Library of Manchester
5. Yeats, *Essays* Op.cit, p.207
6. Letter Horniman to Yeats, 27 February 1908; in Finneran, op.cit.
7. Ibid., 14 May 1908
8. Letter Garnett to Horniman, April 1909; Horniman Collections, John Rylands University Library of Manchester
9. Letter Masefield to Horniman, 21 December 1910; Horniman Collections, John Rylands University Library of Manchester
10. Payne, op.cit., pp.98–9
11. Quoted in Pogson, op.cit., p.72
12. Letter Horniman to Garrod, 4 October 1911; Horniman Collections, John Rylands University Library of Manchester
13. Scrapbook K, Horniman Collections, John Rylands University Library of Manchester
14. Scrapbook L, Horniman Collections, John Rylands University Library of Manchester
15. Letter Connell to Yeats 2 July 1909 quoted in Hogan and Kilroy op.cit.
16. St John Ervine, op.cit., p.425
17. Letter Shaw to Payne, September 1909; in Dan H. Laurence, ed., *George Bernard Shaw. Collected Letters 1898–1910* (Reinhardt, London, 1972)
18. Letter Yeats to Horniman, 15 August 1909; MS 30230, National Library of Ireland, Dublin
19. Letter Horniman to Yeats, 23 December 1909; MS 13068, National Library of Ireland, Dublin
20. Letters Horniman to Yeats, 23 and 31 December 1909; MS 13068, National Library of Ireland, Dublin

13 1910

1. Hone, op.cit., p.239
2. Letter Yeats to Quinn, October 1908; in Wade, op.cit.

3. Quoted in Robinson, op.cit., p.90
4. Quoted in Payne, op.cit., pp.108, 110
5. Scrapbook G, Horniman Collections, John Rylands University Library of Manchester
6. Pogson, op.cit., p.90
7. Payne, op.cit., p.111
8. Letter Galsworthy to Horniman, 20 October 1910; Horniman Collections, John Rylands University Library of Manchester
9. Letter Horniman to Bass, 29 December 1921; MS F92792H01, Central Library, Manchester

14 Legal Battles and Atlantic Crossings

1. Letter Horniman to Yeats, 11 January 1911; MS 13068, National Library of Ireland, Dublin
2. Ibid.
3. Ibid.
4. Letter Horniman to Garrod, 26 May 1917; Horniman Collections, John Rylands University Library of Manchester
5. Murphy, op.cit;, p.264
6. Moore, *Vale*, p.541
7. Quoted in Mary Lou Kohfeldt, *Lady Gregory The Woman Behind the Irish Renaissance*, p.168 (Andre Deutsch, London, 1985)
8. Letter J. B. Yeats to Lily, 22 October 1912; in Joseph Hone ed., *J. B. Yeats Letters to his son W. B. Yeats and Others 1869–1922*, p.151 (Secker & Warburg, London, 1983)
9. Quoted in Elizabeth Coxhead, *Lady Gregory: a Literary Portrait*, p.216 (Macmillan, London, 1961)
10. Scrapbook A, Horniman Collections, John Rylands University Library of Manchester
11. Letter Horniman to Holloway, dated 8 October 1926 in his journal; MS 1803, National Library of Ireland, Dublin
12. Scrapbook F, Horniman Collections, John Rylands University Library of Manchester
13. Letter Pankhurst to Horniman, 5 March 1911; Horniman Collections, John Rylands University Library of Manchester
14. Scrapbook G, Horniman Collections, John Rylands University Library of Manchester
15. Irish Scrapbook F, Horniman Collections, John Rylands University Library of Manchester
16. Payne, op.cit., p.107
17. Letter Payne to Horniman, April 1917; Horniman Collections, John Rylands University Library of Manchester

18. Letter Horniman to Pierce, 4 November 1911; Horniman
    Collections, John Rylands University Library of Manchester
19. Scrapbook H, Horniman Collections, John Rylands University
    Library of Manchester
20. Ibid.

15 Annie's Star in its Zenith, 1912

1. Scrapbook I, Horniman Collections, John Rylands University
    Library of Manchester
2. Letter Houghton to Ellis, 27 December 1911; quoted in Harold
    Brighouse, *What I Have Had*, p.178 (Harrap, London, 1953)
3. Scrapbook I, Horniman Collections, John Rylands University
    Library of Manchester
4. Letter Horniman to Houghton, 13 August 1912; Horniman
    Collections, John Rylands University Library of Manchester
5. Ibid.
6. Letter Stopes to Horniman, 11 May 1915; Horniman Collections,
    John Rylands University Library of Manchester
7. Letter Horniman to Garrod, 12 March 1915, Horniman Collections,
    John Rylands University Library of Manchester
8. *Manchester Guardian* 30 August 1910
9. Letter Houghton to Brighouse, 1 September 1910; in Brighouse,
    op.cit., p.177
10. Quoted in Pogson, op.cit., p.132
11. Letter Houghton to Horniman, 31 August 1912; Horniman
    Collections, John Rylands University Library of Manchester
12. Scrapbook K, Horniman Collections, John Rylands University
    Library of Manchester
13. Letter Phillpotts to Horniman, 14 November 1912; in Pogson,
    op.cit., p.21
14. Scrapbook I, Horniman Collections, John Rylands University
    Library of Manchester
15. Letter Shaw to Horniman 11 June 1912 Horniman Collections John
    Rylands University Library of Manchester

16 Decline

1. Scrapbook K, Horniman Collections, John Rylands University
    Library of Manchester
2. Pogson, op.cit., p.158
3. *Mask*, October 1910
4. Scrapbook L, Horniman Collections, John Rylands University
    Library of Manchester

5. Scrapbook M, Horniman Collections, John Rylands University Library of Manchester
6. Letter Horniman to Bass, 1 April 1934; MS F92792Ho1, Central Library, Manchester
7. Scrapbook G, Horniman Collections, John Rylands University Library of Manchester
8. Letter Rubenstein to Horniman, (no month) 1914; in Pogson, op.cit., p.38
9. Pogson, op.cit., p.171
10. Letter Horniman to Garrod, 15 July 1917; Horniman Collections, John Rylands University Library of Manchester
11. Letters Horniman to Garrod, 14 September and 10 December 1915; Horniman Collections, John Rylands University Library of Manchester
12. Letter Horniman to Garrod, 25 December 1917; Horniman Collections, John Rylands University Library of Manchester
13. Scrapbook P, Horniman Collections, John Rylands University Library of Manchester

17 The Years After

1. Scrapbook P. Horniman Collections, John Rylands University Library of Manchester
2. Letter Horniman to Garrod, 26 May 1917; Horniman Collections, John Rylands University Library of Manchester
3. Letter Horniman to Bass, 27 August 1919; MS F92792Ho1, Central Library, Manchester
4. Scrapbook K, Horniman Collections, John Rylands University Library of Manchester
5. Scrapbook Q, Horniman Collections, John Rylands University Library of Manchester
6. Ibid.
7. Ibid.
8. Ibid.
9. Ibid.
10. Letter Horniman to Manchester Playgoers' Club, 30 August, 1927; MS Th792094273Ma56, Central Library, Manchester
11. Letter Horniman to Bass, 12 April 1928; MS F927092Ho1, Central Library, Manchester
12. Letters Horniman to Garrod, July 1937, May 1923, 26 January 1932, 5 December 1932; Horniman Collections, John Rylands University Library of Manchester
13. Jack Kahane, *Memoirs of a Booklegger* (Michael Joseph, London, 1939)

14. C. E. Montague's review of Shaw's *Major Barbara* at Liverpool Playhouse, 'A City that has a Theatre'; *Manchester Guardian*, 1922
15. Letter Gregory to Yeats, undated; in Coxhead, op.cit., p.185
16. Letter Masefield to Horniman, (no month) 1920; in Pogson, op.cit., p.197
17. Letter Horniman to Garrod, 15 July 1933; Horniman Collections, John Rylands University Library of Manchester
18. Letter Horniman to Garrod, 29 April 1937; Horniman Collections, John Rylands University Library of Manchester
19. MS 30282, National Library of Ireland, Dublin
20. *Manchester Guardian*, 11 August 1937

Select Bibliography

Bax, Clifford ed., *Bernard Shaw, W. B. Yeats: Letters to Florence Farr* London 1946

Brighouse, Harold, *What I have Had* London 1953

Chesterton, G. K., *Autobiography*, London 1936

Coxhead, Elizabeth, *Lady Gregory: A Literary Portrait* 1961

Dean, Basil, *Seven Ages 1880–1927* Vol.1 London 1970

Devlin, Diana, *A Speaking Part: Lewis Casson & The Theatre of His Time* London 1982

Ervine, St John, *Bernard Shaw: His Life, Work and Friends* London 1956

Finneran, Richard J. et al. *Letters to W. B. Yeats* vol.1 London 1977

Flannery, James W., *Miss Annie F. Horniman & The Abbey Theatre* Dublin 1970

Fay, Gerard, *Abbey Theatre: Cradle of Genius* London 1958

Fay, W. G. and Carswell, Catherine, *The Fays of The Abbey Theatre* London 1935

Findlater, Richard, *Banned. A Review of Theatrical Censorship* London 1967

Gilbert, R. A., *The Golden Dawn Companion* Wellingborough 1986

Goldie, G. W., *The Liverpool Repertory Theatre 1911–1934* London 1935

Greene, David H. and Stephens, Edward M., *J. M. Synge 1871–1909* Columbia 1959

Gregory, Augusta, *Our Irish Theatre* New York 1913

Harper, George Mills, *Yeats's Golden Dawn* London 1974

Henn, T. R. *The Lonely Tower* London 1965

Hogan, Robert & Kilroy, James, *The Abbey Theatre: The Years of Synge 1905–09* Dublin 1978

Hogan, Robert & O'Neill, Michael, *Joseph Holloway's Abbey Theatre* London 1967

Holroyd, Michael, *Bernard Shaw* vol.1 London 1988

Hone, Joseph, ed., *J. B. Yeats: Letter to his son W. B. Yeats and Others 1869–1922* London 1944

Hone, Joseph, *W. B. Yeats 1865–1939* London 1965

Howe, Ellic, *The Magicians of the Golden Dawn* London 1972

Johnson, Josephine, *Florence Farr: Bernard Shaw's New Woman* Gerards Cross 1975

Kahane, Jack, *Memoirs of a Booklegger* London 1939

Kane, Whitford, *Are We All Met* London 1931

Kennedy, Dennis, *Granville Barker & The Dream of a Theatre* Cambridge 1985

King, Francis, *Astral Projection, Ritual Magic and Alchemy* London 1972

Kohfeldt, Mary Lou, *Lady Gregory: The Woman Behind the Irish Renaissance* London 1985

Laurence, Dan H., ed., *G. B. Shaw: Collected Letters* London 1972

Mikhail, E. H., *The Abbey Theatre Interviews & Recollections* London 1988

Miller Anna, *The Independent Theatre in Europe 1887 to the Present* New York 1931

Miller, Liam, *The Noble Drama of W. B. Yeats* Dublin 1977

Moore, George, *Hail and Farewell* uniform edition London 1933

Murphy, William M., ed., *Letter From Bedford Park: A Selection From The Correspondence (1890–1901) of John Butler Yeats* Dublin 1972

Murphy, William M., *Prodigal Father: The Life of John Butler Years (1839–1922)* London and New York 1978

Payne, Ben Iden, *Life in a Wooden O* New Haven 1977

Pogson, Rex, *Annie Horniman and the Gaiety Theatre Manchester* London 1952

Plomer, William, *Autobiography* London 1975

Raine, Kathleen, *Yeats, the Tarot and the Golden Dawn* Dublin 1972

Robinson, Lennox, *Ireland's Abbey Theatre A History 1899–1951* London 1951

Rowell, George & Jackson, Anthony, *The Repertory Movement* Cambridge 1984

Saddlemyer, Ann, ed., *Theatre Business* London 1982

Shiublaigh, Marie Nic, *The Splendid Years* Dublin 1955

Trewin, J. C., *The Edwardian Theatre* Oxford 1976

Tuohy, Frank, *Yeats* London 1976

Wade, Allan, ed., *The Letters of W. B. Yeats* New York 1955

Yeats, W. B., *Autobiographies* London 1955

Collected Plays London 1952

Essays and Introductions London 1961

Index

over professionalism within, 80–1, 82;
J.B. Yeats commissioned by Annie to
paint leading figures in, 62; *see also*
Abbey Theatre
Irish Nationalist Society, women's section,
53
Irving, Sir Henry, 113, 134
Jackson, Barry, 119–20, 189–90
Jerome, Jerome K., 182
John Rylands Library, Manchester, 187
Jones, Henry Arthur, 8
Jonson, Ben, *Every Man in his Humour*, 136
Joyce, James, 91

Kahane, Jack, 164, 188–9
Kane, Whitford, 142, 145, 165
Keightley, Cyril, 94
Kohfeldt, Mary Lou, 55

Laconia (liner), 156
Lane, John, publishers, 6
Laughton, Charles, 165
Lecky, William, 49
Leeds, Albert Hall, 86
Legros, Professor Alphonse,, 20–1
Life Study Association, 112–13
Limerick, Mona (Mrs Payne), 111, 112,
120, 155–6
A Little Bit of Fluff, (by Walter W. Ellis)
180
Liverpool: Playhouse, 159; repertory
theatre, 145; St George's Hall, 86
Liverpool Stage Club, 113
Lloyd George, David, 177
Logue, Cardinal, 135
Lomas, Herbert, 161, 172
Lonesome Like, (by Harold Brighouse) 178
Lyric Theatre, Hammersmith, 190
Lyttleton, Lord and Lady Alfred, 133

MacBride, Major John, 74
MacBridge *see* Gonne, Maud
McEvoy, Charles, 18: *David Ballard*, 111,
124; *The Helpmate*, 111; *When the Devil
Was Ill*, 122, 123
Maeterlinck, Maurice, *Interior*, 99, 111
Manchester Chronicle, 183
Manchester Courier, 107, 112, 142, 172
Manchester Guardian, 69, 107, 112, 149,
163, 164, 175, 181, 183, 186, 189
Manchester Independent Theatre Society, 120
Manchester Playgoer, 171
Manchester Playgoers' Theatre Club, 109,
110, 185; Annie elected honorary
member of, 123
Manchester Repertory Theatre (Playgoers'

Theatre Company), 102–3, 105–12, 113,
115–25; American tour (1913), 166–7;
Canadian tour (1912), 154, 156, 157–9,
160; Company disbanded (1917), 180–1,
182; Coronet Theatre seasons, 130–1,
159, 160, 161, 177–8; Heys appointed
business manager, 110; London
production of *Hindle Wakes*, 160–2,
165–6, 171, 172, 173; at Midland Hotel
Theatre (1907), 106–12, 113, 114; moves
to Gaiety Theatre (1908), 115–25; Payne
as artistic director/manager of, 108,
109–10, 116; performs *Measure for
Measure* at Stratford, 119; provincial
tours, 113–14, 120; Royal Court seasons,
171, 172, 173, 180; star symbol of, 110;
see also Gaiety Theatre
Manchester School of Dramatists, 164
Manchester Ship Canal, 107
Manchester University, MA degree
conferred on Annie by, 145–6
Mansfield, Richard, 9
Marjorie, cousin, 11, 163, 179, 182, 185,
191
Marriott, Ernest, 164
Martyn, Edward, 49, 127; *The Heather
Field*, 50
Masefield, John, 69, 145, 190; *Nan*, 130,
158
Matcham, Frank, 120
Mathers, Samuel Liddell (MacGregor), 22,
27, 28, 29–31, 32, 35–6, 40, 41, 42
Maude, Cyril, 161, 162
Maugham, Somerset, 179
Mechanics' Institute, Dublin, 59, 60
Menuhin, Yehudi, 168
Midland Hotel Theatre, Manchester, 86;
Annie's repertory theatre at (1907),
106–12, 113, 114, 117, 118; *see also*
Gaiety Theatre
Milne, A.A., *Mr Pin Passes By*, 183
Molière, Jean-Baptiste, *Les Femmes
Savantes (The Blue Stockings)*, 179
Monkhouse, Alan, 114, 163; *Nothing Like
Leather*, 173; *Reaping the Whirlwind*, 163
Monsell, Elinor, 67
Montagu, C.E., 112, 189
Moore, George, 7, 8, 49, 62–3, 77–8, 127,
150, 174; *Diarmid and Grania* (in
collaboration with Yeats), 50; *The Strike
at Arlington*, 109
Moore, Sturge, 49
Morris, May, 5
Morris, William, 25, 34
Munich, Annie's visits to, 3–4, 22–3